Louis XVI and the French Revolution

D1435060

Louis XVI and the French Revolution

ALISON JOHNSON

McFarland & Company, Inc., Publishers

Jefferson, North Carolina, and London

Table of Contents

Preface

"A weak king." The phrase echoes across two centuries to condemn the man who happened to be king when the French Revolution erupted. Those who admire the Napoleons of history will find little to interest them in the character of Louis XVI, a gentle man whose abhorrence of bloodshed and refusal to use military force against his opponents contributed to the loss of his throne.

Louis XVI may have been a weak monarch, but his personal courage was undeniable. On the day the Bastille fell the mob murdered two of his officials and paraded their heads through the streets of Paris on pikes, but only a few days later Louis XVI rode from Versailles to Paris with no protection to meet with the insurgents. During the first invasion of the Tuileries Palace three years later, he faced armed assassins only a few feet away with unflinching resolve and refused to capitulate to their demands for the deportation of priests unwilling to break with Rome.

Louis XVI did not want to be king. A quiet life spent in pursuit of his interests in locksmithing, carpentry, and geography would have been more to his taste than the luxury and intrigues of Versailles. He accepted the responsibility to rule, however, and attempted to work for the welfare of his people until his government was engulfed by the violent upheavals of the Revolution. Perplexed by the course chosen by so many of his subjects, Louis XVI hesitantly gave way, step by step, to the policies they demanded. Few rulers have acquiesced in such startling changes of government within such a brief span of time as Louis XVI.

Louis XVI remains above all else a very private man. Except for a handful of official letters, he left almost no record of his thoughts and feelings. We get a clear impression of him as a person only at the end of his life through the sensitive record left by the valet who served him in the months he was imprisoned before he was guillotined. During this same period an artist painted a portrait that shows the haunting face of a man who has suffered,

1

contrasting sharply with the impassive and impenetrable visage in the official portraits painted earlier in his reign.

Perhaps no one has offered a more sensitive appraisal of Louis XVI than Malesherbes, a leading liberal intellectual who served him as minister:

> He is a worthy prince ... but in certain situations ... the qualities that are virtues in a private citizen become almost vices in a person who occupies the throne; they may be good for the other world, but they are worth nothing in this one.[1]

In her book *The Deaths of Louis XVI: Regicide and the French Political Imagination*, Susan Dunn introduces her chapter on Albert Camus's reaction to the execution of Louis XVI in this way:

> A few years after the liberation of France, a war-weary Albert Camus, facing new cold war realities, looked back at the execution of Louis XVI and termed it the most significant and tragic event in French history, a turning point that marked the irrevocable destruction of a world that, for a thousand years, had embraced a sacred order. Celebrated by some as man's seizing control of his political and historical fate, the regicide was mourned by others like Camus as the permanent loss of a moral code sanctified by a transcendent God.[2]

Camus's book *The Rebel: An Essay on Man in Revolt* contains a chapter titled "The Regicides" that includes this key passage:

> On January 21, with the murder of the King-priest, was consummated what has significantly been called the passion of Louis XVI. It is certainly a crying scandal that the assassination of a weak but goodhearted man has been presented as a great moment in French history.[3]

In this biography I have chosen to focus primarily on those parts of Louis XVI's life that will help the reader to understand this unassuming man who found himself at the center of one of the most pivotal moments of history. I do not dwell at length upon the complex economic and political causes of the Revolution, which have been covered in great detail during the last two centuries, with nothing close to a consensus being reached. As Bailey Stone noted in his 2002 book *Reinterpreting the French Revolution*:

> The Bicentennial of the French Revolution may have given rise to a flood of commemorative activities, but it has not left in its wake any scholarly consensus on the causation, development, and implications of that vast upheaval. To the contrary, historians barely finished with the pleasurable work of interring a Marxist view of the Revolution regnant in the first half of the twentieth century have turned their spades upon each other, all the while trying to establish their own explanations of cataclysmic events in the France of 1789–99.[4]

Fortunately for posterity, many highly intelligent observers who found themselves at the center of the Revolutionary period kept detailed journals that were printed in the late 1790s and early 1800s. Most of these are now available online in French, and English translations are also available online in some cases. In many sections of this biography, I have chosen to quote extensively from these works that are now in the public domain because they give an immediacy and accuracy that paraphrasing cannot convey. I have provided my own translations.

Another source of primary documents that I used heavily is the very large Arneth collection of correspondence in the Austrian archives between Maria Theresa, the Austrian empress, and her daughter Marie Antoinette, as well as the correspondence between Maria Theresa and her ambassador to France, who was guiding Marie Antoinette in her role as the dauphine and then the queen of France. As Derek Beales points out in his biography of Joseph II (son of Maria Theresa and brother of Marie Antoinette), a bogus collection of letters involving these Austrian principals was published in 1790. According to Beales: "Of the forty-nine letters it contains probably only seven derived from genuine originals. Almost all the remainder are demonstrably pure inventions." As Beales notes, Saul Padover quoted widely from these forged letters in his 1939 biography of Louis XVI, and many other authors then quoted them from Padover's biography.[5] My minimal use of secondary sources helps reduce this kind of error.

With the advent of the Arab Spring in 2011, it is useful to ponder one of the most famous revolutions in history and its unfortunate descent from lofty goals into chaos and extreme violence. As Gouverneur Morris noted in his famous *Diary of the French Revolution*:

> It is not possible to say either to the people or to the sea, so far shalt thou go and no farther, and we shall have I think some sharp struggles which will make many men repent of what they have done when they find with Macbeth that they have but taught bloody instructions which return to plague the inventor.[6]

My love of France has been the outgrowth of a year's study at the Sorbonne after my graduation from Carleton College. I want to express my appreciation for the enthusiastic support for this biography given me by various French friends during my annual April visits to Paris. One year when I was invited to a dinner party in one of their homes, my host, Count Alexis de Berthier, surprised me by saying he was a direct descendant of one of the first victims of the French Revolution. The July 22, 1789, death of his ancestor, who was the chief royal official in Paris, is described in Chapter Ten of this book. His ancestor's death was also memorably described in Charles Dickens's *A Tale of Two Cities*.

The reference librarians of Bowdoin College and Curtis Memorial Library in Brunswick, Maine, have provided useful assistance in this project.

groom. He was so distressed that he gave up hunting for the rest of his life.[4] This traumatic incident in the dauphin's life may well have had a strong influence on his son. Although Louis XVI became an avid and skillful hunter, he always shared his father's abhorrence of shedding human blood, an attitude that would ultimately have a profound effect upon the course of the French Revolution.

Born on August 23, 1754, the future Louis XVI spent the first years of his life in the shadow of his older brother, three years his senior, who was an exceptionally attractive and precocious child who everyone believed would someday be a great king. These hopes were dashed when he died in 1761 after developing tuberculosis. Louis spent a great deal of time with his sick brother to provide him with companionship during the last months of his illness, so the loss was particularly difficult for the shy six-year-old boy who now found himself in a position of unexpected prominence. From that time on, he was taught never to question his duty to someday lead his country as king, but it was never a role he was eager to fill.

From an early age, Louis was trained to participate in court ceremonies. When he was only nine years old, he made a strong impression upon David Hume, the famous English historian and philosopher, who wrote to a friend: "What happened last week, when I had the honour of being presented to the dauphin's children at Versailles, is one of the most curious scenes I have yet passed through. The Duc de B. the eldest, a boy of ten years old [*sic*], stepped forth, and told me how many friends and admirers I had in this country, and that he reckoned himself in the number, from the pleasure he had received from the reading of many passages in my works."[5]

The dauphin supervised his son's education and raised him with firm discipline. When Louis was ten, his father denied him the pleasure of attending the St. Hubert hunt because he had not done some of his lessons correctly. The hunt was an important annual ceremony that courtiers followed in carriages and one that the young boy longed to attend, but despite Louis XV's intercession on behalf of his grandson, the dauphin remained adamant.[6] Through episodes like this he instilled in Louis a strong sense that duty and service were more important than the pursuit of pleasure. The dauphin's direct influence ended abruptly, however, when he died of tuberculosis just a year later, leaving Louis heir to the throne at age eleven. Within a few months Louis lost his mother to the same disease.

Now that Louis was himself the dauphin, one of his chief duties was to eventually marry as his grandfather the king decreed. Louis XV's powerful foreign minister, the duke of Choiseul, was eager to solidify a newly formed alliance with Austria, a former enemy of France. Thus he arranged a marriage between Louis and Marie Antoinette, a daughter of Maria Theresa, the empress of Austria. Having never seen each other, the two young people were thrust together in marriage in April 1770 when Louis was fifteen and Marie Antoinette was only fourteen. Their temperaments were very different. She was rather frivolous, pleasure-loving, and vain and did not like to read, while he was serious, reserved, and had a far better education and more academic interests than did his bride.

The marriage had been promoted precisely because Marie Antoinette was Austrian, but this fact would prove to be a great obstacle to her acceptance by the French people. Because Austria had so recently been one of France's principal enemies, hostile feelings toward the country remained widespread. When Marie Antoinette reached the border between Germany and France, she was subjected to a symbolic ceremony on an island in the Rhine during which she had to remove all her Austrian garments and dress in French clothing.[7] Despite this ritual, the teenager arrived at a court that viewed her with suspicion. As she became increasingly unpopular in the later years of her husband's reign, she was frequently reviled as "the Austrian." Choiseul's fall from power in the interim between the signing of the marriage treaty and Marie Antoinette's arrival in France only served to further isolate her from the courtiers at Versailles.

Count Mercy, the astute and dedicated Austrian ambassador to France, was deeply committed to using Marie Antoinette to further Austria's interests with France; that was after all the reason why Austria had agreed to the marriage. He arranged to have a capable man he could trust, Abbé Vermond, appointed tutor and spiritual adviser to Marie Antoinette, and Vermond conversed with her almost every day. Mercy himself met regularly with Marie Antoinette to discuss court matters and to attempt to guide her behavior so that she would be prepared to be queen someday. His weekly reports to the empress gave her an extremely detailed account of what Marie Antoinette was doing, and Maria Theresa wrote back regularly to confer with him about the best way to guide her daughter. She also wrote frequent letters to Marie Antoinette that are full of kind but firm advice about how she should comport herself in a situation that had enormous implications for the future of both France and Austria. For the sake of privacy, all the important letters were carried by couriers, with the trip between Vienna and Mercy's residence in Paris usually taking about nine or ten days. Fortunately for posterity, this voluminous, intimate, and illuminating correspondence consisting of letters between Mercy and Maria Theresa, as well as letters between Maria Theresa and Marie Antoinette, is available in a collection published by Alfred d'Arneth, who was in charge of the royal archives in Vienna.[8]

Louis wished to be a benevolent ruler, and one of his first actions after his youthful marriage presaged his future concerns. Gala wedding celebrations in his honor were held in Paris at the Place Louis XV (the present Place de la Concorde), where the new Rue Royale leading out of the square contained ditches along the sides that had been left exposed by careless workmen who were still paving the street. Thousands of revelers were jamming the area when for some reason panic broke out and people started pushing their way out of the square. As the crowds poured down the bottleneck of the Rue Royale, many people fell down because of the uneven ground and were trampled. Over a hundred people died in this disaster that cast a pall over the wedding festivities. In retrospect, the episode seemed all too ominous an augury for a reign that would end in mass violence.

This tragedy upset Louis so much that he sent the following note to the Parisian chief of police on June 1, 1770, accompanied by all the money he had at his disposal: "I have learned about the disaster connected to me that happened in Paris, and I am devastated by it. I have just been brought the money that the king gives me each month. It is all that I have available, and I am sending it to you to help those who are most in need."[9]

It is not surprising that Louis already had such a strong sense of duty at age fifteen. His father had dedicated his life to seeing that his sons were given the kind of education that would prepare them to be benevolent rulers of high moral character. He engaged the duke of La Vauguyon to direct their education, and the dauphin himself listened to his sons recite their lessons twice a week so that he would keep abreast of what they were learning. We have an excellent record of what La Vauguyon was teaching Louis XVI during his childhood and teen years because of two booklets written by the future king.

The first booklet was titled *Maximes Morales et Politiques tirées du Télémaque sur la science des rois et le Bonheur des peuples* (Moral and political maxims drawn from Télémaque concerning the science of kings and the happiness of peoples). Twelve-year-old Louis not only wrote this booklet, he also printed twenty-five copies of it on a small printing press that had been used by his father and aunts when they were children. He enlisted the help of his younger brothers in the typesetting.[10]

Louis chose this subject because as part of his education La Vauguyon had asked him to read *Les Aventures de Télémaque*. (Telemachus was the son of Ulysses.) This book was published in 1699 by François Fénelon, an archbishop entrusted with educating one of Louis XIV's grandsons, for whom he wrote the book as an educational tool. When Louis XIV realized that the book was actually a critique of the French monarchy, he was furious and sent Fénelon back to his home diocese. It is curious that some sixty years later La Vauguyon would use *The Adventures of Telemachus* to educate the future Louis XVI.

The title page of the second booklet, which represents an important part of Louis's education during his early teen years, reads: *Réflexions sur mes entretiens avec M. le duc de La Vauguyon*, par Louis-Auguste, Dauphin (*Reflections on My Conversations with the Duke of La Vauguyon*, by Louis-Auguste, Dauphin).[11] This booklet is a series of short essays in which Louis summarizes what he has learned about a particular subject from his instructor. They do not in general constitute Louis's original thoughts, but they do represent his understanding of what he has learned, and the pattern of his life and character would suggest that he internalized what he was taught during his formative years.

One important passage in *Réflexions* states: "A good king, a great king, must have no other goal than to make his people happy and virtuous.... A feeling of tender affection for my people must guide me in the establishment and enforcement of the laws."[12] Another section shows that, like many others in the Age of Enlightenment, the future king was concerned about basic rights: "In France we have neglected too much the study of natural rights, human rights, public and political rights. My late father complained every day about the ignorance in this respect, and he studied the issue and became very enlightened about it."[13] One memorable passage shows Louis's early repugnance for war:

> I will never forget this wonderful statement made by my grandfather [Louis XV], who said to M. the dauphin, my father, on the battlefield of Fontenoy, "Observe the horrors of war! Look at all the blood that is flowing in triumph! The blood of our enemies is still the blood of human beings. The real glory, my son, is to spare it."[14]

The important *Réflexion VI* concerning the use of force contains an important series of statements that not only seem timeless but also indicate the compact style that the future king, always a man of few words, used in writing letters or documents:

1. It is only permissible to take up arms for a good cause.
2. One should go to war only after the most careful deliberation and then only if it is unavoidable.
3. One should go to war only in order to achieve peace.
4. One should take up arms only when the justness of the cause is obvious, and ... not for one's own glory or self-interest.
5. One should wage war only for causes that are not only just, but important.
6. One must weigh the advantages that would be obtained by a victory against the infinite evil consequences of war.
7. In the middle of hostilities, one must always remind oneself that on the

enemy side there are a great many innocent people such as women, children, the elderly, laborers, religious leaders, those who have laid down their arms, prisoners of war, and hostages. Soldiers should not be attacking these people who can do them no harm.

8. One should abstain from all violence that can only cause harm and casualties without contributing to the success of the enterprise.[15]

Although Louis's academic training was excellent, he probably did not receive much guidance about sexual matters. For some reason that will probably forever remain a mystery, it appears that the marriage of Louis and Marie Antoinette in the spring of 1770 was not consummated for a few years. The Austrian ambassador Mercy and his associates were quick to spread rumors that the fault lay with Louis and was perhaps the result of a physical malformation. It was important to the Austrian faction that no one believe the problem could be attributed to Marie Antoinette, for then there might be grounds for an annulment of the marriage. Louis's initial attitude toward his young wife may well have been ambiguous because his father had not only raised him to disdain his grandfather's licentious behavior, but had also conveyed to him his aversion for Choiseul and the Austrians. Moreover, after Choiseul's departure from Versailles, many of his enemies hoped to separate Louis from his new wife and may have discouraged any rapprochement between the pair.

Abbé Véri, who was close to the sources of power at Versailles, kept a detailed journal of life at the court that constitutes one of the most important records of what was transpiring at the court during this period. In June 1774 he wrote a passage that would seem to indicate that the marriage had been consummated by that date: "The queen's influence was increased by a secret success that her husband began to have with her that he had not been thought to be capable of achieving. The joy of such a success and the hope for a dauphin give great power to a princess whose natural graces make her so pleasant and attractive."[16]

As it turned out, Louis and Marie Antoinette did not have a child until 1778, four years after he assumed the throne. There was some talk in letters of 1777 about a possible operation for Louis, but Marie Antoinette wrote at one point that the doctors no longer believed it necessary. In an article published in a urology journal in 2002, George Androutsos, a Greek professor of the history of medicine, suggests that Louis XVI suffered from phimosis, a condition in which the foreskin cannot be fully retracted over the penis. This condition can be corrected by circumcision or making an incision in the foreskin, but as Androutsos notes, there is not enough evidence to conclude whether Louis underwent a surgical procedure or whether the problem disappeared spontaneously, as is sometimes the case.[17]

Marie Antoinette's letters to her mother often mentioned her deep desire to have a child. In a letter that Mercy wrote to Maria Theresa a few months after Marie Antoinette arrived in France, he noted the dauphine's passion for children and said that she had asked to have another chambermaid added to her entourage because the young woman had a lively and pretty four-year-old daughter. Marie Antoinette also let the five-year-old son of her head chambermaid spend all day in her apartment, much to the annoyance of Mercy, who thought the resultant commotion interfered with Marie Antoinette's study with Abbé Vermond.[18] Marie Antoinette's maternal and sexual frustration were undoubtedly one reason why she submerged herself in a constant round of balls, private theatricals, and gambling and devoted much of her attention to fine dresses, elaborate hairdos, and costly jewels. This frivolous and pleasure-seeking behavior would also have been related to her extreme youth because she was only fourteen when she arrived in France.

Louis found pleasure in very different types of activities. His grandfather Louis XV had initiated him into the excitement of the hunt. Louis excelled at this sport and hunted several times a week, exhibiting courage in the face of physical danger that would later stand him in good stead during the Revolution. The duke of Croÿ remarked in his journal in 1780, "The king hunts very frequently and rides with great speed, handling his horse very skillfully."[19] Louis's love of outdoor exercise also prompted him to begin each day with an hour's walk.

It was not unusual in the eighteenth century for gentlemen to take up a craft; Louis had learned to be a good locksmith. Marie Antoinette chided him about his hobby, complaining when he entered her apartments with hands blackened by his work at a forge, but he would not give up this pursuit.[20] Being a methodical and patient person with a strong interest in detail, he found locksmithing a pleasant pastime, preferring the intricacies of a lock to the petty intrigues of court life. Even when he was imprisoned in the Temple before his execution, Louis found diversion one day in showing his son how to use the tools that locksmiths were employing to change the lock on his prison door.[21]

In a letter written in 1773, Ambassador Mercy informed Maria Theresa of another one of Louis's pastimes that Marie Antoinette found annoying:

Despite all the influence she has on the dauphin, she has not been able to turn this young prince away from his extraordinary taste for everything relating to the building trades, like masonry and carpentry, and other similar things. He is always coming up with some renovations to be done on his apartments, and he himself works alongside the workers with the materials such as beams and floor tiles. He spends hours performing this hard work and sometimes ends up more exhausted than a laborer would be who had no choice but to do the work.[22]

Geography was another subject that fascinated Louis, and he devoted so much effort to its study that he was considered one of the best geographers of his day. At the age of eleven, he mapped out the forest of Fontainebleau in great detail in a fifty-eight-page study; a few years later he made a colored map of the Versailles area that is preserved in the Bibliothèque Nationale.[23] As an adult, Louis XVI filled his study with map-making equipment and charts. At Versailles one can still see a large and magnificent globe belonging to him that has a relief map on the outer surface and opens up to reveal a map of the stars and the planets on the inner surfaces of the hemispheres. Geography was not Louis's only academic interest, however; he also eagerly pursued a study of history and languages and learned to read Latin, English, Spanish, and Italian. He was particularly interested in the English political scene and regularly read English newspapers.

Louis XV was no longer popular with his subjects, who resented the fact that his mistresses were running the country, but he wanted the people to love his grandson and Marie Antoinette. Hence he made careful plans for their first official visit to Paris in June 1773. They rode in the royal carriage through cheering crowds to Notre Dame, where they were welcomed by the archbishop of Paris and attended a mass. After a gala dinner in the concert hall of the Tuileries Palace, they walked around the gardens, where the public had been freely admitted. Ambassador Mercy estimated the huge crowd at fifty thousand.[24]

By now the dauphin was almost nineteen and had matured sufficiently to be able to perform his public role on that day to everyone's satisfaction. Even Ambassador Mercy was impressed, and in a letter to Maria Theresa, in which he extolled her daughter's behavior that day, he conceded that the dauphin's conduct had also been excellent.[25] Marie Antoinette was also delighted with the occasion, as she reported to her mother:

> We were honored in every way imaginable, but that is not what touched me the most. That was the love of the poor people, despite the taxes that burden them. They crowded around us, overwhelmed with joy at seeing us. When we went to the gardens of the Tuileries Palace, there was such a huge crowd that for three-quarters of an hour we could move neither forward nor backward. The dauphin and I had several times instructed the guards not to strike anyone, which was much appreciated....
>
> We eventually went up on a terrace, where we spent a half-hour. I can't tell you, my dear mother, the outpouring of joy and affection that we received at this moment. Before leaving, we waved at the people, which made them very happy. How fortunate we are in our position to gain the good feelings of an entire peo-

ple with so little effort. There is nothing more precious; I felt that and will never forget it.

Another point of great pleasure during this beautiful day was the dauphin's conduct. He replied wonderfully well to all the addresses he heard and kept commenting on everything that people were doing for him, in particular the joy of the people to whom he had shown such goodwill.[26]

2

Early Years of Reign

In May 1774, Louis XV died of smallpox, leaving the throne to his grandson, the nineteen-year-old dauphin. The British ambassador, Lord Stormont, wrote the following report to England shortly after the event: "They are all under inexpressible affliction and none more so than the king and queen, who all along expressed the greatest anxiety for their grandfather's recovery, and the utmost apprehension of the load that his death would throw upon them and which their youth and inexperience made them so little able to bear."[1]

Despite his grief, Louis XVI had to make immediate decisions. He promptly sent his grandfather's mistress, Madame du Barry, off to a convent and exiled to the countryside all her relatives who had obtained lucrative court positions. It was customary for the country to present a new king with a monetary gift raised by special taxes, but Louis XVI renounced this practice because he did not wish to add to the already heavy tax burden of the lower classes.[2]

Immediately upon his grandfather's death, Louis XVI read a letter of advice that his father had left for whichever of his sons became king. The letter contained a list of men that he had considered to be honest and capable statesmen. One of the most important names on the list was that of Maurepas, one of Louis XV's early ministers. A man of ready wit, Maurepas had offended Louis XV by writing a set of clever verses deriding his mistress Madame Pompadour, which had circulated widely through the court. As a result, the angry king had dismissed Maurepas and exiled him to his country estate twenty-five years before the end of his reign. Deciding to bring this man of seventy-three back to the court as his chief adviser, Louis XVI wrote him the following letter:

Monsieur:
In the understandable grief that overwhelms me, which I share with all of the realm, I nevertheless have duties I must fulfill. I am the king and this one word

covers a great many obligations, but I am only twenty [*sic*] years old. I do not think that I have acquired all the knowledge necessary for my position. Moreover, I cannot see any minister because they were all shut up with the king during his illness. I have always heard about your honesty and about the reputation that your extensive knowledge of government affairs has rightly earned for you. That is what leads me to ask you to help me with your advice and your insight. I would be obliged to you, sir, if you would come as soon as possible to Choisy, where I will see you with the greatest pleasure.

Louis-Auguste[3]

Maurepas readily accepted the king's offer and was happy to return to power after such a long absence. He acted as minister without portfolio, attending the councils of state with the king and meeting frequently with him to discuss policy. The strengths and weaknesses that Maurepas brought to his high position were described by a contemporary in the following terms:

He was prepossessing and easy, ... flexible, fertile in stratagems for attack, resources for defence, feints to elude, evasions, repartees to laugh down serious opposition, and expedients for retrieving false steps, and surmounting difficulties: he seized, with the eye of a lynx, the weak points, or the singularities of men; was master of the art of imperceptibly drawing them into his snare, or leading them into his views, and of the still more formidable talent of ridiculing everything, even merit, when he wished to depreciate it."[4]

Abbé Véri recorded in his journal an enlightening account of the young king's early interaction with Maurepas after the latter had urged him not to wait any longer to make the important decisions about which ministers he wished to retain in his council and whom he would appoint to replace any ministers whom he did not wish to have continue in their posts.

"But what do you expect?" said the king. "I am overwhelmed with governmental affairs and I am only twenty. All of this upsets me."

[Maurepas replied:] "Only by making a decision can you end this difficult situation. Leave the details and papers to your ministers and limit yourself to choosing men of goodwill and integrity. You have always told me that you wanted to have a council of honest ministers. Is this what you have? If not, change them."

"You are right," said the king, "but I haven't got up my courage to do so. Just four months ago I was accustomed to being afraid when I spoke with a minister."[5]

After Louis XVI made an important decision later that day about whom he would appoint as two of his ministers, Maurepas said to him: "Sire, I am afraid that I spoke with too much force this morning and crossed the boundary of respect. I ask your pardon; I was too worked up." Louis XVI replied graciously: "Oh, don't worry. I am convinced of your integrity and that suffices. You will always make me happy by speaking the truth with vigor; that is what I need."[6]

Another indication of the young monarch's humility appears in the report that Ambassador Stormont sent to London during the early days of the reign:

> His most Christian majesty did by no means ... betray the least impatience to reign; but on the contrary ... a real apprehension of being raised so early to the throne.... He speaks of his inability, inexperience, and total ignorance, in a manner which ... does him honor, and gives room to hope that he will endeavor to learn.... The clear precise manner in which he answered the questions put to him by his ministers, indicate[s] an aptitude to business, and tho' those questions were not very material, carr[ies] marks of a good, plain, natural understanding....
>
> The strongest and most decided features of this king's character are a love of justice, a general desire of doing well, a passion for economy, and an abhorrence of all the excesses of the last reign. He heard much whilst he was dauphin of the consequences of those excesses.... He is strongly bent on correcting those abuses, and sets about it with the eager impatience of a parsimonious son who succeeds to a prodigal father....
>
> He certainly does not consult the queen openly, and he has been heard to say more than once that women ought not to meddle with politics. Were she to attempt to take a decided lead, she would probably lose all her power, but she is too wise and too well advised to take so unguarded a step. She will I imagine employ the much surer arts of insinuation and address, attempt to guide him by a secret line and try to make him follow, whilst he thinks he leads.[7]

In a 1771 journal entry, Abbé Véri noted that those who had previously thought that the young king was lazy and interested only in hunting were mistaken: "Hunting was only one of his occupations; he immersed himself in council business perhaps too much."[8] One of the most important council decisions Louis XVI made was to appoint to the important post of foreign minister the count of Vergennes, who shared his desire to keep France out of any more wars. As Abbé Véri noted in his journal, "Louis XVI's pacific character, which indicates no taste for troops, can only diminish the military spirit."[9] Many of the letters that Louis XVI wrote to Vergennes were preserved by the latter's descendants, who allowed historians Paul and Pierrette Girault de Coursac to photograph these documents, many of which they included in their 1997 collection of letters and speeches of Louis XVI.[10]

Another major office the king had to fill was that of controller-general, or financial director. To this position he appointed Anne Robert Turgot. Turgot was a leading representative of the physiocrats, a group of intellectuals who believed that land was the source of wealth and that revenues should be raised primarily by a tax on land. As a devout Catholic, Louis XVI was troubled by the fact that Turgot did not attend mass, but he was impressed by Turgot's brilliant performance as intendant at Limoges, where he had carried out many innovative reforms in agriculture and grain commerce. Voltaire and other philosophes were delighted with the appointment, thinking it heralded a new age of reform in France.

One of the most pressing issues Louis XVI faced in the early months of his reign was a growing demand for the reinstatement of the Parlement of Paris, a judicial body that had over the years assumed the prerogative of approving governmental edicts before they became law. This power was limited in practice because the king could, through a maneuver called a *lit de justice*, appear in person at a session of the Parlement and overturn its veto. Unfortunately, the Parlements of the eighteenth century had evolved into rather reactionary bodies, with the noble magistrates who made up the Parlements attempting to defend the privileges of the nobility against various reforms proposed by the monarchy. Louis XV had become so exasperated with the Parlement of Paris that in 1771 he had exiled all its members to Auvergne. Voltaire had applauded the king's action, saying: "Have they not often been persecuting and barbarous? ... For myself, I think that the King is right, and since it is necessary to serve, I would rather do so under a lion of good pedigree ... than under two hundred rats of my own kind."[11] Maurepas believed, however, that Louis XVI should reinstate the Parlement of Paris and convinced him that it would be an appropriate measure to mark the beginning of his reign. With great reservations Louis XVI finally agreed to recall the Parlement. He made it clear to the magistrates, however, that they were not to engage in the stubborn opposition that had led to their previous exile.

One of Louis XVI's first public duties was to give a speech to the newly recalled Parlement. Abbé Véri recorded that the king's advisers wished to prepare him thoroughly for the occasion because his grandfather Louis XV had been so timid about public speaking that he could hardly read four sentences at once. To their concerns, Louis XVI simply replied, "Why do you think I would be afraid?" The speech, which he gave from memory, was a great success according to Véri, who praised his "firm and forceful tone" and remarked that the young king's excellent performance was the talk of Versailles.[12]

The Parlement of Paris numbered among its leaders Chrétien de Malesherbes, a liberal thinker of high personal integrity who was not only a talented lawyer but also carried out botanical research. From 1750 to 1763, Malesherbes was director of the press for France and served as the chief censor. He took a very liberal view toward censorship, however, allowing many of the works of philosophes like Voltaire and Rousseau to be published. In fact,

Voltaire commented toward the end of Malesherbes's tenure as chief censor, "Monsieur de Malesherbes has rendered infinite services to human genius by giving a greater liberty to the press than it has ever known before — we are already more than half Englishmen."[13] Malesherbes explained his approach to censorship in this way: "It is not in rigor that a remedy should be sought, but in tolerance. The trade in books today is too widespread and the public is too avid for them for it to be possible to constrain it.... So I only know one way to enforce prohibitions, and that is to issue very few of them. They will only be respected when they are rare."[14]

It was during Malesherbe's tenure in office that many of the volumes of Diderot's *Encyclopédie* were published, although in 1752 the appearance of his second volume elicited sharp criticism because of his statements against religion. Diderot's religious critics pressured Malesherbes to order a search of Diderot's home to seize other manuscripts he was writing. As it turned out, no manuscripts could be found because Malesherbes had offered his own home to Diderot as a place to hide his manuscripts before he ordered the search.[15]

As a leader in the Parlement of Paris and a friend of Turgot, Malesherbes hoped to help marshal support for the latter's programs in the Parlement. Within a few months of the recall of the Parlement to Paris, however, Turgot decided it would be still more beneficial to have Malesherbes in the king's council as minister of the royal household, where he would have control over court expenditures and the lucrative appointments so avidly sought by courtiers. This position would enable Malesherbes to effect the economies that Turgot needed in order to hold down taxes and deficits.

Although Malesherbes had no real desire to become involved in court politics and believed that he had no gift for administrative detail, he retreated to his country estate to consider the matter. Soon after his arrival there, he received letters from both Turgot and the king. Turgot indicated that if Malesherbes did not accept the position, all hope of reform was lost. The king also made a strong appeal in a letter that he asked Abbé Véri to give in person to Malesherbes:

> Turgot has explained to me your distaste for the position I have offered you. I continue to think that your love of the public welfare will conquer your reluctance. You cannot imagine how happy you would make me if you accept this position for at least a while if you are unwilling to commit yourself permanently. I believe that this is absolutely necessary for the good of the country.[15]

Under this pressure, Malesherbes accepted the position, but the rest of the court did not know quite what to make of him. A jovial and friendly person, he did not enjoy court formality. Courtiers raised their eyebrows when he continued to wear his plain magistrate's costume instead of more elaborate court dress. Unfortunately, he began his term of office in the queen's disfavor because she had proposed one of her favorites for the position. In his journal, Abbé Véri quoted Louis XVI's response to her suggestion: "Those are your wishes, Madame; I am aware of them and that suffices. It is up to me to make the decision."[16]

One of the philosophes who was particularly pleased with the appointments of Malesherbes and Turgot was the eminent mathematician d'Alembert, who wrote in a letter to Frederick II of Prussia: "Your praises of our young monarch are justified. He has made an excellent choice of ministers, and he has just named ... the man who is probably the most respected person in the entire nation, Malesherbes, who will work with Turgot for order and economy. There is great alarm in the camp des fripons [of the rascals]. Between Turgot and Malesherbes the future of these persons will be unhappy."[17]

Malesherbes's responsibilities included the supervision of the prison system of the Parisian region, and he began implementing reforms at once. One of the chief abuses he sought to correct was the use of *lettres de cachet*. These sealed orders from the king in most cases condemned the person named to immediate and indefinite exile to their country estate or another part of France. In the more dreaded cases, however, they condemned the person to imprisonment without trial. *Lettres de cachet* were used for a variety of reasons; nobles occasionally even requested them for a family member whose notorious conduct, often of a sexual nature, they did not wish to have openly discussed in a judicial court. In this period *lettres de cachet* were much less frequently abused than they had been in the past, but they still represented an enormous potential for tyrannical use by an unscrupulous minister or anyone else who could persuade the king to sign one. They were a symbol of autocracy that Malesherbes wished to eliminate, asserting that "no citizen is assured that he will not see his liberty sacrificed to personal vengeance, for no one is powerful enough to escape the hatred of a minister or insignificant enough not to merit that of a clerk."[18]

Malesherbes recognized that the abolition of the *lettres de cachet* would both serve the king's self-interest and promote basic principles of justice, as he stated in a memorandum to the king: "Your greatest concern is that your authority should be not only respected but also blessed and cherished, and that it should be no longer the occasion for murmuring and complaints. In rendering it more dear, you will also make it more secure. The justice of kings and the love of peoples are the most solid foundations of authority."[19]

Although Malesherbes would have preferred to have the *lettres de cachet* totally eliminated, Maurepas convinced him that the king's advisers would never allow this to happen. Louis XVI did agree, however, to a compromise whereby a special court was established to review all requests for *lettres de cachet*, thus preventing them from being completely arbitrary. Malesherbes endeavored to have this review procedure formalized by law, but he did not succeed in attaining this goal. In his frustration he wrote to a friend: "I never would have believed that the support of the king is the feeblest of all supports that a reforming minister can have. We had the king on our side, ... but the court was against us, and courtiers are now more powerful than kings."[20]

The *lettres de cachet* were not the only evil Malesherbes wished to correct in the penal system. Conditions within the prisons (with the exception of the Bastille, surprisingly enough) were generally appalling. An English reformer, John Howard, discovered upon visiting the Bicêtre prison in Paris that as many as fifty people might be crowded into a small dungeon. Moreover, there were no fireplaces in any of the rooms where the prisoners were kept; as a consequence hundreds of prisoners died from the cold during the severe winter of 1775.[21] When Malesherbes visited several of these prisons, he was so shocked by the conditions he saw that he declared to Maurepas that Louis XVI himself should see the prisons. But Maurepas's response was: "The king must not go. If he sees the prisons, there will be no more prisoners."[22] The comment reveals much about the king's character. Although Louis XVI did not visit the prisons, he did support Malesherbes in his reform of conditions and authorized him to review the cases of present inmates to ensure no one had been unjustly imprisoned. Several years later Louis XVI abolished the "preparatory question"— the use of torture to obtain confessions from accused persons.

Louis XVI's strong desire for social justice also appears in a 1775 passage from Abbé Véri's journal in which he related that Turgot had told him of the king's wish to eliminate slavery in the colonies by paying the slave owners for their slaves.[23] Louis XVI thought that it would be possible to carry out this plan a decade hence, but by that time, France was in such financial turmoil that this expensive project was not feasible.

Religious intolerance could be dealt with more easily than the slavery question. Malesherbes was responsible for overseeing all religious affairs in the country, and with Turgot's assistance he tried to bring about a greater measure of toleration for Protestants and other religious minorities, a policy welcomed by the king. Turgot and Malesherbes also wished to reduce the financial privileges of the Catholic Church, which controlled vast amounts of property on which it paid virtually no taxes, only making voluntary gifts to the Crown. Voltaire and other philosophes seconded these attempts at reform. The support of the latter men rapidly undermined the cause, however, because it encouraged the Devout party at court to accuse Turgot and Malesherbes of seeking to diminish the power and authority of the church.

In his attempts to reduce court expenditures, Malesherbes fared little better. With a long tradition of ostentatious display in the most dazzling court of Europe behind them, few of the courtiers were willing to adopt a more austere lifestyle. Louis himself had no great love of luxury and would have been willing to cut back on expenditures, but his two brothers, Marie Antoinette, and all their friends did not wish to relinquish their lavish style of life. At last a discouraged Malesherbes reminded the king that he had agreed to serve for only a short time. Taking leave of the artificial life of Versailles, he set off to collect botanical specimens on a walking tour of the Alps and Pyrenees.

Turgot was also having problems achieving his desired economic reforms. One of the chief elements in his plan was to abolish the "corvée," a practice whereby the peasants had to spend a certain number of days every year building and repairing the public roads, without pay for their labor. Turgot planned to eliminate this practice, which amounted to involuntary servitude, by levying a tax on landowners to fund a government department to maintain the roads. But the clergy and nobles, who were the chief landowners of France, rose up in wrath at this suggestion. Representing their reactionary point of view, a member of the Parlement of Paris said: "All public financial burdens should be borne by the lower orders. These are subject by virtue of their birth to the imposition of the taille [a land tax from which the clergy and nobles were exempt] and, without any limitations whatever, to the corvée."[24]

Alexis de Tocqueville, who wrote a fascinating book titled *The Old Regime and the Revolution*, was Malesherbes's great-grandson. The Revolution touched Tocqueville's family deeply because Malesherbes, his daughter Mme. de Rosambo (who was Tocqueville's grandmother), her husband, and her sister and the latter's husband were all guillotined in 1794. (The revolutionaries never forgave Malesherbes for having volunteered at the age of seventy-three to defend the king in his trial.) Tocqueville's mother and father were also imprisoned but were lucky enough to escape the daily roll call announcing the prisoners who were to be sent to the guillotine because the Reign of Terror suddenly ended with the death of Robespierre. Tocqueville wrote to a friend how the tragedy of the king's death had pervaded his childhood: "Everyone wept, not over all the personal hardships we had suffered, nor even over so many relatives that we had lost during the civil war and on the scaffold, but over the fate of that man who died more than fifteen years ago."[25]

Tocqueville notes in his book that in Louis XVI's preamble to his statement suggesting that the corvée be eliminated, he said:

Almost all the roads of the kingdom have been made by the poorest group of our subjects, without pay. All the weight has therefore fallen on those who have nothing but their hands, and are only very remotely interested in the roads; the truly interested are the landowners, almost all privileged, whose property is increased in value by the establishment of roads. In forcing the poor man alone to maintain them, in making him give his time and labor without pay, we take away from him the only resource he has against poverty and hunger, in order to make him work for the profit of the rich.[26]

Turgot also tried to reduce the power of the guilds controlling the various crafts and small manufacturing shops, which decreed such standards as the terms for apprenticeship and the requirements for becoming a master craftsman. In effect, these guilds had acted to restrict opportunity and commerce, but Turgot's proposed reform only created another group of enemies for him among the leaders of the guilds, who held more power than did their workers, as Tocqueville notes:

> When there was an attempt, at the same time, to dismantle the hindrances that the trade-guild system imposed on workers, and it was proclaimed in the name of the king "that the right to work is the most sacred of all properties; that any law which diminishes it violates natural law and must be considered null and void; that the existing guilds are, furthermore, bizarre and tyrannical institutions, the product of egotism, greed, and violence," such words were perilous. What was still more dangerous was to pronounce them in vain. Several months later the corvée and the guilds were reestablished.[27]

The most vital component of Turgot's broad plan for reform was the abolition of the restrictions and duties preventing free commerce in grain among the different sections of France. He received Louis XVI's backing for this policy, but unfortunately its implementation occurred in the fall of 1774 after a bad harvest. By the following spring, severe grain shortages led to widespread fears that speculators would corner the uncontrolled market, thereby driving up prices. Riots broke out in various parts of the country, and in Dijon a mill was destroyed. Demonstrators even marched on the markets of Versailles. Turgot was convinced that the powerful interests aligned against him had fomented these rebellions, and he offered as proof the fact that large sums of money were found on many of the rioters. There were in fact many government officials who had profited heavily by collecting the taxes levied on the shipment of grain from one region to another, and these men were intent upon preventing free trade in grain. The king backed Turgot in implementing strong measures to suppress the riots, but the damage to the grain policy was irreversible.

In his journal, Abbé Véri credits Louis with "a courageous spirit and sangfroid one would not have expected because of his age and his nonviolent temperament." According to Véri, Louis said to Turgot after the Versailles riot, in which several of the rioters were killed, "We have a good conscience on our side and in that position we are truly strong."[28] Louis XVI was only twenty-one at the time; as he grew older, he would become increasingly unwilling to order action that might lead to bloodshed.

Turgot's days were numbered, however. He was increasingly isolated at court, as nearly everyone had some vested interest that would be hampered by his far-ranging reforms. To compound the difficulty of his situation, he was a blunt man, with no gift for the art of persuasion. This rendered his continual lectures to the other ministers in the king's council particularly irksome. Even Louis himself once remarked that Turgot always thought that only his ideas were correct.[29]

In his desire for economy, Turgot even argued against spending the money necessary for Louis to be crowned in Rheims according to the centuries-old tradition. He suggested instead that it would be much cheaper to hold the ceremonies in Paris. Louis insisted, however, upon being crowned in the same cathedral as his ancestors, and the ceremony took place there in June 1775. The duke of Croÿ recorded his impression of that memorable day in his journal:

> I know that I have never before experienced such enthusiasm. I was totally amazed to find myself in tears and to see everyone else in the same state.... The king seemed truly moved by this beautiful moment.... Our king attired with all the brilliance of royalty, on the true throne, was a sight that was so impressive it is difficult to describe.... The king, with the beautiful crown upon his head and the scepter in his hand ... walked down the aisle in a very striking way. [30]

The coronation was a high point in Louis XVI's life. After the exhilarating days in Rheims were over, he had to return to the difficult job of governing France. In early 1776 the king supported Turgot for the last time, sending six of his important edicts to the Parlement of Paris to be registered. When the Parlement refused to approve them, Louis was forced to summon the magistrates to Versailles for a *lit de justice* so that he could through his own presence force the registration of the decrees. It was a victory won by a very young king over an increasingly resentful and recalcitrant Parlement. Support for Turgot had so far eroded that in May 1776 Louis reluctantly dismissed him. It was a move Voltaire deeply regretted, and he expressed himself in strong terms to his correspondents: "It is a disaster. I see nothing before me now but death. I am struck to the heart by this blow, and shall never be consoled for having seen the beginning and the end of the golden age which Turgot was preparing for us."[31]

Many years later, at the height of the Revolution, Malesherbes had begun to question whether some of the physiocratic ideas that he, Turgot, and Voltaire found appealing were in fact appropriate for France at that point.

The free commerce in grain, for example, was a contributing factor to the steep rise in the cost of bread in the summer of 1789 that followed a disastrous harvest the preceding summer and fall. Malesherbes wrote: "Turgot and I were terribly honest men with a passion for good. We knew mankind only from books. Without knowing it and without wishing it, we contributed to the Revolution."[32]

3

Marie Antoinette's Lifestyle

While Turgot was urging economy, Marie Antoinette was spending large sums on balls, gambling, and various court entertainments. In March 1775 the official in charge of royal entertainments recorded in his journal that the queen had spent a huge sum on balls that month; much of the expense was attributable to the lavish use of gold embroidery. Saint-Priest, one of the king's later ministers, was critical of the queen's conduct: "A taste for adornment, the pursuit of luxury, and frivolity increased rapidly. The queen, who was more carried along by the current rather than directing it, let all this happen without much reflection. The king, who preferred a simple, quiet life and liked to avoid unnecessary expenditure, let this torrent flow and stopped nothing."[1]

Marie Antoinette not only dominated the French court, she also left a strong impression upon foreign visitors such as Horace Walpole, who wrote to a friend after attending a ball where she was present: "It was impossible to see anything but the Queen! Hebes, and Floras, and Helens and Graces, are streetwalkers to her. She is a statue of beauty, when sitting or walking; grace itself when she moves."[2] In another letter, Walpole recalled the first time he saw her when she had not yet become queen, "She was going after the late King [Louis XV] to chapel, and shot through the room like an aërial being, all brightness and grace and without seeming to touch earth."[3]

One of the more unusual features of the fetish for adornment that Marie Antoinette encouraged at the court was the creation of elaborate hair styles augmented with false hair pieces, which often rose so high that women had to kneel in their carriages. Abbé Véri wrote in his journal, "Feathers and coiffures that are ridiculously large will end just like all such childish behavior, but in the meantime this style has spread to all corners of the kingdom." Véri also expressed a more general criticism: "The balls, the parties, the adornment, and all the follies of youth have been pushed beyond all reasonable bounds."[4]

Although Marie Antoinette loved the sumptuous pleasures of the court, she found its rigorous etiquette maddening in comparison with the more relaxed life she had known at the Austrian court. The king and queen could not even retire for the evening or get dressed in the morning without following an elaborate and detailed ritual. In her memoirs Mme. de Campan, one of the queen's ladies-in-waiting, described the difficulties to which this etiquette could lead:

> The lady of honor ... handed the chemise. When a princess of the royal family was present for the ceremony, the lady of honor ceded to her this function, but did not cede directly to the princess. In this case, the lady of honor returned the chemise to one of the lesser ladies-in-waiting who then presented it to the princess.... One winter day the queen was undressed, waiting for her chemise. I held it spread out; the lady of honor came in, hurriedly took off her gloves, and took the chemise. Then someone knocked on the door; it was the Duchess of Orléans. Taking off her gloves, she came forward to take the chemise, but the Lady of Honor was not allowed to hand it to her. She passed it to me, and I gave it to the duchess. Once again someone knocked; it was the Countess de Provence. The duchess handed her the chemise. The queen stood there with her arms folded on her chest, looking cold. The countess, seeing how uncomfortable she looked, just threw off her shawl, keeping on her gloves, but while putting the chemise on the queen, she disarranged her hair. The queen began to laugh to cover her impatience, but not before I heard her mutter, "It's disgusting!"[5]

Privacy was not a royal prerogative. All day long crowds of curious people wandered through the rooms of Versailles because it was the custom to allow virtually anyone to enter the palace freely. An English writer named Arthur Young, noted for his works on agriculture, was traveling through France at this time to study its agricultural practices. He recorded in his diary his amazement at such a custom: "In viewing the king's apartment, which he had not left a quarter of an hour, with those slight traits of disorder that showed he lived in it, it was amusing to see the blackguard figures that were walking uncontrolled about the palace, and even in his bed-chamber; men whose rags betrayed them to be in the last stage of poverty, and I was the only person that stared and wondered how the devil they got there."[6]

Mme. de Campan described yet another longstanding but annoying custom that invaded the royal family's privacy:

> One of the traditions that the queen found most disagreeable was that of dining every day in public. Marie Leczinska [the wife of Louis XV] had always followed this exhausting custom; Marie Antoinette observed this practice while she was the dauphiness. The dauphin dined with her, and each household of the family had a public dinner every day. The officials let anyone come in who was properly dressed; this spectacle delighted all the provincials. At the dinner hour, the staircases were filled with people who, after having seen the dauphiness eat her soup,

went to see the princes eat their boullion, and then ran breathlessly to see the king's aunts eat their dessert.[7]

To escape from all this irritating formality and ritual, the queen would frequently retire with her intimate friends to the Petit Trianon, a small château somewhat separated from the main palace. Louis XV had built the Petit Trianon for his mistress Madame de Pompadour, and Louis XVI gave the gem-like little château to Marie Antoinette. In the English gardens nearby, she ordered the construction of a small farm of charming half-timbered and thatched buildings. Here animals were kept so that she and her friends could play at being shepherdesses and milkmaids. This "hamlet" helped Marie Antoinette dispel her boredom for a year or so until she tired of it and turned to other diversions.

The queen was prone to form close friendships, and she became particularly close to two young women. The first was Princess Lamballe, whose devotion to Marie Antoinette eventually prompted her to return from a safe haven abroad to be by the queen's side during the darker days of the Revolution. She met a horrible death during the September prison massacres, probably because she was so closely identified with the queen in the eyes of the mob. Marie Antoinette's other close friend was the duchess of Polignac, a young woman whose striking beauty is evident in her portrait painted by Vigée Le Brun. (Le Brun was the artist who painted the most famous portraits of Marie Antoinette.) The duchess brought to Versailles a whole tribe of family members of limited means, whom the queen provided with lucrative court appointments. The duchess of Polignac eventually held the very high post of governess to the royal children.

Confining herself to a small circle of companions, including Princess Lamballe, the duchess of Polignac, and various lively young people of the court, the queen ignored most of the other courtiers. These courtiers were often offended and began to dislike her and to murmur complaints against her. Many courtiers also resented her steadily increasing interference in matters of state. In Vienna, Maria Theresa was deeply worried about Marie Antoinette's attempts to become involved in French politics and wrote to Ambassador Mercy that she had always been concerned about her daughter's frivolity and lack of application, as well as her headstrong ways.[8]

When Maria Theresa was shown a letter in which Marie Antoinette boasted to an Austrian friend, Count Rosenberg, about unseating a minister she hated, the empress wrote to Mercy to tell him how angry and dismayed her daughter's letter had made her: "What a style! What a way to think! This confirms only too much my concerns that she is running quickly to her ruin."[9] The empress's reaction was not excessive because in her letter to Rosenberg,

Marie Antoinette had gleefully boasted with regard to the dismissal of a minister she hated, "His departure was entirely my doing." She then explained how she had manipulated the king, whom she referred to as "the poor man," into arranging an interview for her with an important statesman who was key to her plot to have her enemy dismissed.[10]

Maria Theresa's son Joseph eventually succeeded his mother to the Austrian throne; he had already become Holy Roman Emperor in 1765. He enjoyed traveling abroad incognito, and in the spring of 1777 he spent six weeks in Versailles under the name of Count Falkenstein so that he could spend some time with the queen and also meet the king. Although he arrived incognito and slept in an inn in Paris during his visit, everyone soon knew who he was and appreciated his open and friendly manner. Joseph had ample opportunity to become acquainted with all the members of the royal family. Shortly after he arrived, he was invited to a private family dinner in the apartments of Provence, one of the king's brothers. Joseph's description of the unusual evening to Ambassador Mercy was part of the long report that Mercy sent to Maria Theresa shortly after the emperor left France.

> The dinner was beyond gay, at least in the conduct of the king and his brothers. They were so much at ease that after everyone had left the table, they amused themselves in childish horseplay, running across the room and jumping on the sofas. The queen and the princesses were embarrassed to have them behave in this way in front of the emperor, but he pretended to ignore their behavior while he continued a conversation with the princesses. Madame [Provence's wife] finally lost her patience and told her husband that she had never seen him act so childishly. All this ended, however, without the emperor letting on how surprised he was by such a strange spectacle.[11]

Mercy's report of what occurred that evening is indeed a startling view of what could occasionally happen behind the scenes in a palace where all public conduct followed a rigid protocol. It is worth noting that at this time the king was 22, his brother Provence was 21, and his brother Artois was 19, while Joseph had reached the more sedate age of 35.

There is at least one other instance in the Vienna archives of a surprising behind-the-scenes event. In June 1772, two years after Marie Antoinette's arrival in France, Mercy wrote to Maria Theresa to tell her about an incident he had just learned about from Marie Antoinette (even though she had told him that on no account was he to mention what had happened in his reports back to Vienna). On the occasion that Marie Antoinette described, she and the seventeen-year-old dauphin were in his brother Provence's apartment when Louis had accidentally dropped a piece of porcelain that Provence had asked him not to touch. Provence was furious to see it smashed into pieces and rushed at the dauphin. They started hitting each other with their fists, to the dismay of Marie Antoinette, who succeeded in separating them with no more damage than a scratch on her hand. Peace was fortunately soon reestablished. When she told Mercy that she had been about to call for help, he replied that it would have been a great mistake to have allowed the incident to become public, given that the consequences for Provence would have been serious because of the special position Louis held as the heir to the throne. Mercy used the incident to impress upon Marie Antoinette that it was very important for Louis and her to always remain aware of their superior position vis-à-vis his brothers.[12]

The position of Louis XVI and Marie Antoinette was also very much in Joseph's mind when he arrived in 1777. While he loved to travel and wanted to gather ideas for improving life in Austria, his trip to France had two principal goals. The first was to attempt to understand why no heir to the French throne had yet been born. The second goal was to try to judge the extent of the queen's gambling and other reckless behavior, reports of which were alarming both Joseph and Maria Theresa. Both issues were of paramount importance not only to France but also to the alliance between Austria and France.

The first goal of Joseph's visit was highly successful because Louis XVI and he quickly established a very friendly relationship and he spent many hours with the king. In their frequent private meetings, their conversation turned on at least one occasion to intimate sexual details about what was happening in the royal marriage bed. Joseph's visit and marital advice apparently had enormous consequences because the king and queen were able to conceive their first child ten months later.

In his long report to Maria Theresa, Mercy noted that the king had explained his sexual problem in graphic detail and had asked his brother-in-law for advice. After remarking that he would let Joseph communicate directly to his mother the intimate details of what the king told him, Mercy stated, "I only wish to remark that despite the king's natural taciturnity and his shy personality he poured out his feelings to his august brother-in-law in a way that no one would have believed possible."[13]

In his biography of Joseph II, Derek Beales includes a very frank letter that Joseph sent back to Austria; this letter was not printed in Arneth and Geoffrey's *Correspondance secrete* because of its extremely graphic sexual detail. As Beales notes, only beginning in the 1950s would anyone have published such a letter:

> Imagine! In his marriage bed — this is the secret — he has strong, perfectly satisfactory erections. He introduces the member, stays there for perhaps two minutes without moving, withdraws without ever discharging but still erect, and bids good night. It's incredible, because in addition he sometimes has night-time

emissions, but in his bed, never when on the job, and he's happy, saying simply that he only does it out of duty and gets no pleasure from it. Ah! If I could have been present once, I should have arranged it properly. He needs to be whipped, to make him discharge in a passion, like donkeys. Further, my sister is pretty placid, and they're two incompetents together.[14]

Louis XVI's failure to engage in what should have been an instinctive rhythmic movement once he had penetrated his wife could be an indication that he did indeed have phimosis, which would have made such movement painful. That pain, as well as the lack of a climax, would probably be reasons that he viewed intercourse as a duty, not a pleasure. Joseph's comment about Marie Antoinette does fit with the impression one receives in various accounts of her life that suggest that she was a charming and beautiful young woman who reveled in the admiration of others but did not have a strong sensual or sexual nature. Twenty-first century readers of the preceding frank letter will undoubtedly be surprised that when these two young people first began their love life (when Louis was fifteen and Marie Antoinette only fourteen) they were extremely naïve about the whole process and that naïveté continued for seven years. It is worth remembering, however, that in the middle of the eighteenth century people were not witnessing scenes of intercourse on television or movie screens or even reading about them in full detail in novels.

The second goal of Joseph's visit to Versailles, his desire to convince Marie Antoinette that her gambling was a dangerous habit, was less successful, although he did establish an excellent rapport with his young sister. In fact, he reported in a letter home that he found her so "pleasant and charming" that he would have liked to have married her had she not been his sister.[15] But even while he was charmed by her, he was extremely alarmed by what he was learning about her behavior. Again Ambassador Mercy's report to Maria Theresa provides us with detail:

His majesty told me that the night before, to please the queen, he had accompanied her to a gathering hosted by the Princess de Guéménée. He reported that he was shocked by the low atmosphere and the licentious behavior at this woman's home. His majesty saw them playing pharon [a card game] and heard people in the presence of the queen accuse their hostess of cheating. The emperor was indignant about this indecent evening and emphatically told the queen that this house was a disreputable gambling den. The queen tried to say otherwise, and she even returned to this princess's party after midnight on the pretext that she had promised to do so. The emperor was mortified by her behavior and discouraged by her obstinacy.[16]

When Joseph left France, he presented Marie Antoinette with a long letter full of extremely perceptive advice about changing her conduct. The letter is of particular importance because if she had taken its advice to heart and changed her lifestyle, she would not have been so hated by the people of France and the course of the Revolution might well have been different. The following excerpts indicate the many topics covered in the letter:

What are you here in France to accomplish, what right have you to respect and honor except as the king's companion? You run the risk of being humiliated, beautiful as you are, and such a fall would be frightful for you. What is your place in the king's heart, and especially in his esteem? Are you doing everything possible to please him? Do you analyze his desires and his character so that you can conform to them? Do you try to make him prefer above every other object or pastime your company and the pleasure you can provide him? ... Do you make yourself essential to him? Do you persuade him that no one loves him more sincerely and has his glory and happiness more at heart? Does he see your affections uniquely concentrated on him so that you make him shine without regard to yourself? ... Are you totally discreet about his faults and weaknesses? Do you excuse them and silence anyone who dares to comment upon his faults? ...

When you are with him do you try to be sociable and tender? Do you seek out such opportunities, do you try to react to the feelings he shows? Are you cold and distracted when he caresses you or talks to you? Do you appear bored, even disgusted? If that is the case, how would you expect a cold man to try to get close to you and finally love you? This point requires all your attention, and everything you can do to achieve this great goal will be the strongest element in your future happiness. Never let yourself become discouraged and always sustain in him the hope that he may yet have children, so that he never gives up on the idea or despairs of ever having any. You must avoid such negative thoughts and the habit of sleeping in different beds with all your power, which rests in your charms and your friendship....

Have you weighed the frightful consequences of games of chance and the company associated with them, the atmosphere surrounding them, the disruption that they cause in every way to the fortunes and the habits of an entire country?

How can you ignore the fact that the sensible people in Europe hold you responsible for the ruin of many young people because of the evils associated with gambling, the abominations that result from it, if you protect and expand these games, or even worse if you seek them out. It is a question of such great consequence and such obvious danger that I leave it to your judgment to ponder it further. Remember the incidents that you have witnessed and then consider that the king does not gamble and that it is scandalous that you alone support these games. Make a noble effort to stop your gambling and all the world will approve your action.

Similarly, take a moment to consider all the disadvantages that you have already incurred by attending the opera balls and the adventures there that you told me about. I can't conceal from you my opinion that of all your dubious pleasures this one is undoubtedly the most inappropriate, especially in the way you attend, for having Monsieur [Provence] accompany you counts for nothing. Why do you want to go there incognito and pretend to be someone else? Do you really believe that you aren't recognized? ... The place is notorious. What are you seeking there? ... Why these adventures, this debauchery? Why mingle with these libertines, prostitutes, and strangers? ...

I must tell you that I have observed that this is the behavior that most scandalizes all those honorable people who love you. The king abandoned all night at Versailles while you mingle with the riffraff of Paris....[17]

Frank as it was, Marie Antoinette tried to accept her brother's advice with a good grace, but it had no lasting effect on her behavior. After he left Versailles, she wrote to her mother:

The emperor's departure has left me feeling an emptiness that I have had trouble shaking off. I was so happy during the short time he was here, and it now seems like a dream to me. But what will never be a dream to me is all the good advice that he gave me, which will be forever written in my heart.

I want to let you know that he gave me something at my request that has given me the greatest pleasure: his advice in writing. That will be my chief reading at present, and if I ever can forget (which I doubt that I will) everything that he has told me, I will always have this paper before me that will remind me of my duty.

My dear mother will have seen by the letter I sent yesterday that the king conducted himself very well during the last moments that my brother was here. I want to assure you that he was deeply affected by my brother's departure.... After he left, when I was most in despair, the king was so attentive and comforted me with such tenderness that I will never forget it. That would make me love him if I didn't already do so.[18]

Although Marie Antoinette spent a considerable amount of time with the king's brothers, Provence and Artois, because she found their company entertaining, while she was still the dauphine she made a very interesting statement in a letter to her mother: "While we [Provence and I] continue to maintain a tone of friendship and cordiality, in fact those feelings are not sincere on either side. I am more and more convinced that if I had to choose a husband among these three brothers, I would still prefer the one that heaven gave me. His character is excellent, and although he is awkward, he always tries to do things that will please me."[19]

While one is entering dubious territory when trying to unravel the psychology of someone who lived over two centuries ago, it is worth considering whether Marie Antoinette might have been a compulsive gambler. The Mayo Clinic's website lists the following as "Signs and symptoms of compulsive (pathologic) gambling":

• Gaining a thrill from taking big gambling risks
• Taking increasingly bigger gambling risks
• A preoccupation with gambling

- Reliving past gambling experiences
- Gambling as a way to escape problems or feelings of helplessness, guilt or depression
- Taking time from work or family life to gamble
- Concealing gambling
- Feeling guilt or remorse after gambling
- Borrowing money or stealing to gamble
- Failed efforts to cut back on gambling
- Lying to hide gambling

All but perhaps the last of these signs and symptoms seem to apply to Marie Antoinette. Mercy had mentioned to Joseph that the queen was running up debts that the king had to find funds to cover.[20] It is worth observing that according to the Mayo website, "Compulsive gambling typically begins in the late teen years." As noted earlier, the queen's deep unhappiness and embarrassment about her failure to become pregnant year after year when all France was impatiently awaiting an heir would certainly be relevant to the fifth sign listed above.

Joseph's failure to change Marie Antoinette's behavior was just one of many failures he may have had in mind when he asked on his deathbed to have the following epitaph placed on his tomb: "Here lies Joseph II, who failed in all he undertook."[21] His bitter request was not carried out, but is of interest in light of his report to his mother that he considered Louis XVI to be a weak king. As Joseph approached the end of his life, a decade of rule during which he had introduced widespread reforms, such as the abolition of the death penalty, had shown him that ruling a large country or empire was not as easy as he had once assumed. A month before his death in 1790, having lost Belgium from his vast empire and facing unrest in Hungary, Joseph II wrote to his brother, who succeeded him as Leopold II:

> I confess to you ... that, humiliated by what has happened to me, seeing that I am unfortunate in everything I undertake, the appalling ingratitude with which my good arrangements are received and I am treated — for there is now no conceivable insolence or curse that people do not allow themselves to utter about me publicly — all this makes me doubt myself, I no longer dare to have an opinion and put it into effect, I allow myself to be ruled by the advice of the ministers even when I don't think it is the best, since I dare not hold out for my own view and indeed I haven't the strength to impose it and argue for it.[22]

Much of Joseph II's bitter statement can also be applied to Louis XVI, particularly during the last two or three years of his reign, but in contrast to the emperor the king never became bitter and he faced death with great equanimity, having been much less ambitious and egotistical than his brother-in-law and more willing to focus on the world beyond politics and government.

One of the reasons that Maria Theresa and Joseph had been so concerned about Marie Antoinette's behavior was that they frequently read French newspaper accounts describing her love of gambling and her attendance at masked balls in Paris. This period was also unfortunately characterized by an abundance of scurrilous anonymous pamphlets, and many began to appear that attacked Marie Antoinette in gutter language and spread scandalous lies about her conduct. Her close friendships with women were frequently attacked as suspect. In early 1778 Abbé Véri described one pamphlet published in London that focused on Marie Antoinette, Princess Lamballe, and some of her other close female friends.[23] This pamphlet was almost certainly one of those making the accusation that the queen had lesbian relationships with these women because she asked the king to buy up the entire edition. He did so and had it stored under seals in the Bastille. It was a very expensive maneuver, however, and even such a purchase could not guarantee that copies would not continue to circulate. Marie Antoinette was also reputed to have many male lovers. One pamphlet appearing after the Revolution began accused her of having slept with many of the officers in the National Guard.

There has been some speculation that the king's brothers, Provence and Artois, may have secretly been behind some of these pamphlets. Provence was a brilliant but rather sly young man, while Artois was an athletic dandy and libertine. Because neither shared Louis XVI's high moral character, it is conceivable that they could have lent themselves to this kind of intrigue. By implying that the king would not be the father of any children the queen would bear, they could put themselves and Artois's sons in line to succeed him. Louis XVI's cousin, the duke of Orléans, clearly did everything he could for many years to undermine the position of the king because he hoped that as the representative of the other Bourbon line descended from the Sun King, Louis XIV, he might someday replace his cousin.

The venomous tone of most of the pamphlets is so extreme, however, that it suggests that there was also a darker psychological motivation on the part of people who resented the queen as a symbol of beauty, wealth, and power. The many pamphlets suggesting that Marie Antoinette was carrying on lesbian relationships with her close friends, the duchess of Polignac and Princess Lamballe, clearly had a homophobic impetus. One pamphlet was even illustrated with an engraving of Marie Antoinette kissing one of these women in an erotic way. No evidence has surfaced, however, of any such lesbian relationship, although cinema directors sometimes cannot resist the appeal of the topic. A veritable sewer of slurs and slanders was to follow Marie Antoinette to her death, culminating in the terrible accusation during her trial before a Revolutionary court that she had had incestuous relations with her eight-year-old son to sap him of the strength he would need to rule France.[24]

The only man other than the king who may have been Marie Antoinette's lover was the handsome Swedish officer, Count Axel de Fersen. As part of his education, Fersen's father, a field marshal in the Swedish army and a former ambassador to France, sent his son to France for a five-month visit. It was in 1774 during this trip that Fersen first encountered Marie Antoinette when they were both only eighteen and her husband had not yet succeeded to the throne. She approached the handsome and charming young Swede at a masked ball at the opera in Paris and spoke with him at some length.

Four years later Fersen returned to France to continue his military training. In a 1778 letter to his father, he called Marie Antoinette "the most beautiful and agreeable princess that I know."[25] By this point, she had included Fersen in her circle of close friends who gathered for special parties at the Petit Trianon. Her marked interest in him and his own attraction to the queen were probably strong reasons why Fersen decided that it would be prudent to leave Versailles to pursue his military career elsewhere. After spending a while on the coast of the English Channel as part of a French military group that was pondering an attempt to cross the Channel and invade England, Fersen left France to fight in the American Revolution as an aide-de-camp to General Rochambeau.

After Fersen made his decision to part with Marie Antoinette by leaving the court at Versailles, the Swedish ambassador reported to the king of Sweden, Gustavus III: "I must admit that I can't help believing that she has taken a strong liking to him. I've seen too many undeniable indications of this to doubt it.... The queen has been unable to keep her eyes off of him for the last few days; her eyes filled with tears when she looked at him."[26]

Fersen distinguished himself in the American conflict, particularly during the Battle of Yorktown. He also served during the war as a translator between George Washington and General Rochambeau. After the war he returned to France, where he was made a colonel in a French regiment known as the Royal Suédois. In 1783, however, King Gustavus III of Sweden, who had earlier relied upon the military talents of Fersen's father, required Fersen's presence as an aide-de-camp during his extended tour of Italy. The Swedish king wrote: "I am very pleased with Count Fersen. In meeting him I experience all the pleasure and interest one feels on seeing a friend from whom one has long been parted; who has been exposed to great danger and who deserves all one's sympathy."[27]

Before he left France for Italy, Fersen disclosed his feelings for the queen in a letter to his beloved sister Sophie, with whom he kept up a lifelong correspondence that has enabled posterity to realize the depth of his devotion to Marie Antoinette:

> I cannot leave Paris without regret. You will think it quite natural when you learn the cause of this regret. And I will tell you, for from you I will have no secrets.... I have made up my mind never to contract conjugal ties.... I cannot give myself to the only woman I desire, to the only woman who really loves me; therefore I will give myself to no one.[28]

After a prolonged absence spent in Italy and Sweden, Fersen was sent back to Paris in October 1788 by Gustavus III, who wanted to be kept abreast of the rapidly deteriorating situation in France on the eve of the Revolution. From this point forward, Fersen did everything he could to help protect the king and queen's safety, often exposing himself to great danger through his valiant efforts.

4

Deteriorating Financial Situation

With France's financial problems more pressing than ever, the king had to find a competent controller-general to succeed Turgot. Little less than a financial wizard was needed to maintain a regime that was unable to raise money effectively because the nobles and clergy contributed so little to the revenue raised. In the eighteenth century, the lower and middle classes supplied the bulk of the tax revenue. Historically, the nobility had argued that their role was to serve as military officers, and the Catholic Church considered its role to be to handle all the spiritual needs of the country. The Church was a huge center of wealth in France because it owned vast amounts of land and these holdings were being steadily increased by legacies. Nevertheless, it contributed to the state coffers only a voluntary monetary gift from time to time. It did, however, permit the king to use its land as collateral for raising loans.

After two men had filled the position of controller-general inadequately for brief periods, Louis XVI chose Jacques Necker to direct the finances of the country in late 1776. Necker was a Swiss banker who had become rich by shrewd speculation in the Parisian banking world. His brilliant and charming wife greatly increased his personal influence because she hosted one of the leading salons of Paris, which was frequented by many of the philosophes. Necker was not of noble birth, however, and he was also a foreigner and a Protestant. Louis XVI at first appointed him only as "director of finance" because it would have been highly unusual to have a non-Catholic in the king's council.

Soon it became even more essential for the regime to have efficient financial management because the Americans were prevailing upon Louis XVI and his foreign minister, Vergennes, to help finance their war for independence. Still smarting from her defeat by the English in 1763 at the end of the Seven Years War, when she lost Canada to England, France viewed support for the American Revolution as a chance to reduce England's power. The king and Vergennes, however, did not wish to declare war on England openly or even to make it evident that they were aiding the rebels. Hence they set up a trading company under Beaumarchais (the author of *The Marriage of Figaro*) and supplied the American rebels through this channel. By the end of the war, however, France was openly providing troops and naval support for the American cause. The six thousand men whom France eventually sent to fight in the American conflict included several idealistic young noblemen such as the marquis of Lafayette, only nineteen at the time, who went to America as officers.

The French attitude toward the American Revolution was a curious one. The sophisticated and wealthy French nobles idolized Benjamin Franklin, who arrived at the court of Versailles without a wig, wearing a plain brown suit. The jaded and bored courtiers viewed him as a Natural Man, stepping forth from the pages of Rousseau. Franklin came looking for money and support for the American cause, and his enormous popularity helped procure both. No small part of his success resulted from his ability to charm the women of the court and the salons of Paris, who helped to shape official attitudes.

Of course, it was ironic that one monarchy would give aid to rebels against another monarchy, as the king's brother Provence and the queen were quick to point out. Liberals in France, however, viewed the American struggle as a great experiment in the assertion of the rights of citizens against arbitrary power. The writings of Voltaire, Rousseau, and the other philosophes had prepared them to support the American cause, and the young nobles who crossed the Atlantic to help fight returned full of new ideas about freedom and eager to reform France.

One such young nobleman was the count of Ségur, whose father became Louis XVI's minister of war. In his memoirs Ségur describes how he and his close friends, the viscount of Noailles and the marquis of Lafayette, all of them of high rank and wealth and linked by family ties, were so inspired by the American cause that they wanted to leave immediately to fight in the American War for Independence. Not yet knowing what the reaction of their families would be to their desire to join the American battle, the eager young men began to talk secretly with the American commissioners sent to negotiate with the French government — Silas Deane, Arthur Lee, and Benjamin Franklin. They were particularly amazed by the Americans' frankness in admitting that things were going badly for them in the field:

> What added considerably to our esteem, our confidence and our imagination, was the good faith and the simplicity with which the deputies, disdaining all diplomatic artifice, made us acquainted with the frequent and successive reverses experienced by their yet undisciplined troops; for at this early stage of the contest, the numbers and tactics of the English gave them a temporary triumph over the bravery of the Americans, yet unskilled in the profession of arms.[1]

Despite the attempts of the three young noblemen to keep their plans secret, word soon reached the court when they began to urge other young officers to join them in the American cause. The foreign minister formally forbade them to leave because he was "apprehensive that the departure to America of volunteers, distinguished by their rank, and who, it could not be supposed, would take that step without his permission, might open the eyes of England to the views which he still wished to conceal." Their families were also opposed to their plans. With great reluctance, Ségur and Noailles had to renounce their project because they could not obtain money to fund their departure to America from their parents, who in Ségur's words, "warmly reproached us for our rash spirit of adventure."[2]

Lafayette's parents were no longer alive, however, and he possessed an enormous fortune that he was free to spend as he wished. While appearing to acquiesce in the foreign minister's orders for a couple of months, Lafayette secretly announced to his friends Ségur and Noailles that he was about to leave for America on a ship that he had purchased, which was awaiting him in a Spanish port. He also used his vast fortune to purchase arms and ammunition to take to America, to hire a crew for his ship, and to provide funds for military officers who wanted to fight with him in America. When the court learned of Lafayette's activity, he was arrested so that he could be prevented from leaving France. Within only a few days, however, he escaped from his guards and crossed the Pyrenees into Spain, where he joined his ship and immediately set sail for America.[3]

Because Lafayette became such a major player not only in the American War for Independence but also in the French Revolution, it is worth noting the assessment of his personality and character provided by Ségur:

> At every period of his life, and above all in his youth, La Fayette displayed a cold and grave exterior, which sometimes gave to his demeanor an air of timidity and embarrassment, which did not really belong to him. His reserved manners and his silent disposition, presented a singular contrast to the petulance, the levity, and the ostentatious loquacity of persons of his own age; but, under this exterior, to all appearance so phlegmatic, he concealed the most active mind, the most determined character, and the most enthusiastic spirit.[4]

It was not long before Lafayette distinguished himself in the Battle of Brandywine, in which despite a serious wound to his leg, he managed to rally the American forces he commanded. His early success caused the opinion of courtiers to swing to his side, as Ségur noted:

> As soon as Paris rang with reports of the first battles in which La Fayette and his companions in arms had raised the reputation of the French name, the approbation of his conduct became general. The very persons who had most blamed his

adventure applauded him; the court itself appeared proud of his achievements, and he became the object of envy to our young men. Thus, public opinion, declaring itself still more exclusively in favor of war, rendered it inevitable, and drew after it, as a matter of course, a government which had not strength enough to resist the impulse.

In conformity with this view, the old Count de Maurepas, the first minister, said more than once to my father that it was the impetuous ardor of the young courtiers and officers which had overcome the wiser deliberation of the council of state, and, in a manner, compelled the government to declare war."[5]

Abbé Véri described in his journal the enthusiastic welcome Lafayette received from Louis XVI and his court on a return visit in early 1779. On this occasion Benjamin Franklin presented to Lafayette a gift from the Continental Congress—a sword on which were engraved the names of the five battles where Lafayette had distinguished himself.[6]

France did indeed declare war on England in 1780, and by 1781 Noailles and Ségur were both distinguishing themselves in the American combat, where the leadership and manpower provided to the Americans by the French played a large role in the success of the American War for Independence. The money drained from France to support the American cause contributed directly, however, to the downfall of the French monarchy because large sums had to be raised at a time when the regime was already dangerously short of funds.

The new director of finance, Jacques Necker, wanted above all else to remain popular with the people and was therefore reluctant to raise taxes. His only other alternative was to borrow the money, and he was indeed an expert at obtaining loans and instilling confidence in France's creditors. In his book *Origins of the French Revolution*, William Doyle discusses the huge amount of money borrowed by Necker between 1777 and 1781 in order to finance the American revolt against the British:

> But most of this money was borrowed for relatively short periods, less than twenty years, and offered a return of anything up to 10 percent per year. All this made Necker's loans extremely profitable ways of investing money. It also made them ruinously expensive to the state; but the potential economic gain of shattering the British Empire seemed ample justification for such a special war effort. And so all Necker's loans were subscribed within days.... His success meant that he was able to achieve what had hitherto been thought impossible — to finance a major war without any new taxation.[7]

To pay the mounting interest on the debt, Necker took out new loans. Between 1774, when Louis XVI ascended to the throne, and 1789, when the Revolution broke out, the interest on the national debt more than trebled.[8] By 1786 half of the entire French revenue was required to pay the interest on the debt.[9]

While France was spending itself into a financial crisis by financing the American War for Independence, a long-awaited child was at last born to the king and queen in December 1778. When the queen's labor began, all the family members and important people of the court gathered in the rooms adjoining hers to attend the event. According to custom, everyone of consequence who wished to be present was allowed to enter the queen's bedroom to witness the delivery of the baby. This long-standing practice insured that a royal heir had in fact been born and that no substitution had occurred. Mme. de Campan has left a vivid account of the birth scene:

> The waves of curious people who rushed into the bedroom were so numerous and excited that they almost killed the queen. During the night, the king had taken the precaution of having the tapestry hangings that surrounded the bed tied up. Otherwise, they would certainly have fallen down upon her. It was no longer possible even to move in the room, which was filled with such a mixed crowd, you would have thought yourself in a public square. Two Savoyards climbed up on the furniture in order to see better. The noise, the sex of the baby ... or a fault of the attending doctor suddenly caused a sharp deterioration in the queen's condition.... The doctor cried, "Air, hot water, we must bleed her by the foot." The windows had been sealed [against the cold]; the king opened them with a strength only his tenderness for the queen could give him, since these windows were very tall and had been taped all along their edges.[10]

This birth greatly enhanced the king's reputation and standing, and the future of France now seemed more secure. For seven long years the royal couple had awaited a child, while throughout the country they had been the subject of gossip and ridicule as people debated Louis XVI's ability to father an heir.

Louis XVI was not a ruler who insisted upon the constant attention and flattery of his courtiers. On one occasion early in his reign, he entered a crowded reception unannounced and unattended. Because all the seats were already occupied, he simply opted to share a large footstool with a lady of the court. Maurepas was so shocked by this behavior that he lectured the young king about the respect he should demand from his subjects.[11] In his journal Abbé Véri criticized Louis XVI for failing to assert his royal authority over his servants on another occasion. The king had found that one of his valets shaved him better than any of the others. When he requested that this man always shave him, the other valets complained that the job should be rotated. To avoid further argument, Louis XVI learned to shave himself.[12]

After a lapse of more than two centuries, it is difficult to evaluate the personality and manner of this unfortunate king because his contemporaries have left sharply differing assessments, biased by their own positions or prejudices. One of Louis XVI's earlier ministers, Mirosmenil, for example, left the following evaluation of him: "I have never known anyone whose character was more contradicted by outward appearances than the king.... He is good and tender-hearted; you can never speak to him of disasters or accidents to people without seeing a look of compassion come over his face, yet his tone is brusque, his replies are often hard, his manner unfeeling. He is, however, firm and courageous in making decisions."[13] The count of Ségur used similar words to describe Louis XVI, "It is well-known that the benevolence, and we may add, the good nature so remarkable in the character of this monarch, were usually concealed under an exterior somewhat rude, a harsh look, and a very abrupt address."[14]

The duke of Croÿ's memoirs are of particular interest because he died before the Revolution with its resultant reevaluations. He described the night when he found himself to be the only courtier present at the king's evening retiring ceremony: "He spoke with me and with his servants in a way that was both kind and appropriate; he couldn't have been more pleasant on this private occasion and demonstrated both good-will and good sense." Croÿ also described the king's deportment at the more formal occasion of a public dinner: "He spoke with everyone ... with an air of the greatest kindness and familiarity and was always eager to laugh at some small joke." One wonders if the shy king would sometimes try to cover his social unease with jokes because Croÿ also notes: "The king ordinarily tried to tease and joke with everyone, ... making jokes about tiny things. I would have rather seen him adopt a better tone, but he spoke with so much kindness and affability that one couldn't help liking him."[15]

Quite the opposite evaluation comes from Saint-Priest, who was serving as a council minister when the Revolution broke out: "He made no effort to please or encourage people and said nothing to anyone to indicate either his esteem or disapproval. He was not welcoming to any strangers presented to him and rarely spoke a word to them. Never was a man less fit to reign, although he could have filled other roles because he was well versed in literature, knew several languages, had some astronomical knowledge, and had an extensive knowledge of geography and marine affairs."[16]

Although it is impossible at this point in time to arrive at a view of Louis XVI's personality that cannot be disputed, his benevolence and goodwill are illustrated in a striking fashion by the preparations he made for the voyage of La Pérouse, a French explorer who made an important expedition to the South Seas in 1785. The king himself wrote a note to his chief botanical expert, asking for a list of fruits and vegetables to send on the voyage whose cultivation could be of permanent benefit to the peoples visited by La Pérouse. After receiving the list, the king himself added to it some of his own favorite flowers—lilacs and a special variety of rose. He also sent with the expedition various medicines that would be of benefit to the native peoples, including mercury for the treatment of the venereal diseases that English and Dutch sailors had already carried to the South Sea Islands. But Louis XVI's character is best revealed by his strict instructions to La Pérouse:

> If urgent circumstances ... ever force the said La Pérouse to employ the superiority of his arms against the native peoples in order to procure over their opposition the necessities of life such as food, water, and wood, he will use force only in the greatest moderation and will punish with extreme rigor any of his crew who exceed his orders. In all other cases ... he will turn to armed force only as a last resort to defend his crew.... His majesty considers one of the most desirable results of the expedition to be its accomplishment without the loss of the life of a single person.[17]

5

The Necklace Affair

In 1781 Necker startled France by publishing his famous *Comte-Rendu*, or accounting, a blue-covered book of over a hundred pages purporting to be a faithful record of current government receipts and expenditures. By juggling the figures, Necker was able to state that despite the burden of the interest on the loans that had financed the American War for Independence, the French treasury would actually have a small surplus in 1781. The book sold thirty thousand copies in the first week; according to one courtier, it was "in the pocket of every abbot and on the dressing table of every woman."[1] Most readers were convinced that Necker was a financial genius to be able to finance a war without raising taxes.

The other ministers in the council were not so easily fooled. As the various experts began to analyze the document, they realized that it was obviously fallacious because it discussed only "ordinary" accounts and concealed the fact that there was a large deficit for the year. As William Doyle notes, "He said nothing about *extra*ordinary accounts, from which the bulk of the war effort was financed; but nobody noticed this omission."[2] The famous mathematician and philosophe Condorcet complained of its "insolence of tone" and asserted: "[It says] stupid things about each detail of administration that it discusses. Never was the pride of an upstart so brutally expressed."[3] More and more courtiers began to turn against Necker in the wake of this episode. They finally found just the instrument to bring about his downfall — a private memorandum he had written to the king, suggesting that the financial powers of the Parlement of Paris be reduced.[4] The king's brother Provence, who held a grudge against Necker, managed to obtain a copy of this memorandum. Aware of the reaction that would ensue, Provence released this document to the magistrates of Parlement, who were outraged by Necker's suggestions. To make matters worse, Necker was now demanding financial control over the navy and war departments and insisting upon a seat on the foreign policy council. Maurepas informed the king that if these requests were met, the rest of the ministers would depart. Some historians have suggested that Necker may have in fact made these demands so that he would have an excuse to resign before it became obvious that he could do nothing to save the country from bankruptcy. When he departed in 1781 after having spent five years in office, he left France in a perilous financial position.

Shortly after Necker's departure, Maurepas died at the age of 83. Louis XVI ruefully remarked how much he would miss hearing his old friend walking around in the apartment he had occupied directly above him. A long relationship was now ended, and the king was left to make his decisions without the advice of his beloved mentor.

Despite his own long friendship with Maurepas, Abbé Véri believed the minister had been too inclined to let matters drift along, perhaps being unwilling because of his advanced age to urge controversial reforms. Véri recorded these impressions in his journal: "If Louis XVI had been guided by a minister as wise as M. de Maurepas but more active and firm about eliminating abuses, the reign of this prince would have been the finest in the history of the monarchy. He had no vices or tastes that would have put any obstacle in the way of these reforms. His character would have naturally encouraged such a program if it had been directed by a vigorous impetus, but without this strong guidance he was unable to make the required effort."[5]

Governing France was not, however, an easy matter. The French tradition of royal government revolved around the king's council, which was formed of the ministers he appointed. As William Doyle notes: "Since the only title to power was the favour of the king, the life of a minister was a constant struggle to retain or enhance royal favour, and to limit or diminish the credit of others. Council meetings were the scene of acrimonious clashes as ministers denounced each other's policies in front of the monarch.... Nor were ministers above engineering obstacles to the success of their colleague's policies after they had gone into effect."[6]

Louis XVI's problems in governing France were greatly compounded when an amazing story broke in August 1785 that would shake the very foundations of the French monarchy. The court suddenly learned that Cardinal de Rohan had been accused of procuring a diamond necklace worth a fabulous sum from the queen's jewelers by falsely representing himself as her agent.

As Grand Almoner of France, Rohan was one of the highest religious leaders in the country, despite his rather dissolute personal conduct. He also belonged to one of the wealthiest and most powerful families in France and was allied by marriage to most of the other leading families in the country. While ambassador to Austria many years earlier, he had clashed with Maria Theresa, who wrote to Mercy in 1773, "I am impatiently awaiting the moment when Rohan will be recalled; he is an impossible man."[7] The empress obviously communicated her vehement dislike for Rohan to her daughter. This was a serious problem for the ambitious Rohan, who was seeking to attain even more power in the government but recognized that the queen's aversion to him stood in the way of his further advancement.

Into this situation came an adventuress named Jeanne de la Motte, who had a peripheral position at court as a descendant of an illegitimate son of Henry II. Convincing Rohan that she was an intimate of Marie Antoinette, she passed notes to him that were supposedly from the queen but had actually been forged by La Motte's lover, a man by the name of Vilette. Finally, La Motte had the audacity to disguise a Parisian courtesan as Marie Antoinette and invite Rohan to a midnight assignation in the gardens of Versailles. The gullible Rohan duly met the veiled imposter in the shrubbery and was convinced on the basis of a few murmured words that he had been in the presence of the queen.

Soon La Motte began passing notes to Rohan purporting to be requests from the queen for substantial loans. He turned these sums over to La Motte in the hopes of ingratiating himself with Marie Antoinette. Emboldened by her easy success, La Motte came up with an even more audacious scheme.

A jewelry firm in Paris that often served the queen had hoped to tempt her to purchase an elaborate diamond necklace that included over seventeen diamonds that were five to eight carets each and a couple that were twelve carats each.[8] Thinking it too extravagant, she had refused to buy it. When La Motte heard of this fabulous necklace, she approached Rohan and told him that the queen wished him to obtain the necklace for her on credit. Rohan accepted this story and obtained a contract from the jewelry firm, which he gave to La Motte. She soon returned it to him with a forged signature of Marie Antoinette. Despite the fact that the forgery read "Marie Antoinette de France," while the queen's official signature was only "Marie Antoinette," Rohan did not suspect the fraud. He presented the signed contract to the jewelers, who gave him the necklace. He then took it to La Motte's home, where he gave it to Vilette, whom La Motte passed off as Marie Antoinette's valet. After Rohan's departure, Vilette and La Motte passed the necklace on to her husband, who broke it up and sold the stones in London.

When the first installment payment on the necklace came due in the summer of 1785 and the jewelers received no money, they contacted Breteuil, minister of the royal household at Versailles. He immediately made inquiries of the queen and found that she was ignorant of the whole affair. The two of them then alerted the king.

On the morning of August 15, 1785, as Rohan arrived in the king's apartments dressed in his ornate robes and cassock, ready to say mass, the king and queen confronted him with the question of the necklace. In one horrible realization he knew he had been duped. "Ah, Sire," he cried, "I see too late that I have been tricked," and then proceeded to protest his innocence.[9]

Louis XVI asked Rohan to go into the adjoining room, where he would find a pen, ink, and paper with which to write out his deposition stating all that had occurred involving the necklace. When Rohan finished writing, the king told him that he was to be arrested. Rohan asked that he be spared the humiliation of being arrested in his robes in view of the court, but Louis XVI was adamant and gave orders for his immediate arrest. Unfortunately, the soldier who arrested Rohan thoughtlessly let him write out a message in German to one of his subordinates. It was an order to destroy all documents relating to the necklace, so this evidence disappeared before the king's officers could search through Rohan's papers.[10]

The king was understandably furious because the whole affair cast grave aspersions on Marie Antoinette's character. Had Rohan not so readily believed the many rumors about her, he would never have allowed himself to become involved in such a scheme. He had all too quickly given credence to the suggestion that she was scheming behind the king's back to obtain a necklace that he did not wish to purchase for her. But far more reprehensible was Roland's easy acceptance of the idea that the queen would compromise herself by meeting with him in the middle of the night in the shrubbery of the palace gardens. Rohan had clearly been influenced by the many slanderous verses and pamphlets that had long made the rounds of Parisian society, detailing assignations the queen supposedly gave to numerous lovers on the palace terraces and in the surrounding woods. He must have thought it not unusual that he too would be summoned. For a man of Rohan's high spiritual office to have simply believed the worst about the queen, however, was a blatant insult to her and was received as such by the irate king.

The foreign minister, Vergennes, wanted the matter hushed up for the good of the country and all concerned, but Breteuil encouraged the king to bring the whole matter out into the open and prosecute Rohan. Over a decade earlier Breteuil had been replaced by Rohan at the embassy in Vienna, which may have been one reason why Breteuil was so eager to disgrace him publicly. There was also some speculation in the king's circle that Rohan might have misused funds from an institution he directed and then used the necklace maneuver to raise cash that he intended to pay back at a later time. At any rate, the decision was made to handle the whole inquest publicly, a procedure that turned out to be disastrous. The king offered Rohan the choice of which court he wished to be tried by, and he shrewdly chose the Parlement of Paris. In the meantime the clergy vehemently insisted that they alone had jurisdiction over one of their own, but their protests were ignored.

While awaiting trial, Rohan was confined in the Bastille, which actually offered quite comfortable quarters to prisoners of his rank. La Motte was also imprisoned, but her husband managed to escape to England. The third party to the intrigue to be arrested was an Italian charlatan by the name of Cagliostro, who was popular in society as a clairvoyant and alchemist. Although this was supposedly the Age of Enlightenment, many people in France were fascinated by the supernatural. This interest culminated in the great success of Mesmer, who had half of Parisian society coming to him to participate in his strange mesmerizing rituals. Despite his high church office, Rohan was as susceptible to these influences as the rest of French society and had consulted Cagliostro about the success of his efforts to ingratiate himself with Marie Antoinette. When Cagliostro assured him that his fortunes were about to rise, Rohan decided to follow La Motte's plan to procure the necklace for the queen.

Rohan had chosen his law court well. The Parlement of Paris had long been antagonistic to the power of the Crown, and its members found Rohan not guilty. He left the trial surrounded by cheering crowds, although the king at least had the satisfaction of dismissing him from office and banishing him to his country estate. Even then he was widely criticized for punishing a man who had been found innocent by the Parlement. La Motte did not fare so well; she was sentenced to be publicly flogged, branded with a "V" for "voleuse" (thief), and imprisoned for life. Her husband was condemned in absentia and Vilette was exiled, but Cagliostro was released.

It was a resounding victory for the Rohan family, but the queen, who had been totally innocent in the affair, found her reputation besmirched by the sensational trial. Many people were only too eager to believe that she had in fact negotiated with Rohan to obtain the necklace in return for sexual favors. To add to the scandal, La Motte escaped from prison within a year and fled to England, where she at once published libelous memoirs attacking the queen. Five thousand copies were quickly sold in France because of such titillating accusations as the following:

> To my dying breath, I will maintain that illicit relations existed between the Cardinal and the Queen.... A physical as well as a moral wreck at the age of fifty-one after a life of excess and debauch, His Eminence found it strenuous to live up to the amatory standards of his royal paramour and made arch admission that he resorted to a variety of stimulants: first fortifying himself with a dose of Cagliostro's famous aphrodisiac, then stimulating himself further by a visit to the love nest he maintained in Passy, where the fledgling occupant obliged by parading before him costumed as Mother Eve — all this elaborate ritual to perk him up, to put him "in the proper mood," as he put it, "to keep a rendezvous with the royal redhead in the Salon de Venus."[11]

The devastating effect of these slurs on Marie Antoinette's reputation cannot be underestimated. The respect of the French people for the Crown was so severely undermined by the episode that later observers as diverse as Napoléon and Goethe would date the beginning of the French Revolution from the necklace scandal.[12]

6

Attempts to Avoid Bankruptcy

The next controller-general of major stature after Necker's departure was the viscount of Calonne, a man of considerable ability who took office in 1783. Unfortunately, he possessed limited political acumen, a quality that was especially necessary at this point because the government had to raise money to deal with the financial crisis in a society in which the wealthy refused to pay any significant amount of taxes.

Calonne began his term by obtaining further loans and engaging in extensive public works, hoping to stimulate the economy through projects like the construction of a new naval harbor at Cherbourg. The harbor at Cherbourg was considered very important for the protection of the French fleet in any naval conflict with England because there was no sheltered deep harbor on a large stretch of the Channel coast, but the project was extremely expensive. When Arthur Young visited Cherbourg to view the famous project, which involved building a huge seawall based on a series of enormous cones, he was greatly impressed with the French engineering talent represented but remarked: "The whole scheme will prove fruitless, unless such an expence [sic] is bestowed on the remaining cones as would be sufficient to exhaust the revenues of a kingdom."[1] Young's assessment was accurate; construction had to be stopped in 1788. Even Napoléon was unable to complete the seawall, which was finished only in 1853. In retrospect, it was of course a great mistake for France to sink money into this project at a time when the country was already staggering under a huge debt.

By 1786 the interest on the national debt alone was more than half the annual budget. Court expenditures were only six percent of the annual revenue, so no amount of economizing on balls or banquets at the court was going to remedy the financial situation. In *Origins of the French Revolution*, William Doyle states:

> The revolution that was to sweep away the political institutions of old France, and shake her society to its foundations, did not begin on 14 July 1789 [fall of the

Bastille]. By that time the old order was already in ruins, beyond reconstruction. This was the result of a chain of events that can be traced as far back as 20 August 1786. For it was on that day that Calonne, comptroller-general of the royal finances, first came to Louis XVI and informed him that the state was on the brink of financial collapse.[2]

Knowing that large sums of money had to be raised quickly, Calonne returned to one of the proposals that had led to Turgot's downfall ten years earlier. This was a tax on land proportionate to the size of the holding, a tax from which neither the church nor the nobles were to be exempt. With the king's approval, Calonne joined to this plan a proposal for the creation of provincial assemblies to administer the tax. These assemblies were to be elected without regard to social status, a concept that was highly innovative. Realizing that these proposals had no chance of getting by the Parlement of Paris, whose privileged members would never consent to an increase in taxation of the upper classes, Calonne asked Louis XVI to appoint an Assembly of Notables to consider his new measures. This was a device that had been successfully employed by Henry IV almost two centuries earlier. Calonne hoped that this hand-picked group of nobles and prelates could be persuaded to endorse his program.

But when the Assembly of Notables met in February 1787, almost all of them were reluctant to accept the principle of significant taxation of the church and nobility. Calonne alienated the Assembly of Notables in his opening speech by denouncing the various abuses that weighed upon the working classes of France. Unfortunately, the Assembly was full of Necker's supporters, and these men did not think that the financial crisis was real. Believing that Necker's *Comte Rendu* had made it clear that there was no intrinsic problem with the French financial situation, they asserted that Calonne's ineptitude had caused the current temporary crisis.

Public opinion had turned sharply against Calonne, and as Alexis de Tocqueville noted, public opinion was of great importance to Louis XVI, who liked to think that he was in touch with what his subjects wanted:

> The king continued to speak as a master, but in reality he himself obeyed a public opinion which inspired him or carried him along every day, which he consulted, feared, and constantly flattered; absolute by the letter of the laws, he was limited by their execution. From 1784, Necker said in a public document, as an uncontested fact: "Most foreigners can hardly have any idea of the authority that public opinion today exercises in France: they find it difficult to understand what this invisible power is that commands even in the king's palace."[3]

Unfortunately, the respected foreign minister, Vergennes, who might have been able to help Calonne get his program approved, had died a few days before the Assembly opened. Finally, Calonne's popularity dropped so low that in April 1787 the king dismissed him. He retired to his country estate, but when the Parlement of Paris began to take legal action against him in August for supposed criminal mismanagement of public funds, he fled to England.

One of Calonne's principal opponents in the Assembly of Notables had been the archbishop of Toulouse, Loménie de Brienne, who was a protégé of the queen. Despite his high church office, he was reputed to be virtually an atheist. Nevertheless, Louis XVI appointed him to succeed Calonne and even named him prime minister, a post that had not existed in France for many years. In his biography of Louis XVI, historian John Hardman makes an important point about this decision:

> Brienne's appointment was preceded by an exchange of memoranda with the King which amounted to a negotiation. Louis's marginal comments on Brienne's first memorandum and his own memorandum would be sufficient in themselves to dispel the notion that the King was stupid and ill-informed. His remarks are precise, clear, at times sardonic, and display a thorough mastery of the complex financial and administrative issues involved.[4]

Brienne was intelligent and flexible, but the members of the Assembly of Notables were in no mood to endorse the modified land tax that he believed was necessary. They insisted instead that the king provide them with regular financial reports. Finally Louis XVI gave up and dismissed the Assembly of Notables in May 1787.

On August 6 the king presided at a *lit de justice* session of the Parlement of Paris to force it to accept a stamp tax so that badly needed money could be raised. The Parlement had previously maintained that it had no power to approve new forms of taxation and that for this purpose it was necessary to convoke an Estates-General. The last time an Estates-General had met was in 1614. It was an elected deliberative body composed of three separate "orders" representing the clergy, or First Estate; the nobility, or Second Estate; and lastly the Third Estate, comprising everyone else in the country.

On August 7, 1787, the Parlement of Paris declared the stamp tax void, at which point the king exiled all its members to Troyes. Later in August, when the king's youngest brother, the count of Artois, went to the Palace of Justice to register further edicts with a subsidiary court that was still functioning, he was booed by a crowd of ten thousand demonstrators. Finally the French Guards charged the crowd, and several people were killed or wounded.

At this point Brienne decided to give in to Parlement, and its exiled members returned to Paris in triumph in September 1787. But in November yet another crisis occurred when the king held another *lit de justice* to register an edict enabling the government to borrow a large sum because the royal treasury was virtually empty. As a concession the king promised at the same time to convoke an Estates-General by 1792. During this tumultuous session, his cousin the duke of Orléans, who had ambitions of becoming regent if Louis XVI was forced out, stood up and protested that the king's action was illegal. The king angrily retorted, "The registration is legal because I have listened to everyone's opinion."[5]

For the next several months, the conflict between the king and the Parlement of Paris continued to smolder. In May 1788 Lamoignon, the strong minister whom the king had recently appointed to head the judiciary, advised the king to move forcefully against Parlement. Lamoignon proposed a series of sweeping judicial reforms that would greatly limit the power of the Parlement of Paris, replacing it by a plenary court closely controlled by the Crown, a court that would receive the power of registering edicts.

Learning of these proposals in advance, the Parlement of Paris made a formal declaration of its rights and of the rights of its members as French citizens. The members insisted that only they had the authority to register laws, demanded the abolition of *lettres de cachet*, and asserted that only an Estates-General had the power to consent to new forms of taxation. Finally, on May 5, 1788, royal troops surrounded the Palace of Justice in Paris to arrest the two most radical members of Parlement. The other magistrates at first refused to yield their colleagues, saying they were all equally involved, but after a standoff of several hours, the two leaders gave themselves up. The arrest of two leaders was not going to quell the opposition, however. As Malesherbes noted, "The Parlement of Paris is ... merely the echo of the Parisian public and ... the Parisian public is the echo of the whole nation."[6]

On May 8, 1788, Louis XVI suspended both the Parisian and provincial parlements and put into effect Lamoignon's edicts for new courts. The nobility of France immediately made common cause with the parlements because they wanted to remain immune from taxation. It was a summer of sporadic violence throughout France, with supporters of the provincial parlements organizing revolts against the Crown. In Grenoble, for example, where members of the local parlement had been ordered into exile because they had protested against the royal edicts, a major riot broke out on June 7. Demonstrators attacked the headquarters of the royal representative, the duke of Clermont-Tonnerre, by throwing paving stones ripped from the street at the troops guarding the building. Other protesters threw down tiles pulled loose from the roofs above, giving the episode the name "the day of the tiles." Clermont-Tonnerre was forced to surrender, and the magistrates of the Parlement of Grenoble made a triumphal return to the Grenoble Palace of Justice with the bells ringing out their victory.

Finally the protests could no longer be ignored. On August 8, 1788, the king advanced the date for convening a meeting of the Estates-General by three years, moving it to May 1789. Within a few days Brienne and Lamoignon resigned. There was little else Louis XVI could do but recall Necker, who still enjoyed enormous popularity with most of his countrymen. Using this popularity and his connections with the chief financiers of the realm, Necker was able to take out additional loans to enable the government to limp along until the Estates-General could vote new taxes.

Before leaving office, Lamoignon prophetically declared, "The privileged orders have dared to resist the king; in two months there will be no more parlements, nobility, nor clergy."[7] A few years later Robespierre echoed his words:

> Thus it was that in France the judiciary, the nobles, the clergy, the rich, gave the original impulse to the revolution. The people appeared on the scene only later. Those who gave the first impulse have long since repented.... But it was they who started it. Without their resistance, and their mistaken calculations, the nation would still be under the yoke of despotism.[8]

7

Composition of the Estates-General

On September 23, 1788, the Parlement of Paris, which had once again been recalled by the king, returned in triumph and registered the edict convoking the Estates-General. In announcing their action, the magistrates stressed that the Estates-General should be constituted just as it had been in 1614, with three separate orders—the First Estate, made up of the clergy; the Second Estate, made up of the nobility; and the Third Estate, which included everyone else in the country. Each order was to deliberate separately, with all voting done by order. This meant, of course, that the clergy and nobility would outvote the Third Estate on any issue affecting their interest.

The bourgeoisie were furious to hear that voting would be by order and believed that they had been betrayed by the magistrates of the Parlement of Paris, whom they accused of seeking to limit the king's power only to assume it for themselves and the rest of the aristocracy. All over the country there was a sudden reversal of opinion and an outcry against the Parlement of Paris. In January 1789, Mallet du Pan wrote: "Public discussion ... no longer troubles itself except secondarily with the king, with despotism or with the constitution; it has become a war between the Third Estate and the two other classes."[1]

After taking the initial step of convoking an Estates-General to be held the following spring, Louis XVI had invited the scholars and educated people of France to send him their opinions about the organization and purposes of the Estates-General. This request brought forth a flood of pamphlets discussing all aspects of French political life. The most famous of these pamphlets was written by Abbé Sieyès, who was a canon of the cathedral of Chartres. As a commoner, he knew he could never aspire to become a bishop because high offices were reserved exclusively for the nobility. Like so many other well-educated and talented members of the bourgeoisie, he deeply resented the class structure of France in which birth counted for everything. In his

trenchant pamphlet, he argued: "What is the Third Estate? Everything....
What has it been heretofore? Nothing.... The lucrative and honorific positions
are held only by members of the privileged order.... We are told: 'Whatever
your services have been, whatever talents you have, you shall go only so far
and no further. It is not appropriate for you to be honored in this way.'"[2]
Sieyès argued that the real power lay not with the king but with the nobles:

> In one way or another, all the branches of the executive power are controlled by
> the caste that supplies the clergy, the magistrates, and the military officers. A
> spirit of fraternity or complicity causes the nobles to prefer their own company
> to the rest of the nation. Their usurpation is total; they reign everywhere.... It is a
> great mistake to believe that France is ruled by a monarchical regime.... It is the
> court that has reigned and not the monarch. It is the court that takes action,
> appoints and dismisses ministers, creates and distributes positions. And what is
> the court, if not the head of this immense aristocracy that covers every part of
> France, which through its members attains everything and controls all the essen-
> tial parts of the public domain?[3]

It was particularly galling to men like Sieyès that the noble class constituted such a tiny fraction of the country's inhabitants. Out of a French population of about 23,000,000, no more than 100,000 were members of the clergy
and 400,000 were nobles. The remaining 22,500,000 people—bourgeoisie,
artisans, workers, and peasants—constituted 98 percent of the population.[4]
The time had come when this overwhelming majority no longer wished to be
suppressed by a few aristocrats who for the most part performed no useful
work. (Nobles by tradition were not supposed to engage in manufacturing or
commerce, although there were occasional exceptions.)

One of the most hotly debated issues related to the calling of the Estates-
General was the number of representatives for each order. The Third Estate
insisted that it should be given twice as many delegates as each of the other
two orders and that all voting should be done by head, not by order. In this
way the Third Estate could hope to dominate the Estates-General because
many of the parish priests and a few of the nobles were likely to join them
on various issues. The clergy and nobility were in general strongly opposed
to this doubling of the Third Estate. Finally, Necker announced in December
1788 an edict from the king's council calling for the election of twice as many
representatives for the Third Estate. The edict was ambiguous, however, on
the question of voting by head. The Third Estate hoped that the doubling of
the Third implied voting by head because otherwise the move seemed meaningless. The first two orders feared that voting by head might indeed be a
result of this doubling. Because neither side could be sure how to interpret
the doubling announced by Necker, this crucial issue remained unresolved
when the Estates-General opened.

Once this question of the number of representatives for the Third Estate had been decided, royal instructions for the elections were issued in January 1789. A wide franchise was extended to include almost all male taxpayers over the age of twenty-five. Because no real machinery existed for holding these elections, a selection process of several steps was initiated for the Third Estate. Local villages and regions sent delegates to secondary assemblies, which then elected deputies to the Estates-General. As the lawyers were among the most articulate and well-known people at these meetings, large numbers of them were elected to represent the Third Estate. A substantial proportion of delegates were local government officials, and many came from the ranks of merchants and financiers. A few farmers with large holdings were elected, but there were no peasants among the representatives.

Patched together though it was, the election process for the Third Estate yielded a group of dedicated, well-educated men, many of whom were highly gifted individuals. One of the most brilliant and unusual delegates of the Third Estate was actually a renegade nobleman from Aix-en-Provence, Count Mirabeau. Mirabeau's personal appearance was arresting, for he was a large man with a massive head covered with a shock of bushy hair. His personal life was scandalous, and he had been imprisoned for long periods by means of *lettres de cachet* for licentious behavior. Despite these personal deviations, he was an enormously gifted writer and orator and was to have a great influence on the course of the Revolution. No one ever really trusted him, however, because he was known to take bribes.

Abbé Sieyès was not elected to represent the clergy, so he ran in the Paris elections and became a deputy to represent the Third Estate for that city. Two lawyers from the Dauphiny region who were elected for the Third Estate, Jean Mounier and Antoine Barnave, became leaders as the Estates-General evolved into the National Assembly. Barnave's motivation was based in part on a deeply resented personal snub. One evening while his mother was attending the opera in the city of Grenoble, she had been forced to leave her box because a nobleman arrived who demanded it.[5] This kind of incident, occurring all too frequently in the lives of the bourgeoisie, had created a large base of smoldering resentment whose force was a major impetus to the Revolution. Barnave expressed the frustration of talented members of the Third Estate when he complained, "The roads are blocked at every turn."[6]

The king had asked the local gatherings not only to elect delegates to the Estates-General, but also to draw up grievance lists stating everything they thought should be considered by the Estates-General. The very process of drawing up these lists caused a great amount of political discussion and analysis of the existing problems of France and thereby produced within the Third Estate a kind of consensus about the major changes to be sought.

There was a considerable Parisian influence on these grievance lists because by this point there was a group of people known as the "patriot" or "national" party who were working to channel in an effective way all opposition to the ancien régime, with its privileged orders. Within this party there was a small but very influential group of men known as the Committee of Thirty, which met in Paris at the house of Adrien du Porte, a magistrate of the Parlement of Paris. Other members included Lafayette, the mathematician Condorcet, the very wealthy duke of Aiguillon, and Mirabeau, as well as some representatives of the church, such as Abbé Sieyès and Bishop Autun, better known as Talleyrand. These men circulated model grievance lists to the provinces and maintained political contact with provincial leaders. One circular that was disseminated by some members of a provincial assembly in early 1788 was described by Tocqueville in this manner:

> "We know, in a general way," it [the provincial assembly] says, "that the majority of taxes, especially the taille and the salt tax, have disastrous consequences for the farmer, but we want to know further about each abuse in particular." The curiosity of the provincial assembly did not stop there; it wanted to know the number of people who enjoyed tax privileges in the parish, nobles, clergy, or commoners, and what exactly those privileges were; what the value of the property of these tax-exempts was; whether they resided on their lands or not; if there were many church lands, or as they said then, property in entail, which was out of circulation, and their value. All this was still not enough to satisfy the assembly; it wanted to be told at what sum one might estimate the taxes, taille, other dues, corvée, which the privileged should have paid, if equality of taxation existed.
>
> This was to inflame each and every individual by the recitation of his miseries, to point a finger at their authors for him, to embolden him by the sight of their small number, and to penetrate his very heart to inflame his greed, envy, and hatred.[7]

Tocqueville was able to locate several of the reports which peasants sent in, and their importance as a background to the violence that would before long erupt is clear. He described their contents in this way:

> In these diatribes, the name of every privileged person, noble, or bourgeois, is carefully indicated; his way of life is sometimes described and always criticized. The value of his property is sought with interest; the number and nature of his privileges are described at length, and above all the harm that they do to all the other inhabitants of the village. The bushels of wheat which must be paid to him in feudal dues are listed; his income is guessed with envy.... As for the taxes, they are all badly established and oppressive; there is not one which finds grace in their eyes, and they speak of them all in hot-headed language which breathes fury.[8]

All this political activity during the winter of 1788–89 took place against a backdrop of growing hardship in France. Harvests had not been good since the eight-month eruption of the Laki volcano in Iceland in 1783–84. Over two centuries later, in response to the famous 2010 volcanic eruption that had disrupted air travel throughout Europe, the *Guardian* printed a fascinating online article titled "How an Icelandic Volcano Helped Spark the French Revolution."[9] The article quotes Benjamin Franklin, who wrote of "a constant fog over all Europe, and a great part of North America." The haze of dust and sulphur particles affected weather patterns throughout the northern hemisphere. In France the spring of 1788 brought excessive rain and floods; these were followed by droughts and a widespread July hailstorm so bad that the giant hailstones killed animals and men and ruined large amounts of grain about to be harvested.[10] The harvest was disastrously bad that year, and to make the situation even worse, the winter of 1788–89 was bitterly cold. The countryside and towns were filled with beggars. Disturbances often broke out when grain was shipped around the country because bands of hungry people sometimes tried to intercept the shipments, while others complained that speculators were hoarding grain. This widespread suffering created an atmosphere in which everyone looked forward to the Estates-General as a great opportunity to create a better society in France.

8

Opening of the Estates-General

When the Estates-General opened in early May 1789, it was at once evident that the Third Estate wished to assert its equality with the nobility and the clergy. But the ever-present court protocol only served to remind the delegates of the Third Estate of their inferior social status. Even the costumes the delegates wore were rigidly prescribed, as had been the case when the last Estates-General met in 1614. The clergy wore their robes and the nobles were elegantly dressed in suits of black silk and wore white-plumed hats, but the men of the Third Estate were required to wear plain black cloth suits and tricorn hats.

On May 4 there was a grand procession of all the delegates of the Estates-General to the Church of Saint Louis. The delegates of the Third Estate marched farthest from the king, and when they arrived at the church, they were irritated to find that the clergy and nobles had clearly marked seats, while they were left to fend for themselves. To their further chagrin, the officiating bishop presented to the king "the homage of the clergy, the respect of the nobility, and the very humble supplications of the Third Estate."[1] The well-educated lawyers, merchants, and others who formed the bulk of the Third Estate were anything but humble at this point. The bishop's statement only served to underscore the basic injustice of the class system they were so eager to change.

One of the people watching the grand procession to the church that day was Necker's daughter, Germaine de Staël, who had recently married the Swedish ambassador. She was later to become one of the most famous chroniclers of the period, leaving a beautifully written and widely cited record titled *Considérations sur la Révolution Française.* On this momentous day she was sitting in a window next to Mme. Montmorin, whose husband had succeeded Vergennes as foreign minister. Mme. de Staël, who was only twenty-three at the time, expressed all her youthful hopes for the benefits that would come from this historic assembly. By contrast, Mme. Montmorin announced in a decided tone of voice, "You are wrong to rejoice; from this event will come great disasters for France and for us."[2] The truth of her words was all too sadly confirmed. Mme. Montmorin died on the scaffold with one son, her other son drowned himself, her husband's throat was cut in the September prison massacres, and a daughter died in a prison hospital.

Another observer who shared de Staël's enthusiasm had just arrived that spring from America. This was Gouverneur Morris, one of the leaders of the American Constitutional Convention. He was largely responsible for putting the ideas the delegates had agreed upon into a final document written with clarity and style. Morris is usually credited with having written the Preamble to the Constitution.

Morris arrived in Paris in 1789 to represent the interests of Americans wishing to sell grain to the French; three years later he was appointed minister plenipotentiary to France. Fortunately for historians, he kept a daily journal written in engaging and memorable prose that is an important record of revolutionary events as seen by an astute and witty foreign observer. On May 4 he recorded his impression of the day's events: "The procession is very magnificent, through a double row of tapestry. Neither the king nor queen appear too well pleased. The former is repeatedly saluted as he passes along with the Vive le Roi but the latter meets not a single acclamation. She looks, however, with contempt on the scene in which she acts a part and seems to say: for the present I submit but I shall have my turn."[3]

On May 5, the king formally opened the Estates-General with a short speech, saying: "Gentlemen, the day I have been eagerly awaiting has at last arrived, and I see myself surrounded by the representatives of the nation it is my glory to command."[4] Gouverneur Morris found the speech very moving: "The tone and manner have all the fierté [pride] which can be desired or expected from the blood of the Bourbons. He is interrupted in the reading by acclamations so warm and of such lively affection that the tears start from my eyes in spite of myself."[5] The king was at this point still very popular with his countrymen, most of whom believed that he was a good monarch who was misled by bad advisers.

Necker presented a very long speech, most of which was read by an assistant. In this three-hour discourse on the financial state of the realm, he dwelt chiefly upon the need for the Estates-General to vote new taxes to save the country. He said nothing about the possibility of a constitution and barely alluded to the question, so crucial to the Third Estate, of voting by head.

This question of voting by order or by head immediately paralyzed the Estates-General. The next day the clergy and the nobility each met separately and began to verify the credentials of their delegates. The Third Estate, however, refused to do this, saying that all voting, including verification of credentials, should be by head, with all three orders united into a single assembly.

As the weeks went by, the nobility remained intransigent, insisting that the preservation of the monarchy depended on voting by orders. The clergy remained divided on the issue. The parish priests were sympathetic to the Third Estate, but the bishops sided with the nobility. Meanwhile, the members of the Third Estate were becoming increasingly impatient. The Parisian delegation had been delayed by various election problems, but at last they arrived on June 3, adding a large number of activist delegates eager to reform France.

During the meetings of the king's council in late May and early June, Necker promoted a program that included several important concessions to the Third Estate. First, all taxation was to be levied according to a vote by head. Another major part of the Necker plan was for the king to suggest that any future legislative body would be organized into two houses, following the English pattern. Necker also urged that the tax exemptions of the nobility and clergy be eliminated and that admission to civil and military positions be open to all, regardless of rank. Necker believed that the king was on the verge of accepting his program when an event occurred that may have changed the course of French history.

The eight-year-old dauphin, a child of great promise, died after a long illness, which was probably tuberculosis of the bones. Louis XVI was a very loving and devoted father and was overwhelmed by grief at a time when it was paramount for the country to have strong leadership. On June 14 he withdrew with his family to the seclusion of his château at Marly, where he fell more directly under the reactionary influence of Marie Antoinette and his brothers, who wanted him to assert royal authority against the Third Estate, using force if necessary to subdue it.

After several days Necker and other council members, including the liberals Montmorin and Saint-Priest, were called to Marly for a royal council. Nothing was decided at the first meeting and before the second could take place, death once more intervened to change the balance of the discussions when Necker was called to the bedside of a dying relative in Paris. In his absence many conservatives vigorously attacked his program, and he returned to find the council had been enlarged by the addition of several of his opponents.

In the meantime, events at Versailles were moving quickly. On June 13 three priests abandoned their colleagues and joined the Third Estate; within the next two days sixteen more priests came over. On June 17 the influential Abbé Sieyès proposed a motion that the Third Estate declare itself to be the National Assembly because it represented 98 percent of the population of the country. When this bold motion carried, it was clear that the Third Estate had assumed for itself a large share of the governmental power in France. It was the first formal step in a movement that became the Revolution.

Other decisive acts soon followed. When the deputies from the Third Estate arrived at their hall on the rainy morning of June 20, they found it closed, ostensibly for alterations before the imminent royal session. Being denied entrance by the royal troops guarding the building, the deputies sought shelter in a large building nearby that was used as a tennis court. Believing that their political existence was being threatened, the deputies swore an oath, henceforth famous as the Tennis Court Oath, in which they pledged to work together until they had written a new constitution and established it on a solid foundation. Despite their audacious move, those assembled still viewed themselves as loyal to the throne and finished their meeting by shouting, "Long live the king."

When the newly declared National Assembly met in the Church of Saint Louis on June 22, several nobles and 149 members of the clergy, including 2 archbishops, joined it. The bold initiatives of the Third Estate were rapidly drawing support. In the face of these developments, the conservative members of the king's council wanted him to assert his royal authority and stand firm against this usurpation of power by the Third Estate. They urged upon him a show of force, but Necker continued to plead the danger of such a course, particularly with the loyalty of the army in doubt. When the conservatives triumphed in the council and plans were made for a royal session of the Estates-General on June 23 to proclaim their position, Necker announced he would not attend.

On the morning of June 23, the hall was surrounded by four thousand soldiers as Louis XVI entered to proclaim his position. The mood of the deputies of the Third Estate was not good because they had waited for an hour in the rain while the nobles and clergy were being seated. They were also uneasy because troops were present and their trusted Necker was conspicuously absent. Their fears were confirmed when the king's representative stated that the recent decrees of the National Assembly were nullified. The king suggested that the nobles and clergy should give up their exemption from taxation but stopped short of ordering this. No mention was made of equality of access to posts of military command or civil positions, an issue of great concern to members of the Third Estate, who saw men of talent continually denied access to high office. The king's program also promised control of taxation by the Estates-General, reform of the judiciary system, abolition of *lettres de cachet*, and more freedom for the press. But the king did not offer voting by head on any question of importance, and this issue was central for the Third Estate.

In his final words, Louis XVI stated that if the Estates-General could accomplish nothing, he would proceed to act alone for the welfare of the French people. Many viewed this as a veiled threat of dissolution. The king then ordered the delegates to leave for the day and to assemble the next morning in their respective meeting halls to deliberate as separate orders.

After the king left the hall, most of the nobles and some of the clergy followed him, but the delegates of the Third Estate remained in their places. Before long, the master of ceremonies advanced to repeat the king's orders that they disperse. Bailly, the Parisian astronomer who was now president of the National Assembly, asserted, "No-one can give orders to the nation in assembly."[6] But the most dramatic response came from Mirabeau, who announced, "We will leave our places only at the point of a bayonet."[7]

The king made an attempt to have the troops move the delegates out of the hall, but the soldiers were sympathetic to the cause of the Third Estate and the hostile attitude of the crowd outside the hall made it difficult for the troops to enter the building. Louis XVI gave up the attempt when he saw that it would lead to bloodshed. A witness quoted him as saying, "Oh, well, devil take it, let them stay."[8] This became a characteristic pattern of behavior with the king as the Revolution progressed. He hoped to discourage opposition by a show of force, but if this force met with resistance, he could not bring himself to shed blood to assert his will.

Since the Third Estate had won this round, more and more members of the clergy and nobility joined them in the next few days. On June 27, Louis XVI finally gave up and suggested that the remaining members of the first two estates also join the Third Estate. The National Assembly thus became the sole legislative body of France. The English traveler Arthur Young summed up the day's events in his diary entry for June 27:

> The whole business is now over, and the revolution is complete. The king has been frightened by the mobs into overturning his own act of the *séance royal* ... full in the teeth of what he had ordained before. It was represented to him, that the want of bread was so great in every part of the kingdom, that there was no extremity to which the people might not be driven: that they were nearly starving ... that Paris and Versailles would inevitably be burnt; and in a word, that all sorts of misery and confusion would follow his adherence to the system announced in the *séance royal*.... He was thus induced to take this step, which is of such importance, that he will never more know where to stop, or what to refuse.[9]

From his vantage point many decades later, Tocqueville would offer the following perceptive analysis:

> It is not always in going from bad to worse that one falls into revolution. It more often happens that a people who have borne without complaint, as if they did not feel them, the most burdensome laws, reject them violently once their weight

is lightened. The regime that a revolution destroys is almost always better than the one that immediately preceded it, and experience teaches that the most dangerous moment for a bad government is usually when it begins to reform itself. Only great genius can save a ruler who tries to help his subjects after long oppression. The inevitable evil that one bears patiently seems unbearable as soon as one conceives the idea of removing it. Every abuse that is then eliminated seems to highlight those that remain, and makes them feel more biting; the evil has decreased, it is true. But sensitivity to it is greater. Feudalism in all its power never inspired as much hatred in the French than at the moment it was about to disappear. The smallest arbitrary acts of Louis XVI seemed more difficult to bear than all the despotism of Louis XIV.[10]

9

Fall of the Bastille

On June 26, 1789, the king ordered six regiments to march to the area between Versailles and Paris to help maintain order in Paris, where the hungry populace was demanding bread. The harvest of 1788 had been disastrous and the new crop would not be ripe for another month, so there was still a desperate shortage of grain and what was available did not always reach Paris. The price of bread shot up during the summer of 1789, reaching a peak on July 14, the day the Bastille fell, exactly one year after the hail storm that destroyed the 1788 crop. Adding to the unrest was the widespread unemployment caused both by the crop failures and by recent trade agreements admitting English goods, which had led to the closing of various workshops. In Paris orators and pamphleteers stirred up the populace from the safe haven of the Palais Royal, an area in the center of the city that was the private domain of the duke of Orléans. Its gardens, which were surrounded by cafes, shops, and gambling dens, had become a popular place for people to gather and engage in political discussions and protest. The duke of Orléans, the king's cousin, was enormously wealthy but a man of licentious personal morals and unscrupulous political ambitions. Because he hoped that if Louis XVI were dethroned he would succeed him as regent, he was eager to foment unrest and rebellion among the Parisians.

On June 30 a group of angry citizens attacked a jail and freed ten French guards who had been imprisoned for insubordination. After this June 30 riot, the king ordered another ten regiments to the outskirts of Paris, this time mostly Swiss and German troops, which were considered more reliable than the French ones.

The queen, the king's brothers, Provence and Artois, and other leading courtiers wanted to use military force to subdue the rioters and control the National Assembly. Necker believed that there were many secret plots to which the king himself was not a party. Knowing Louis XVI's reluctance to kill any of his subjects, those close to him may well have worked behind his back in

plotting any decisive use of force, hoping that if a military action were initiated, he would have to back it. At any rate, alarming rumors were sufficiently widespread that the deputies of the National Assembly feared that all these troops had been gathered to dissolve their body. Some stories even circulated that alleged that explosives had been placed in tunnels under the hall of the Assembly. Becoming increasingly concerned that the monarchy was indeed plotting a counterrevolutionary move, the deputies demanded that the king remove the troops. He replied that the soldiers were there only to keep order in Paris and suggested that the Assembly could move to Noyon or Soissons if it felt threatened by their presence.

On July 11 the king, succumbing to pressure from Necker's enemies within the court, dismissed him and sent him into exile. By July 12 news of Necker's exile reached Paris. Already feeling threatened by the encircling troops, the Parisians viewed Necker's dismissal as a signal that the king was about to move against them. Rumors flew that another St. Bartholomew's Massacre was about to take place. The Parisian bourgeois also feared that bankruptcy would soon follow Necker's departure. Thousands of people poured into the streets, carrying statues of Necker and the duke of Orléans borrowed from a wax museum. While a journalist named Camille Desmoulins was haranguing the crowd, he pulled some oak leaves from a tree and stuck them on his cap as a green cockade because green was the color of the livery of Necker's servants. Soon all the protesters were wearing green cockades.

In response to these demonstrations, Baron de Besenval, the commander of the Swiss Guards and other royal troops assembled at the Champ de Mars just outside Paris, marched part of his forces into the city in an attempt to restore order. He later described this pivotal day of July 12, 1789, in his memoirs:

> On the way to Place Louis XV [the present Place de la Concorde], my troops were assailed with insults, rocks, and pistol shots. Several of my men were badly wounded. Nevertheless, the troops made no menacing gestures to their attackers, so much did they respect the order that not a drop of the demonstrators' blood should be shed....
>
> The disorder was growing from hour to hour, and my concern was greatly increasing. What should I do? If I used the troops in Paris, I would ignite a civil war. Blood that was precious no matter from whom it flowed would be spilled without achieving public calm. People were accosting my troops almost under my very eyes with all the usual seductions. I received intelligence about their loyalty that alarmed me. Versailles was leaving me to my own devices in this cruel situation and insisted on regarding three hundred thousand mutinous men as a mob and the revolution as a riot.
>
> Everything considered, I believed that the wisest course was to withdraw my troops and leave Paris to itself.[1]

Besenval's decision to march his troops out of Paris was key to the events that unfolded over the next few days and had a great influence upon at least the near term of the French Revolution. As the commander in the field who had been sent by Louis XVI to control the disorders in Paris, it seems odd that Besenval assumed that the king would rather have him leave Paris than kill a single person. Communication over the twelve miles that separated Versailles from Paris was dependent upon couriers on horseback, and at least one courier was intercepted by the rioters. Since events were happening very rapidly in Paris, it seems self-serving of Besenval to blame his inaction on the lack of updated orders from Versailles. Oddly enough, historians writing about this crucial day at the beginning of the Revolution have in general simply quoted Besenval's account without much analysis or efforts to find alternative accounts of his fateful decision not to fight. Such research seems particularly important because many observers have reservations about the veracity of various passages in Besenval's memoirs. Some even question whether he was the person who wrote them.

At any rate, once Besenval withdrew his troops, Paris was left in a chaotic situation with no military or police control over the populace. On the night of July 12, crowds destroyed the customs posts at the entrances to the city and roamed the streets looking for arms and food. Gouverneur Morris noted in his diary that evening: "These poor fellows have passed the Rubicon with a witness. Success or a halter must now be their motto. I think the court will again recede and if they do, all farther efforts will be idle. If they do not, a civil war is among the events most probable. If the representatives of the Third have formed a just estimate of their constituents, in ten days all France will be in commotion."[2]

The middle classes of Paris quickly saw that a civil force was needed to fill the vacuum and protect life and property in the city. Drawing on the electoral districts that had been set up to choose the deputies to the Estates-General, they called upon each of the sixty districts to supply two hundred men to form a military force to resist any attacks from the aristocrats and to prevent looting by the hungry mobs. These soldiers were to wear a red and blue cockade because these were the colors of the city. Within a few days this force evolved into the National Guard and chose Lafayette as its commander. He added the royal color of white to the cockade to symbolize the union of Paris and the Crown, producing the tricolored cockade. The act was consistent with Lafayette's attempt over the ensuing years to support both the king and the Revolution.

On the morning of July 14, the Parisian crowds broke into the Invalides and armed themselves with thirty-two thousand muskets and four cannons that they found stored there. Thus armed, they decided to march to the

Bastille, a large medieval fortress on the eastern edge of Paris that had been built during the Hundred Years War to defend the eastern approach to the city against the English. The rioters attacked the Bastille in order to seize the large amount of gunpowder stored in the fortress, which they needed for the weapons they had taken from the Invalides. But another very important motive for the attack was that the Bastille, with its forbidding towers and surrounding moat, was a prominent symbol of royal military power and had been a hated prison over the centuries. Historian Alfred Cobban notes, "Rumour and pamphleteers had for years been disseminating a picture of its dungeons packed with wretched state prisoners."[3] Ironically enough, however, the situation had significantly changed during the reign of Louis XVI. By the late 1780s the Bastille was used for only a handful of prisoners, and once the decision was made in June 1789 to abolish *lettres de cachet*, which were the chief source of prisoners held in the Bastille, the decision was also made to demolish the outmoded fortress so that it could be replaced by a public square with a column and fountain in the middle. In his engaging book *Citizens: A Chronicle of the French Revolution*, historian Simon Schama notes: "Just a few weeks before it fell to the citizens' army, then, the Bastille had already been demolished in official memoranda."[4] Only seven prisoners were found still incarcerated in the Bastille when it fell: a depraved nobleman imprisoned at the request of his family, two lunatics, and four forgers. Schama includes in his book many interesting details about imprisonment in one of the eight towers of the Bastille during the reign of Louis XVI:

> Most prisoners were held in octagonal rooms, about sixteen feet in diameter, in middle levels of the five-to-seven-storied towers. Under Louis XVI they each had a bed with green serge curtains, one or two tables and several chairs. All had a stove or chimney.... Many were permitted to bring in their own possessions and to keep dogs or cats to deal with the vermin. The Marquis de Sade, who was held there until the week before the Bastille fell, took full advantage of these privileges. He brought in (among other things) a desk, wardrobe, ... a full complement of shirts, silk breeches, ... dressing gowns, several pairs of boots and shoes; his favorite firedogs and tongs; four family portraits, tapestries to hang on the white plaster walls; velvet cushions and pillows, mattresses to make the bed more comfortable; ... a library of 133 volumes....
>
> Some of the literary inmates even thought a spell in the Bastille established their credentials as a true foe of despotism. The Abbé Morellet, for example, wrote, "I saw literary glory illuminate the walls of my prison. Once persecuted I would be better known ... and those six months of the Bastille would be an excellent recommendation and infallibly make my fortune."[5]

Schama notes that de Sade and others imprisoned in what was known as the "Liberty" tower, were accorded the privilege of walking in the garden and on the tower ramparts. The infamous de Sade, whose depraved and violent sexual activities gave us the term "sadistic," sometimes amused himself during his walks on the tower ramparts by shouting obscenities to people passing below.[6] After the prison authorities restricted him from walking on the towers, he resorted to using an improvised megaphone to shout out his window. He carried this too far in early July 1789, after he learned from his wife during one of her weekly visits that revolutionary ideas were sweeping Versailles and Paris. According to Schama:

> From de Sade's window, at regular intervals, like news bulletins on the hour, came broadcast announcements to the effect that governor de Launay planned a massacre of all the prisoners; that they were at this minute being massacred and that the People should deliver them before it was too late. Already in a state of jitters, de Launay had the troublemaker removed on about the fifth of July to Charenton, where he raged at the indignity of being shut up with so many epileptics and lunatics."[7]

Although de Sade was no longer in the Bastille when it was attacked on July 14, his shouted cries for help during the first few days of July may well have helped inflame the Parisian crowds. At any rate, on the fateful day of July 14 the rioters were joined in their attack upon the Bastille by three hundred French Guards under the leadership of officers Pierre Hulin and Jacob Elie. At first the leaders of the attacking forces attempted to negotiate a surrender by the fortress's governor, Marquis de Launay, who had neglected to lay in sufficient supplies and had no orders from Versailles. De Launay invited the delegates into the fortress to discuss the various issues and suggested they have lunch with him. When these representatives did not return promptly, those left waiting outside feared that they had been imprisoned. A few of the attackers managed to lower one of the outer drawbridges, and the crowd swarmed over it into the outer courtyard. Feeling themselves threatened, some of the soldiers on the ramparts started to fire, and the enraged crowd below then attacked with a vengeance.

De Launay considered setting a match to the vast store of gunpowder, an act that would have killed everyone in the area, but he was restrained by one of his officers. When it became clear to de Launay that he and his 110 men could not successfully resist the large number of soldiers and angry rioters who surrounded the fortress, he surrendered. An eyewitness described the crowd's triumphant departure from the Bastille with de Launay:

> Hulin, Elie, and a few others undertook to guard him and succeeded in getting him out of the Bastille, though he was roughly handled by the people, who were calling for his death.... Some of the crowd tore out his hair, others threatened him with their swords and tried to run him through. The wretched man, feeling

the agony of death coming over him, said in a faint voice to Hulin, "Ah, Monsieur, you promised not to leave me, stay with me till we get to the Hôtel de Ville [City Hall]...."

But the fury of the crowd continued to increase and their blind wrath did not spare de Launay's escort. L'Epine received a blow on the head with the butt of a musket, which would have stretched him out dead, if he had not been wearing a hard round hat that saved his life.... Hulin himself, in spite of his vigor and his powerful frame, could no longer resist the violence of the mob. Exhausted by his efforts to defend his prisoner and overwhelmed by the rough treatment he had himself received, he had to separate from M. de Launay at la Grève in order to take some rest. Hardly had he sat down when, looking after the procession, he saw the head of M. de Launay stuck on the point of a pike. His last words had been, "Oh, my friends, kill me, kill me at once and don't keep me suffering like this!" The people, fearing that their victim might be snatched away from them, hastened to cut his throat on the steps of the Hôtel de Ville.[8]

It should be noted in passing that various commentators have ridiculed Louis XVI because of his journal entry for July 14, which consisted of one word: "rien" (nothing). This journal was, however, only a hunting journal in which the king listed what game had been killed that day, not a place where he usually recorded what else was happening in his life.

In his diary Gouverneur Morris commented upon the events of the momentous day: "Yesterday it was the fashion at Versailles not to believe that there were any disturbances at Paris. I presume that this day's transactions will induce a conviction that all is not perfectly quiet."[9]

10

Accommodating the Revolutionaries

The Bastille was not only captured, within four months there was hardly one stone left standing on another. The fortress had been a symbol of a society of privilege. Its destruction seemed to portend the lengths to which the revolutionaries would go in their desire to reshape France.

Amid the shocked disbelief with which the inhabitants of the dream world of Versailles viewed the fall of the Bastille, the king's advisers once again offered sharply conflicting suggestions. His brother Artois and Marie Antoinette urged him to go to Metz, a French city close to the border of Germany and Luxembourg, where he could count on loyal troops and could also quickly cross the border into the territory ruled by Marie Antoinette's brother Joseph II if his life was threatened. But Louis XVI's other brother, Provence, and the duke of Broglie, the commander of the army, both thought he should remain at Versailles. After some debate, Louis XVI decided to stay and attempt to conciliate the various antagonistic forces. It was a decision that would ultimately cost him his life.

On July 15, Louis XVI went to the National Assembly accompanied only by his brothers, leaving his guards behind as a gesture of goodwill. He announced an important decision to the deputies:

> Gentlemen, I have assembled you here to consult you on matters of the highest importance for the state. None is more urgent and affects me more deeply than the dreadful disorders taking place in the capital. As head of the nation, I come confidently into the midst of its representatives to express the pain I feel because of the present situation and to invite you to find means to reestablish order and calm. I realize that you have heard erroneous information; I know that some people have proclaimed that you are in personal danger. Is it really necessary for me to reassure you that such terrible rumors are totally inconsistent with my known character? I am one with the nation, and I join with you. Help me in these circumstances to assure the safety of the state. I count upon the zeal of the

representatives of my people constituting the National Assembly, who are united to attain the security of all. That is a sufficient guarantee for me, and counting upon the loyalty of my subjects, I have ordered the troops to leave Paris and Versailles.[1]

Once again Louis XVI rejected the use of force at a critical juncture, relying instead upon the goodwill of subjects who would before long turn against him. On this occasion, however, his speech was so well received by the deputies that they all escorted him triumphantly back to the palace. The procession took an hour to move slowly to the palace, as it passed through streets of Versailles that were lined with crowds of townspeople shouting, "Long live the king." Some even climbed trees to have a better view of the occasion.

On July 16 the king attempted to placate his opponents by recalling Necker to power to handle the financial crisis. This day also saw the first wave of emigration. Those who had unsuccessfully urged Louis XVI to stop the disorders by the use of force now decided to leave the country, knowing full well that unchecked violence would sooner or later endanger their lives. Many conservative members of the court fled France at this point, including the king's younger brother, the count of Artois, and the countess of Polignac, who was one of the queen's closest friends and also the governess for the royal children.

In their fascinating pictorial record titled *La Révolution: Des Etats Généraux au 9 Thermidor* (The Revolution: From the Estates-General to the 9th of Thermidor), François Furet and Denis Richet describe the resultant scene as people began to flee: "At Versailles the immense château was now half deserted.... The north wing, which had been occupied by the Condé family, was now virtually empty. The south wing, known as the pleasure wing, where Comte Artois and the Polignac family lived, was closed forever."[2]

Louis XVI agreed to go to Paris on July 17 in the company of fifty deputies from the National Assembly to meet with the representatives of the city. Because he had given orders for the troops near Paris to disperse in an attempt to placate the Parisians, he went to the volatile city without protection. Being only too well aware of the massacres of de Launay and another high official of Paris only a few days earlier, Louis XVI made a will before he left Versailles. As always, however, he faced danger with an unusual degree of courage. Mme. de Staël later described his demeanor on that day: "His religious calm preserved his personal dignity on this occasion as on all the succeeding ones, but his authority no longer existed."[3]

Bailly, the astronomer who had been presiding over the National Assembly, had just been chosen mayor of Paris by the district councils, and he met Louis XVI at the outskirts of Paris to present to him the keys of the city. As he offered them to the king, he said: "Sire, I bring to Your Majesty the keys of his good town of Paris; they are the very keys presented to Henry IV. He had reconquered his people, and today the people have reconquered their king."[4] In his memoirs Bailly enthusiastically described the events of this memorable day, little realizing that the revolution he fostered would eventually claim him as a victim.

> The route ... was lined by men of the National Guard and behind them stood the crowd, three and sometimes four deep armed with muskets, swords, pikes, lances, scythes, sticks, and whatnot. I believe ... there were a hundred thousand armed men in Paris that day.... I was the first to arrive at the Hôtel de Ville and it was suggested that I should present to the king the tricolored cockade which the Parisians had adopted since the Revolution as a symbol.... I offered him the cockade, saying, "Sire, I have the honor to offer to your Majesty the distinctive emblem of the French." The king took it in very good humor and fastened it onto his hat. He then went up the steps leading into the Hôtel. He was guarded and surrounded by a number of citizens representing the town. They were all carrying swords which they crossed over his head, making a trellis of steel. The clashing of the swords, the hubbub of voices, and even the cries of joy reverberating through the vaulted building sounded somehow frightening. I would not have been surprised if the king had felt somewhat alarmed at that moment. But thronged as he was by the crowd, he marched along with the assurance of a good king in the midst of a friendly people.... As he entered the council-chamber, there was a burst of applause and cries of "Long live the king" were heard everywhere. The people, with tears in their eyes, turned to look at him and stretched out their hands towards him.... M. de Corny asked that a statue be erected to Louis XVI, the restorer of public liberty and father of the French nation, and, immediately, by universal acclamation, it was voted that this statue should be set up on the site of the Bastille.[5]

The desire of those assembled to erect this statue to Louis XVI makes it clear that at this point the revolutionaries' hatred was directed toward the ancien régime, not the king. This warm reception must have surprised Louis XVI. Before leaving Versailles, he had not only executed his will but had also made his confession to his priest and given temporary powers to his brother Provence, in the event that he was killed or held hostage by the Parisians. He did not arrive back at Versailles until 9 o'clock that evening, leaving those awaiting him prey to the gravest apprehensions. Everyone in the palace was overjoyed when he at last returned. Marie Antoinette and the children ran to embrace him on the staircase, so great was their relief at his safe return. Mme. Campan reports that Louis XVI kept saying, "Happily no blood has been shed, and I swear that never shall a drop of French blood be spilled by my order."[6]

The king had been fortunate on his trip to the capital. A few days later two of his officials fell to the fury of the Parisian mob. On July 22, Berthier de Sauvigny, the intendant of Paris, and his father-in-law, Fouillon de Doué, one of the new council ministers, were both brutally killed, despite the efforts of Lafayette, Bailly, and other authorities to save them. The Parisians attacked these men because they blamed them for the shortage of bread in the city. One preposterous rumor circulating through Paris charged that Berthier had ordered wheat to be cut down while it was still green to diminish the supply. Another rumor asserted that Foullon had said that the starving people could eat grass. The furious people in the mob hanged these men from Parisian street lamps called "lanternes," and "à la lanterne" quickly became a rallying cry for the masses in pursuit of their aristocratic enemies. Upon this occasion the rioters decapitated their victims and stuffed their mouths with grass. Gouverneur Morris confided to his diary his sense of horror at the events of the day:

> In this period the head and body of M. de Fouillon [*sic*] are introduced in triumph. The head on a pike, the body dragged naked on the earth. Afterwards this horrible exhibition is carried thro the different streets. His crime is to have accepted a place in the ministry. This mutilated form of an old man of seventy-five is shewn to Berthier, his son-in-law, the intendant of Paris, and afterwards he also is put to death and cut to pieces, the populace carrying about the mangled fragments with a savage joy. Gracious God, what a people![7]

The disturbances in Paris that summer were paralleled by troubles that erupted throughout the countryside of France. The phrase "the Great Fear" has been used by historians to describe the mood of mass hysteria that swept across the land during the late summer. Most of the common people believed they were about to be attacked by counterrevolutionary aristocratic forces, and rumors flew that an English force was ready to land at Brest, on the Brittany coast.[8] Large numbers of vagabonds roamed the countryside because food and employment were both extremely scarce. As the unrest increased, more and more nobles emigrated, adding to the ranks of the unemployed not only their large numbers of servants, but also the artisans who had supplied them with luxury goods. The peasants feared that aristocrats were paying the roaming bands of hungry people to steal or destroy their crops.

The convoking of the Estates-General and the drawing up of the grievance lists had led the lower classes of France to hope for an immediate and great amelioration of their lives. This belief created a state of perpetual excitement throughout France, and people thus reacted quickly to the news of the fall of the Bastille. In cities and towns across the country, demonstrators demanded a share in the local government. Sometimes, as in the city of Strasbourg, they engaged in violent attacks on the royal representatives. By the end of the summer of 1789, new local citizen governments and hastily organized National Guard units had virtually assumed control of provincial France. During the summer many peasants also attacked various châteaux, primarily to destroy the official records formalizing their duties and financial obligations to the nobles.

On August 3 a spokesman for the National Assembly's reports committee reported: "By letters from every province, it appears that properties of whatever sort are falling prey to the most disgraceful brigandage; on all sides castles are being burned, monasteries destroyed, farms given up to pillage. Taxes, payments to lords, all are destroyed; the law is powerless, magistrates without authority, and justice is a mere phantom sought from the courts in vain."[9]

The bourgeois deputies of the National Assembly could see that the revolution they had started might progress far beyond any stage they believed desirable, endangering the whole concept of private property. They were faced with two alternatives, neither of them attractive. One was to urge the king to put down the disorders by force. But in this case, they would be in effect reinstating Louis XVI in his full power, which they feared he might then use against them. On the other hand, they could accept the effects of the peasant rebellions as a fait accompli and move to drastically reduce the power of the nobility. It was this latter course that the majority of the delegates chose during the month of August.

Realizing that the most important issue to be joined was the whole question of the rights and privileges that were a holdover from feudal society, a group of deputies from the Breton Club took a bold step. They arranged to have the duke of Aiguillon, one of the greatest landholders in France, address the Assembly to make a sweeping renunciation of his rights as a member of the nobility. As it turned out, before he could be recognized to speak, the viscount of Noailles, Lafayette's brother-in-law, mounted the podium to offer up his rights as a nobleman. As a younger brother, his fortune was limited, so his renunciation of rights was necessarily less striking than that of the very wealthy Aiguillon, who followed him to the podium. The delegates showered both men with applause and voted to eliminate all labor services, any vestiges of serfdom, and other personal obligations of the peasants to the nobility. Financial obligations to the nobility, such as various fees and crop-sharing procedures, were to be settled once and for all by cash payments to the nobility. As it turned out, these payments never took place, but the feudal obligations did eventually disappear. All tax exemptions were also eliminated.

In the highly emotional atmosphere of this evening session of the National Assembly, other nobles rushed to offer up various rights such as their exclusive hunting privileges, the monopoly of military commands, and the right to administer manorial justice. Various rights of the church also vanished in the frenzy, including the tithe and the right of clergymen to hold multiple offices. By the time the session closed at 2 A.M, the various resolutions had swept away most of the old hierarchical order of France. In closing, the Assembly proclaimed Louis XVI to be the "regenerator of French liberty," and to solemnize the great occasion a Te Deum mass was arranged.

Interestingly enough, neither Mirabeau nor Sieyès chose to be present for this crucial session. In commenting afterward upon the hectic event, Mirabeau said, "That's just like the French; they spend a whole month debating about syllables and then in one night they overturn the entire ancien régime." Abbé Sieyès later spoke to denounce the abolition of the tithe without compensation to the church, closing his speech with a line that became famous, "They want to be free, but they don't know how to be just."[10]

In the days following this historic session, many noblemen and members of the court expressed their total disagreement with these resolutions. Louis XVI declared that he would not allow his nobility or the Catholic Church to be despoiled. Once again, however, events were moving beyond his control. The Assembly proceeded to refine the hastily passed resolutions into more detailed laws and then demanded the king's participation. He consented only to publish the laws, without stating his approval.

In the meantime the National Assembly was devoting much of its attention to the creation of a declaration of rights. On the basis of his American experience, Lafayette strongly urged the passage of such a document, and he asked Thomas Jefferson, who was serving as ambassador to France, to help him prepare a draft version. Mirabeau, on the other hand, argued that the constitution should be written before any such declaration of rights was made. Many deputies argued that too much talk of equality might lead the lower classes to demand economic equality. But on August 26 the National Assembly finally passed its famous Declaration of the Rights of Man, which begins with the words "All men are born and remain free and equal in rights." Its articles abolished imprisonment without trial, proclaimed freedom of speech and of the press, and asserted the right of citizens to approve all taxes through their chosen representatives. Taxation was henceforth to be allocated according to one's ability to pay. The religious question had produced considerable debate, which resulted in a somewhat ambiguous article providing that no one could be "disturbed" for his or her religious opinions, if their practice did not trouble the public order. The declaration ended with an affirmation of the right to hold property.

Also at issue as the Assembly tried to write a constitution was the question of a veto for the king. Mirabeau and many other deputies favored an absolute veto, while others such as Barnave favored a suspensive veto, which could be overturned by the will of three successive legislatures. In mid–September, Barnave attempted to work out a compromise whereby Louis XVI would accept the August decrees and the Declaration of the Rights of Man in exchange for obtaining a suspensive veto. Necker tried to persuade the king to agree to this plan but was unsuccessful. In the meantime the Assembly passed the suspensive veto, and many delegates felt betrayed when the king did not then promulgate the August decrees.

In the middle of this impasse, Louis XVI brought the thousand-man Flanders regiment to Versailles on September 23. This regiment was ostensibly brought in as protection against possible disorders, but the National Assembly viewed the troops as a direct threat. As in early July, the king and the National Assembly found themselves on opposite sides of momentous issues, with the presence of troops once again inflaming an already tense situation. In Paris, demonstrators were again thronging the gardens of the Palais Royal, demanding that the king end his opposition to the will of the National Assembly. To insulate the National Assembly from the disturbances in the capital, its conservative and moderate members urged Louis XVI to move the Assembly to Soissons or Compiègne, but he refused to do so and also vetoed proposed plans for his personal flight from Versailles. It was a decision he would soon regret.

Finally matters came to a head on the evening of October 1, when the officers of the king's bodyguards gave a banquet for the officers of the Flanders regiment. During the festive evening the king, the queen, and the dauphin greeted the men and were entertained by patriotic songs. By the end of the evening, many soldiers had drunk too much, and the national cockade was insulted by a few of the revelers. It was just the kind of incident the orators of the Palais Royal had been awaiting.

11

Mob Takes Royal Family Captive

Events were moving at a faster pace than anyone at the court of Versailles realized. On the morning of October 5, Louis XVI went hunting as usual, but the streets of Paris were thronged with people eager to avenge the insult to the national cockade that had occurred at the officers' banquet on October 1. In the midst of the turmoil, a mob of poor women from the volatile Faubourgs St. Antoine and Les Halles, joined by a few men disguised as women, decided to march on Versailles to bring the king to Paris as a guarantee against further famine. Shortly before noon, a crowd of almost six thousand women left Paris armed with pikes, scythes, and a pair of cannons taken from the Hôtel de Ville. The surprising fact that almost all the marchers were women suggests that the march had been orchestrated in advance by certain Parisian factions.

By the time the women left Paris, the troops of the National Guard were demonstrating at Place de la Grève (site of the present Hôtel de Ville), insisting that their commander, Lafayette, lead them to Versailles to help the women bring the king to Paris. Lafayette remained out of sight until midday but finally could delay no longer and appeared before the Guardsmen on his horse. Always a powerful orator, he tried to persuade the troops not to leave the city. But in reply to his words, the soldiers only shouted, "To Versailles." Finally the revolutionary government of Paris, called the Commune, ordered him to lead the troops to Versailles. Gouverneur Morris, a close friend of Lafayette, wrote in his diary that day: "Lafayette has marched by compulsion, guarded by his own troops who suspect and threaten him. Dreadful situation, obliged to do what he abhors or suffer an ignominious death, with the certainty that the sacrifice of his life will not prevent the mischief."[1]

When Lafayette left Paris at 4 o'clock in the afternoon at the head of fifteen thousand troops of the National Guard and a few thousand men from the streets of Paris, the women's march was already drawing close to Versailles.

During the twelve-mile walk to Versailles, the marchers had made frequent stops at wine shops and were soon intoxicated. Because it rained all day, they had to wade through puddles and thick mud, and their anger grew as they toiled toward Versailles.

By early afternoon, word had reached the palace that the mob of women was on its way. Marie Antoinette sent men off at once to find the king and bring him back from his hunt. One of the most complete accounts of these fateful days comes to us from the duchess of Tourzel, who had been appointed to the important position of governess to the royal children when her predecessor, the countess of Polignac, emigrated immediately after the fall of the Bastille. In her memoirs, Mme. Tourzel described the climactic scene when the king returned to the palace:

> M. de Narbonne Fritzlard ... begged his Majesty to give him a few troops and some guns, assuring him that he would soon rid him of this band of robbers. "It is necessary," he said, "to hold the bridges of Sevres and Saint Cloud. They will either abandon their project or advance by Meudon. Stationed on the heights, I will open fire on them, and I will pursue them with the cavalry in their flight in such a way that not one of them will reach Paris." The king, who always hoped by kindness to recall the wandering spirits to himself, could not make up his mind to adopt a plan which would cause bloodshed among his subjects, and he placed no obstacle in the way of this army of brigands.[2]

Because Louis XVI did not wish to defend himself against the marchers, one of his ministers, Saint-Priest, urged him to leave Versailles. It appeared at first that the king would follow his advice, but unfortunately, Saint-Priest left the palace for a short while to take his pregnant wife to safety in a nearby convent. In his absence Necker argued that the king should not leave because there was no money available to pay for the troops to accompany him. He seems also to have convinced Louis XVI that he would lose face by becoming a "fugitive king." Louis XVI feared, moreover, that if he left, the National Assembly would appoint as regent his cousin the duke of Orléans, who many believed had been busy behind the scenes helping to organize these latest attacks.

All was chaos and confusion as everyone thronged around the king, trying to decide what to do before the mob arrived. When the king's grooms tried to bring him the royal carriages, men from the National Guard of Versailles unharnessed the horses. At one point Marie Antoinette sent word to her servants to prepare for immediate departure. Shortly thereafter, she sent word that the decision had been made to remain at Versailles.

In her memoirs Mme. Tourzel bitterly regretted that no one had had the foresight to send the queen and her children to join the king where he was hunting, so that they could all escape while there was still time.[3] Every hour that passed increased the danger to the royal family. Joseph Weber, an Austrian friend of the queen, later wrote that by the end of the afternoon the situation had deteriorated to the point that regardless of what road the queen had taken to leave Versailles, she would have been assassinated.[4]

Mme. de Staël hurried from Paris to Versailles when she learned of the women's march and joined her parents, the Neckers, at the palace in time to witness the crucial deliberations of the king. In her memoirs she described the problems Louis XVI faced in meeting the threats against the monarchy: "Even though he had decided to remain at Versailles, the king could have used his bodyguards to meet force with force. But Louis XVI had religious scruples about risking French lives for his personal defense, and his courage, which no one who saw him die could ever doubt, never led him to any spontaneous action."[5] It is interesting to note that Mme. de Staël did not believe that a temporary military success that day would have saved the king anyway because she was convinced that the Revolution was by now inevitable.

In his reluctance to shed blood, Louis XVI went so far as to order his bodyguards not to fire on the demonstrators. By midafternoon the soldiers of the Versailles National Guard, spurred on by the news from Paris, began sporadic attacks on the bodyguards, who were left in an intolerable position because they had orders not to shoot. To save these loyal men from being massacred by the approaching Parisian mob, the king sent most of his bodyguards away from Versailles to safety. This left the palace virtually undefended because by this point the loyalty of the Flanders regiment was clearly in doubt.

Shortly before 5 o'clock that afternoon, the horde of Parisian marchers descended upon Versailles. They first invaded the chamber of the National Assembly, rendering further discussion there almost impossible, as an observer reported:

> I went into the Assembly at about 8 P.M. It presented a strange spectacle.... The galleries were full of women and men armed with scythes, sticks and pikes.... I was in a gallery, where a harridan was directing the movements of about a hundred women and a number of young people who shouted or kept silence as she ordered them. She addressed the deputies with coarse familiarity. "Who's that talking down there? Make the chatterbox shut up. That's not the point: the point is that we want bread. Tell them to put our little Mother Mirabeau up to speak."[6]

The women insisted on seeing the king, and a dozen were admitted to the palace to present their demands to him. He was conciliatory to the point of embracing one of them, so they returned with a positive report to the throngs waiting outside. Their confederates wondered suspiciously, however, if they had gone over to the other side and came close to attacking them.[7]

In the middle of the evening, Louis XVI also acceded to the demands of the Assembly that he sign the Declaration of the Rights of Man. It is possible that some of the more radical deputies of the Assembly had encouraged the Parisians to march to Versailles precisely to force the king's immediate acquiescence. He had earlier that same day stated his views on the subject: "The Declaration of the Rights of Man contains some very good principles that will help guide your work ... but it also includes some statements that are ambiguous and open to different interpretations. These can only be properly evaluated when their exact meaning has been established by laws based upon the Declaration."[8]

As all the members of the court thronged around the king and queen in a state of extreme agitation and foreboding, the gathering darkness only augmented everyone's fear that they would be slaughtered before morning. The rioters had already killed one of the bodyguards and wounded others, showing only too clearly the fate that might await the palace residents. Word arrived at last from Paris that Lafayette was leading the National Guard to Versailles, and everyone was relieved to think they would soon have some protection against the hostile crowd.

Lafayette needed all his usual self-assurance and diplomacy on this dangerous night, as he sought to maintain control of the men of the Parisian National Guard, whose sympathies were inclining toward the demonstrators. At the outskirts of Versailles, he stopped the troops and insisted that they swear an oath of allegiance to respect the National Assembly and the law and to obey the king.

When Lafayette entered the palace shortly before midnight, everyone pressed around him, knowing him to be their only protection against the mass of Parisian women armed with their frightful pikes and scythes. He asked the king for permission to take charge of the outer defenses of the château, a permission at once granted. He calmly and forcefully reassured all present that he had full control of the situation and urged everyone to retire for the evening. Totally exhausted by his day-long efforts to maintain control of a National Guard on the verge of rebellion, Lafayette announced that he would leave the palace to sleep in his quarters in the town. The disastrous results of this decision were apparent within a few hours.

Marie Antoinette's advisers, knowing all too well that the mob's fury was directed particularly against her, suggested that she would be safer if she spent the night in the king's suite. Upon reflection, she decided to remain in her own room, confiding in Mme. Tourzel that she would rather expose herself to danger than draw the rioters' vengeance upon the king and her children.[9]

While the royal family and courtiers slept in the palace and Lafayette retired to the town, the throngs of Parisian women had little choice but to stay awake all night. They warmed themselves at bonfires in the streets as they sang revolutionary songs and listened to orators who inflamed them to an even greater fury. By the time the sun rose, they were in a murderous mood and streamed around the palace, looking for a possible entrance. Finding an unlocked gate, they rushed through it, meeting with resistance only from two bodyguards. One of the men of the mob was an infamous character with a long beard, who was known to all of Paris as "Coupe-tête." He proceeded to justify this title by chopping off the heads of the unlucky pair of bodyguards with an axe. Encountering no further resistance, a group of sixty men and women followed a soldier of the Versailles National Guard, who led them to the queen's apartments. As they approached, one of them shouted, "We are going to cut off her head, tear out her heart, fry her liver and that won't be the end of it."[10] Two bodyguards were on duty protecting the entrance to her apartments. They had just time to shout a warning through the door and turn to face the mob. In the few moments it took their assailants to overpower them with sword thrusts and blows from pikes, the queen had just time enough to leap from her bed and run down an interior passage leading to the king's apartments. Even then, she had to wait for several interminable minutes outside a barred entrance before she could finally make herself heard and flee her pursuers, who would soon discover her escape route. Fortunately, they had stopped to vent their rage on her empty bed, stabbing it with pikes and slashing the hangings with their scythes, making it only too clear what fate she had narrowly escaped.

The marquis of Ferrières, a moderate deputy to the National Assembly, wrote a record of these events that incriminates the king's cousin, the duke of Orléans. Ferrières noted that the duke mingled with the rioters, receiving their cries of "Long live King Orléans":

> While the conspirators ... were flooding through the apartments, men dressed as women were spreading the word ... that M. Lafayette was a traitor.... One of the leaders ... was advising a group of men and women who thronged around him and to whom he was handing money to spare no one but the dauphin and the Duke of Orléans. "We want the heads of the queen and M. Lafayette." At these words a man with a frightful face disguised as a woman displayed a sort of sickle and swore that he would be the one to cut off the old bitch's head.[11]

As the rioters were surging toward the king's apartments, members of Lafayette's National Guard at last arrived and forced them to leave the palace. The intruders then ran throughout the courtyards, gathering all the hapless bodyguards they could find. They brought them to the marble courtyard below the king's windows, where they engaged in a tumultuous discussion of whether they should behead their terrified victims, hang them, or cut their throats. In the midst of the turmoil, constant shouts of "the king to Paris" rang out. Within the palace Lafayette was trying to convince the king to go to Paris to avert further bloodshed. Fearing for the lives of his faithful body-guards being held by the mob, Louis XVI reluctantly agreed. The rioters beneath his window demanded to see the king on the balcony to hear his pledges themselves. When he appeared and agreed to go to Paris with them, shouts of "Long live the king" accompanied those of "Long live the nation." In order to save their comrades trembling below, those bodyguards still with the king appeared on the balcony with him, throwing down their bandoliers and putting on the caps of the National Guard. Lafayette also addressed the mob from the balcony and sent his troops down to take custody of the belea-guered bodyguards.

Meanwhile the crowd was shouting for the queen to appear on the bal-cony. Although she had many faults, cowardice was not among them. All who witnessed her behavior from this moment until her ultimate death have testified to her great courage. She walked out onto the balcony, knowing full well that she was the special object of hatred of those clamoring below, many of them holding guns in their hands. Perhaps hoping to soften the wrath of the crowd by the sight of the children, she led out onto the balcony the four-year-old dauphin and his ten-year-old sister, Madame Royal. When voices from the crowd at once shouted, "no children," she sent them back inside and faced the crowd without flinching. One of the bystanders later testified that he saw a man aim his gun at the queen before his companion pushed down the barrel. Marie Antoinette's unusual bravery in this terrifying situ-ation struck the emotions of the crowd, several of whom suddenly shouted, "Long live the queen."[12]

Having gained its objective of forcing the king to leave Versailles, the mob erupted into a holiday mood. Not long after noontime a bizarre pro-cession set off for Paris. Next to the royal carriage rode Lafayette, seated on his magnificent white charger. Behind the carriage walked a few dozen dis-armed bodyguards. The soldiers of the National Guard were everywhere, each carrying a loaf of bread on his bayonet. Bringing up the rear of the procession were carts filled with wheat and flour from the palace stores. As a grisly reminder of their power, the people carried aloft on pikes the heads of the two bodyguards slain defending the entrance to the queen's apartment. In celebration of their victory, the marchers had entwined their weapons with oak leaves, and they waved branches of poplars, causing one observer to remark that the procession resembled a slowly moving forest. Some women rode astride the cannons, while others found horses. Weber has left a moving account of the trip:

> [A]s they stopped occasionally to fire other vollies [sic], the fishwomen alighted
> from their cannon and horses, forming rings before the carriage of the king,
> embracing the soldiers, and singing in horrid discord songs the chorus of which

was: "Here is the baker, the baker's wife, and the baker's boy." The horror of a dark, cold, rainy day, that infamous militia muttering in the dirt, those harpies, those monsters with human faces, and amidst his captive guards, a monarch ignominiously forced away with all his family, inspired such a sad mixture of grief and shame, and formed altogether so dreadful a scene, that I cannot even now recal [sic] it to my imagination without experiencing the greatest agitation.[13]

Proceeding at a walking pace, the entourage took almost six hours to reach Paris. The procession was all the more bizarre because not only was Louis XVI being taken captive to Paris by Lafayette and his troops, but Lafayette himself was in effect the captive of his own soldiers and the Parisian mob. During these long hours, vulgar insults shouted at the queen and the lurid sight of the two bloody heads of their faithful bodyguards bobbing on long pikes above the crowd could only have produced feelings of extreme horror and apprehension in the occupants of the royal carriage.

At the outskirts of Paris, Mayor Bailly met the royal family. With a notable lack of sensitivity, he welcomed the king by saying, "What a glorious day is this, Sire, on which the Parisians are going to receive your Majesty and your family into their city."[14] Being totally exhausted by the events of the last two days, the royal family wished to retire immediately to the Tuileries Palace, where they were to reside. Lafayette insisted, however, that the king go to the Hôtel de Ville to pay his respects to the Paris Commune. Cries of "Long live the king" accompanied his progress through the streets of Paris, but to Mme. Tourzel, "They were more noisy than hearty, and in them a certain amount of violence, painful to hear, was perceptible."[15]

Perhaps realizing the damage done by her previous careless behavior, Marie Antoinette now became more aware of the necessity of placating the people of Paris. When the king said to the members of the Commune, "I come with pleasure into the heart of my good city of Paris," she added, "and with confidence," a phrase that seemed to please those assembled.[16]

At last the royal family was allowed to retire to the Tuileries Palace, which had lain unused for so many years that it had fallen into a musty state of neglect. Rooms had been hastily prepared for everyone, but the one assigned to the dauphin had no locks and was unguarded. Mme. Tourzel barricaded the doors with what furniture she could find and sat up all night by his bedside.[17] At the end of that day, Gouverneur Morris wrote in his diary:

What an unfortunate prince! The victim of his weakness, and in the hands of those who are not to be relied on even for pity. What a dreadful lesson it is for man that an absolute prince cannot with safety be indulgent. The troubles of this country are begun, but as to the end it is not easy to foresee it.[18]

12

Life of the Royal Family in Paris

The next morning the royal family awoke to the cries of hundreds of people who filled the courtyards and gardens of the Tuileries Palace, having come to see for themselves that the king and queen were now in Paris. Many shouted, "Long live the king and the royal family!" whenever a family member appeared at the windows of the apartments, but others were clearly antagonistic to the new inhabitants of the palace. To satisfy the crowds, the family members all had to put on the national cockade. At one point a group of fishwives even entered the ground-floor apartments of the king's sister, Madame Elisabeth, who in dismay asked for new quarters.

A few days later a Parisian newspaper published a report that the queen was going to redeem all the articles that poor women had been forced to pawn in order to buy food. A large group of these women soon gathered outside the Tuileries, loudly demanding this charity until Louis XVI finally suggested that Marie Antoinette redeem all articles below a certain value.

Life was far different here from what it had been at Versailles, where the vast gardens filled with flowers and magnificent fountains had provided pleasant diversions for the royal family. None of them could even set foot in the Tuileries Gardens without being attended by a half dozen soldiers of the National Guard. For the last twenty years, Louis XVI had hunted several times a week, but he now had to give up his horses and dogs and renounce his favorite recreation. Suddenly reduced to an inactive life, he obtained exercise only through occasional rides in the Bois de Boulogne with National Guardsmen as an escort or games of billiards with Marie Antoinette in the evening.

After a few days a routine of life was established at the Tuileries that included the daily rising and retiring ceremonies. Twice a week a court was held, and many nobles came to show their sympathy and support for the king. Among them was his former minister, Malesherbes, who wrote to a friend:

> Although I hate to dress myself up and although I abominate that cursed sword which gets between my legs when I go upstairs and which will make me break

my neck some day, I attend the king's levee regularly every Sunday. For the greatest pleasure of the whole week is when I see with my own eyes that this *brav homme* [good man] is still all right. I never talk to him, but that is nothing; it is enough for me to have seen him, and I think, too, that he is glad to have seen me there.[1]

At the time that the king had convoked the Estates-General, Malesherbes had presented him with a memorandum emphasizing how important it was for him to take control of the situation in a decisive way. "You read a great deal, Sire," he stated, "and you are more learned than people think. But reading is nothing unless it is accompanied by reflection. I have recently been rereading the section on Charles I in David Hume's *History of England*. Read it again, reflecting upon it. Your positions are similar."[2]

Malesherbes had earlier assured Louis XVI that because of the "gentler manners of the times," he would not meet the same fate as the English king. Now events were giving the minister cause to reconsider that assessment. He had been confident about the future when the National Assembly was established through the Tennis Court Oath, but as violence broke out that summer and fall, he became increasingly uneasy. As noted in the Preface, Malesherbes was not optimistic: "I pity him indeed. I fear that he will have a hard time escaping those scoundrels, and it is a shame, for he is a worthy prince.... But in certain situations ... the qualities that are virtues in a private citizen become almost vices in a person who occupies the throne; they may be good for the other world, but they are worth nothing in this one."[3]

The man who was now most responsible for maintaining the safety of the king was Lafayette, commander of the National Guard. Known as the "hero of two worlds" because of his brilliant military assistance to the American cause, he also attempted to bridge the gulf between the worlds of the court and the Third Estate. The king and queen never entirely trusted him, but they realized that he protected them by maintaining an uneasy control over the wilder Parisian factions. Lafayette was a man of high character, but he was an ambitious leader who imagined himself the savior of the French people.

The other main source of official power lay in the National Assembly, which followed the king to Paris a few days after his forced departure from Versailles. It was to prove an unfortunate move because it made the deputies even more susceptible to the radical influence of the Parisian crowds. After meeting temporarily in various buildings, the Assembly set itself up permanently in the Manège, a former royal riding school on the edge of the Tuileries Gardens. Located on what is now the Rue de Rivoli, it was just across the street from the Tuileries Palace where the king resided.

The long and narrow building was in no way suited to a legislative assembly. Tiers of seats were hastily installed at each end for the deputies, and the president's chair and the speaker's podium were located on opposite walls in the middle of the room. Before long, the deputies fell into a pattern of sitting in the left or right ends of the room, depending upon their political sympathies. This practice gave rise to the modern usage of the terms "left" and "right" to indicate political allegiance. The visitors' galleries were always filled with Parisians who alternately cheered and jeered the various speakers, creating an atmosphere of constant crowd pressure.

Shortly after the move to Paris, many of the leading moderates in the Assembly resigned in dismay at the extreme turn of events and escaped to the provinces or abroad. Among them was Jean Mounier, a lawyer from Grenoble who was a strong proponent of a constitutional monarchy based on the English system. He had rallied the deputies to swear the famous Tennis Court Oath and had also been president of the Assembly before it left Versailles. With the departure of these moderate deputies, the Assembly was left in the hands of men who wished to set up a constitutional monarchy in France but acted in such a way as to severely limit the king's power. Louis XVI was now chief executive of France in name only. Although his council ministers were supposedly in charge of the executive powers of the government, in actual practice the situation was very confused. The National Assembly set up committees to oversee all functions of the government, and these committees encroached to a large extent on the powers of the king's ministers. This period was one of great frustration to the king, who no longer had any real power to control events but had grave reservations about the headlong course of the Revolution.

Violent incidents always distressed Louis XVI. Soon after his arrival in Paris he was dismayed to hear that a mob had hanged a baker and then shown his head on a pike to his wife, who died of grief soon afterward. Louis XVI sent money to help the family but could do little to prevent this kind of violence.[4] Lafayette and the members of the National Assembly were also becoming apprehensive about the growth of mob violence, and the governmental authorities apprehended and hanged three of the men who had killed the baker. On October 21 the National Assembly passed a decree giving the authorities the power to declare martial law when mob disorders arose. In such a case a red flag was to be displayed as a warning that any further demonstrations would be suppressed by the National Guard.

From the moment the king was brought to Paris in captivity, there were many nobles who conceived various plans for helping him to escape to the provinces or abroad. Most of these plans did not materialize, primarily because Louis XVI realized that if he were to escape to the provinces and try to rally those still loyal to him, then a civil war would almost certainly break out. As Mme. Tourzel relates in her memoirs: "The king took no part in the intrigues formed in his favor. This good and excellent prince was so afraid of the misfortunes which a civil war would cause that he preferred to prolong his sufferings rather than witness the employment of a means which might occasion so many evils."[5]

One nobleman, the marquis of Favras, who was formerly in the service of the king's brother Provence, was arrested in December 1789 and charged with conspiring to help the king escape. There were many rumors that Provence himself was heavily involved in the plot and perhaps even hoped to succeed to the throne after his brother's departure, but Favras limited himself to saying only that he had acted upon the orders of a "great lord." To protect himself from the suspicions thus aroused, Provence went to the Hôtel de Ville to make a public declaration of his loyalty to the Revolution. Favras was brought to trial in February amidst a tremendous Parisian outcry for vengeance. Every day the magistrates of the court of Châtelet passed through crowds of people shouting: "Off with Favras's head! Hang the judges!" In this highly charged atmosphere, the judges sentenced Favras to death by hanging, a form of execution previously reserved for the lower classes.

At this point the king decided that the time had come to assert himself. On February 4, 1790, he walked across the Tuileries Gardens to the adjacent Manège to address the National Assembly in a speech designed to place himself in a position of leadership of the Revolution. His speech covered many important issues:

> Gentlemen, the gravity of the circumstances in which France finds itself brings me to your midst....
>
> You have a great goal before you, but it is important to reach it without increasing the current unrest or producing new convulsions....
>
> You will recall, gentlemen, that over ten years ago, at a time when the desire of the nation for provincial assemblies had not yet been expressed, I had begun to substitute this type of administration for that which a long tradition had established. The outcome having made me realize that I was not mistaken in the utility of such bodies, I sought to produce the same benefit for all the provinces in my realm. To assure general confidence for these new administrations, I wanted their members to be freely chosen by all the citizens. You have improved upon these ideas in various ways....
>
> Time will reform what is defective in the collection of laws that you are producing, but any enterprise that has a tendency to undermine the principles of the constitution itself, any effort which has as its goal the overthrowing of such principles or the weakening of their good influence will serve only to introduce among us the frightful evils of discord....
>
> Let us thus attempt in good faith to implement our dreams and to realize them with a unanimous accord. Let everyone know that the monarch and the

representatives of the nation are united in the same cause with a single desire so that this firm belief spreads throughout the provinces a peaceful spirit of good-will....

I like to believe that one day all Frenchmen without distinction will recognize the advantage of the complete suppression of the differences in rank and condition when it is a matter of working together for the public good and our country's prosperity, which concerns all of our citizens equally. I hope that everyone will see that henceforth to be called to serve the state in some way, it will suffice to have shown oneself to have remarkable talents or virtues....

I will defend and maintain the constitutional liberty whose principles have been consecrated by the general will, in addition to mine. I will also, in concert with the queen, who shares my beliefs, prepare my son from an early age for the new order that circumstances have produced. I will train him throughout his early years to find his happiness in the happiness of the French people....

I trust that as you carry out your work, you will with wisdom and candor concern yourselves with strengthening the executive power, which is a necessary condition for a lasting order.... I also hope that you will not forget that administrative confusion, which leads to a confusion of powers, often degenerates through blind violence into the most dangerous and alarming of all tyrannies.[6]

Almost all the deputies responded to the king's speech with great enthusiasm. After the king left the hall, a deputy proposed the following oath: "I swear to be faithful to the nation, the law, and the king, and to maintain by all means in my power the constitution decreed by the Assembly and sanctioned by the king." Almost all the deputies swore to this oath, and the spectators in the galleries raised their hands to signal their acquiescence. Those present were as usual carried away by their emotions, but the event nevertheless indicates that at this date almost all the members of the National Assembly remained optimistic that they could work with the king to produce a stable and desirable system of government for France.

Taking advantage of the wave of good feeling that followed his speech that spring, the king announced his intention to take his family to spend the summer as usual at the château of St. Cloud on the outskirts of Paris. Many Parisians were reluctant to see them go even this far from the heart of the city, but Lafayette insisted that it was important to prove to the world that the king was not a prisoner in Paris. They left accordingly in late May to spend the summer at St. Cloud but returned to Paris from time to time. It was a welcome respite for the king and queen, for they had far more personal liberty there and no longer felt the constant pressure from the populace of Paris. As she stood one day with Mme. Tourzel on the terrace at St. Cloud looking at the view of Paris in the distance, Marie Antoinette commented how ironic it was that in earlier days she had stood on the same spot and wistfully dreamed of living in Paris.[7]

One visitor who came privately to visit the king and queen at St. Cloud was Mirabeau, now the most powerful man in the National Assembly. He remains one of the most enigmatic figures of the French Revolution. His libertine personal life and the obscene writings of his youth shocked normally tolerant French society, but even his enemies conceded the brilliance of his intellect and the astuteness of his political intuition. By employing a coterie of assistants, Mirabeau was able to speak with authority on all aspects of the French situation, maximizing to the fullest extent his great oratorical powers. His demagogic speeches pleased the more radical elements of the Assembly, yet at the same time were designed to strengthen the monarchy because Mirabeau was convinced that only a strong constitutional monarchy could offer France a promising future.

When he came to St. Cloud in May 1790, Mirabeau entered into private relations with the king and queen, attempting through a long series of memoranda to persuade them to various courses of action. In return for his services, they paid his huge debts and gave him a large monthly retainer. This venality was one of the qualities that caused more upright men like Lafayette to view Mirabeau with distaste. Mirabeau rationalized his acceptance of this kind of fee by saying he would take money only to promote positions he favored. Although they paid him to work to strengthen the monarchy, Louis XVI and Marie Antoinette never trusted Mirabeau or implemented his advice.

The chief thrust of Mirabeau's advice was that to save the monarchy, they should flee to a provincial capital where they could rally about them all those loyal to their cause. Initially, Mirabeau proposed that they go to Rouen in Normandy, where support for the royal cause was particularly strong; later he suggested other cities, such as Compiègne. Marie Antoinette, however, wrote to one of her correspondents, "We will never be so wretched ... as to be reduced to the painful extremity of having recourse to Mirabeau."[8] It was an assertion of pride and disdain she may later have regretted.

13

Bastille Anniversary Celebration

In order to keep control over the Revolution, the bourgeois National Assembly limited the number of French citizens who could vote by setting up a distinction between "active" and "passive" citizens. Active citizens were men who paid an amount in annual taxes equal to at least three days' wages. Only these people were allowed to vote. Even then, they could vote only for the electors of a secondary assembly, who in turn elected the deputies to the National Assembly. To be eligible to be an elector in the secondary assembly or to hold local office, a man had to pay taxes amounting to more than ten days' wages. Making the system even more restrictive was the law that a person could be elected as a deputy to the National Assembly only if he paid a fee equal to fifty days' wages. A further curious distinction stated that domestic servants could not be active citizens. As a result of this limitation of the franchise, approximately two million potential male voters were excluded, leaving some four million eligible male voters.

There were some who objected to this policy, urging a more democratic attitude. Camille Desmoulins, one of the more vocal of the radical journalists, protested in vivid words: "You would relegate Christ himself to the canaille; the active citizens are those who took the Bastille."[1] He further objected that under this decree neither Rousseau nor Corneille would have been eligible for the National Assembly. Among the handful of deputies opposing these voting restrictions in the National Assembly was Robespierre, a lawyer who had embraced the cause of the poor and believed that they had an equal right to vote.

Property qualifications also limited membership in the political clubs that were becoming a powerful force in the capital. The Jacobin Club was an outgrowth of the Breton Club, which had helped initiate the Revolution at Versailles. The Jacobins included many prominent deputies to the Assembly and others in positions of power, who gathered every evening to discuss the current political issues, including the agenda of the National Assembly for the following day. More radical and less wealthy politicians met in the Corde-liers Club on the Left Bank under the leadership of Danton and Marat. These clubs were an outgrowth of the tremendous intellectual excitement that had seized France on the eve of the Revolution. Mme. de Staël described the atmos-phere created by the opening of opportunities to men of talent, the liberty of the press, and the brilliant discussions in the National Assembly: "[These things] freed from their chains the French spirit and patriotism, in short all those energetic qualities that later led to results that were sometimes cruel, but always tremendous. Everyone breathed more freely, and the vague hope of a happiness without shackles seized the country with all its power, as men are moved in their youth by illusions, without thought for the future."[2]

One of the most important results of this mood of enthusiasm was the decision of the revolutionary leaders to celebrate the first anniversary of the fall of the Bastille by holding a Festival of Federation to which all regions of France were invited to send delegates from the National Guard and regular army units. The aim of the Federation was twofold: to replace narrow sectional interests with a feeling of national pride and unity and to consolidate the Revolution. As a site for the celebration, the organizers chose the Champ de Mars, a large field near the Ecole Militaire on the southwestern edge of Paris. In order to provide seating for the vast number of spectators anticipated, the planners decided to dig out the center of the Champ de Mars and pile up the dirt all around the periphery in order to create a huge amphitheater.

Twelve thousand men were employed to prepare the area, but as the cru-cial date approached it was obvious that the work would not be finished on time. At this point, in a great surge of patriotic enthusiasm Parisians flocked to the area to help move dirt. Even Lafayette wielded a shovel for two hours. Fashionably dressed ladies came out from Paris to push wheelbarrows, and every day after their regular work was done, people would march out from the city to help move earth for a couple of hours before dark. Those who were particularly zealous saw to it that the less enthusiastic also did their part. Monasteries were forced to send their monks to labor alongside the rest of the citizens. While they worked, the people sang the new patriotic songs like "Ça Ira," and at the end of the evening everyone marched back to the city by torchlight, carrying patriotic banners.

With this extra labor, the project was completed in time for the July 14th anniversary of the fall of the Bastille. The huge amphitheater was ready with its tiered seating of thirty rows, with space at the top for people to stand. In the center was a large altar upon which mass was to be celebrated, and at one end was a platform for the king, the royal family, the president of the National Assembly, and other dignitaries.

Some Parisians were so eager to have a good seat for the festivities that they camped out at the Champ de Mars the night before the Federation event. The official celebration began on the long-awaited day at 6 A.M. when the various Federates, as they were called, assembled in their units and started marching through the streets of Paris toward the Champ de Mars, carrying the banners of their eighty-three departments. It rained heavily throughout the day, but even the weather could not depress the Parisians, who were in a holiday mood. The parade route was lined with enthusiastic crowds, and many citizens watching from their windows gave food and wine to the soldiers. At the Place Louis XV (Place de la Concorde), the troops were joined by the deputies of the National Assembly, who marched with them to the Champ de Mars, crossing the Seine on a bridge of boats. The marquis of Ferrières wrote a vivid account of the arrival at the Champ de Mars:

> The first Federates who arrived began to dance the farandole; others as they arrived joined them, forming a circle that soon enclosed a large area of the Champ-de-Mars. It was a spectacle worthy of an observant philosopher to see this crowd of people who had come from the far corners of France, drawn by the impulse of a national identity, banishing all memory of the past, every concern about the present, and every fear for the future. They yielded themselves to a deliciously carefree mood, and the 300,000 spectators of every age and both sexes who were watching them, followed their movements, beating time to the dance with their clapping. They forgot the rain, their hunger, and the boredom of the long time they had had to wait. Finally the cortege entered the Champs de Mars, the dancing stopped, and each Federate soldier rejoined his unit.[3]

When all had arrived, Talleyrand, the bishop of Autun, celebrated mass on the huge altar, which was flanked by three hundred priests wearing white robes belted with tricolored sashes. It seems particularly appropriate that Talleyrand officiated on this occasion so highly ambiguous for the cause of religion in France because he was a cynic who had entered the church reluctantly as a young man and had risen to a position of power only through his wiles as a politician. He was competing with Gouveneur Morris for the attentions of a prominent Parisian beauty and was far more interested in living the good life than in contemplating the life hereafter. In fact, it was Talleyrand who coined the phrase "la douceur de vivre" to refer to the lifestyle of the ancien régime, now gone forever. On the night after the Federation celebration, he twice broke the bank at a Parisian gambling house.[4]

LaFayette, as representative of the assembled troops, went to the altar after the mass and swore an oath to be faithful to the nation, the law, and the king. Then the president of the National Assembly swore the same oath, and the troops and spectators in turn shouted, "I swear it!" Finally it was the king's turn, and in a strong voice he stated, "As king of the French, I swear to use the powers delegated to me by the constitutional act of the State and to maintain the Constitution decreed by the National Assembly and accepted by me." Marie Antoinette then held up the dauphin to the people and said, "Here is my son, who joins me in the same sentiments." The crowd broke forth in wild cheers of "Long live the king," "Long live the queen," and "Long live the dauphin." In his account, Ferrièrres wrote, "At this point the sun broke through the clouds in all its glory, making it seem as if the Eternal itself wanted to be a witness to this mutual engagement and to ratify it by its presence."[5]

Mme. de Staël also vividly described the events of the day: "The spectators were deliriously happy. The king and liberty seemed to them at that point to be completely united. A limited monarchy has always been the true wish of France, and the last wave of a truly national enthusiasm happened at this Federation of 1790."[6]

During the days that the Federates remained in Paris, they showed their devotion to the king and his family. When they passed in review before him at the foot of the grand staircase of the Tuileries Palace, he spoke to as many soldiers as possible. They idolized the dauphin, who was a charming and attractive little boy. One day one of these men saw the dauphin pull a leaf off a lilac bush and asked if he could have it as a souvenir. At once the dauphin was besieged with soldiers all clamoring to have a leaf he had picked. Within a few minutes the lilac bush was bare.[7]

In a special review of the regular army troops and the Federates at the Etoile, the king found himself urged by all the soldiers to visit them in their provinces. Mme. Tourzel recognized the pivotal character of the moment:

> If the king had taken advantage of this opportunity ... and had announced at this review that he was about to respond to the wish expressed by the deputies ... if he had elected to be accompanied in his visits only by the good Federates who evinced such attachment for him, he would have disconcerted the Assembly.... The king unfortunately did not realize the effect his presence would produce in the provinces; he feared that the zeal of his faithful servants would carry them too far and that the opposition of the malcontents would bring about a civil war. All these considerations prevented him from following the advice that he should take advantage of so favorable an opportunity to leave Paris. The majority of his ministers lacked energy and were always afraid of making any attack on that direful liberty which existed only in name.... The fault of the king was that he had too little confidence in himself. Persuaded that others saw more clearly than himself, he dared not take the course indicated to him by the uprightness of his mind and the goodness of his heart. Discontented with the education he had received, he judged himself unfavorably, and he did not do himself the justice he deserved."[8]

Mme. Tourzel's evaluation of the king's character is particularly relevant because she was one of the few people who remained in close proximity to him throughout the Revolution. She was not alone in her realization of the importance of the Federates' devotion to the king during that summer of 1790. A year later Barnave, one of the leaders of the National Assembly, admitted to the king's sister that this period of Federate support for Louis XVI had had the potential to change events in his favor. "We should have been lost, if you had known how to profit by it," he told her.[9]

14

Civil Constitution of the Clergy

A few days before the great Federation celebration, the National Assembly had passed a law that soon divided the French people. This was the Civil Constitution of the Clergy, a decree that in effect placed the control of the clergy under the government of France instead of the Vatican. Church property had already been confiscated in the fall of 1789. The new law contained some needed reforms such as the abolition of absentee bishops, but one of its most controversial provisions called for bishops and priests to be elected in the same manner as government officials. After much hesitation, the king acted upon the advice of two leading bishops whom he respected and reluctantly signed the bill, hoping by his action to avert a break between church and state. He had written to Rome to ask for guidance, but the Pope remained silent on the issue for several months, leaving Louis XVI to agonize whether he had made the right decision. In *The Oxford History of the French Revolution*, William Doyle provides a likely reason for the Pope's surprising delay in responding to the king's urgent plea for guidance: "[T]he news from Avignon and the Comtat, coming in when the debate was at its height, suggested that if he [the Pope] did prove recalcitrant a French threat to agree to the annexation of these territories would blackmail him into compliance."[1]

In November 1790 the National Assembly passed another law giving priests only two months to swear an oath to support the Civil Constitution of the Clergy or else forfeit their parishes. This bill, as usual, was then sent to the king for his signature. He held it during the early weeks of December, struggling with his conscience. As a devout Catholic, he wanted to do nothing to weaken the church, but some of his advisers were asserting that his signature would avert mob violence and bloodshed. On the day after Christmas, he finally capitulated and signed the decree.

Instead of averting a crisis, the king's signature precipitated one. On January 2, 1791, the National Assembly met to witness the taking of the oath by the large number of its members who belonged to the clergy. The hall was surrounded by a noisy crowd of people threatening to hang those who would not swear the oath, but to the surprise of most of those present, only Talleyrand, one other bishop, and one-third of the priests belonging to the Assembly took the oath. Most of the other priests attempted to make a statement explaining their dissent; the elderly bishop of Poitiers stated that he would not dishonor his gray hairs by swearing the oath. The session became uproarious as the priests tried to explain the dictates of their conscience, while opposing deputies insisted they be allowed to state only whether they would swear or not swear. One indignant priest pointed out that even the Romans had allowed the Christian martyrs to make a statement of their faith before they were executed.

Sunday, January 18, had been designated as the day on which each priest would at the end of his sermon either swear the oath or state that he refused to do so. The pressure upon the priests was enormous because many Parisians flocked to the churches to insist that they swear the oath, while others urged them to remain true to their conscience. At St. Sulpice in Paris, the priest had announced in advance his decision to refuse to swear the oath, and a mob of angry people filled the huge church. After the sermon they all started shouting, "Take the oath!" and "Hang him from the lamppost!" As the priest tried to make a statement of his beliefs, the organist pulled out all the stops and drowned him out with the patriotic song "Ça Ira," whose new refrain now included the words "hang the aristocrats from the lamppost." Some of the demonstrators even began to dance to the music. Others attempted to attack the priest when the municipal authorities and other clergy tried to lead him to the vestry. According to Mme. Tourzel: "One of them gave him a blow with his fist, a second tore his hair, and a third put a pistol to his head. The Marshal de Mouchi, who was at mass, never left the priest, and even parried several blows that were aimed at him. M. Bailly [the mayor] arrived as usual when the danger was over."[2]

It was a particularly depressing period for the king, who viewed with anguish all the violence toward the priests who were trying to remain loyal to their faith. Most of the bishops and almost half the priests of France refused to swear the oath and were replaced by elected clergy. Thus deep divisions were set up within the population throughout France, with the members of rural parishes in general remaining loyal to their nonjuring priests. The king's signature, given at such a cost to his conscience, had not achieved the peace he had hoped, and the refusal of so many priests to swear the oath seemed to imply that the king should never have signed the law.

Most of the king's ministers who had served him after July 1789 had been hounded out of office during the fall of 1790, leaving him increasingly isolated and powerless. Even the once so popular Necker parted company with the National Assembly when they printed paper money "assignats" backed by church property in an attempt to solve the financial problems facing the country. The king was forced to appoint a new council comprised of men chosen by Lafayette and thus became more than ever simply a puppet of the Assembly.

As the mood of many Parisians turned ugly over the religious question, demagogues stirred up the populace with their talk of an aristocratic plot against the Revolution. Wild rumors spread through the city. One of the most inflammatory was a story that the towering bastion of the Château of Vincennes on the outskirts of Paris was being fortified for use against the revolutionaries and that a tunnel was being dug to connect the tower with the Tuileries Palace to afford the king a means of escape. There was increased fear of a royal escape because the king's two elderly aunts, who were both deeply devout, had fled to Italy on February 20 in order to have access to priests still in good standing with the Vatican.

On February 28, 1791, a thousand armed citizens marched on Vincennes to destroy the tower. As word of the march spread through Paris, an angry crowd also assembled outside the Tuileries. Many supporters of the king feared a repetition of the October 1789 mob violence when the royal family was taken captive and brought from Versailles to Paris. These men hurried to the Tuileries to help protect the king and gained access to the palace through a passage that was not manned by the National Guard. In the meanwhile Lafayette rushed National Guard troops to Vincennes and arrested over sixty men who were attempting to knock down the tower. Hearing then of the disturbances at the Tuileries, he hastened there, where a witness saw him "mounted on his white charger, galloping to and fro, as if the fate of the world depended on him."[3] He insisted that the noblemen who had come to the king's defense with pistols and daggers should all be disarmed to avoid a confrontation. Louis XVI reluctantly asked his supporters to leave their weapons in his private room, and most then departed, although a few who refused to be searched were arrested.

Nothing was going well for the monarchy at this point. Although Mirabeau's support of the Crown had had its dubious aspects, the king was deprived of his services when Mirabeau suddenly fell gravely ill and died in early April 1791. On his deathbed he said, "I carry in my heart the funeral knell of the monarchy."[4] He was the first Frenchman buried in the Pantheon, which was still under construction. On the day of his funeral, Gouverneur Morris recorded his impressions:

> The funeral of Mirabeau (attended it is said by more than 100,000 persons in solemn silence) has been an imposing spectacle. It is a vast tribute paid to supe-

rior talents, but no great incitement to virtuous deeds. Vices both degrading and detestable marked this extraordinary creature. Compleately [*sic*] prostitute, he sacrificed everything to the whim of the moment. Cupidus alieni prodigus sui. Venal. Shameless; and yet greatly virtuous when pushed by a prevailing impulse, but never truly virtuous because never under the steady control of reason nor the firm authority of principle. I have seen this man, in the short space of two years, hissed, honored, hated, mourned. Enthusiasm has just now presented him gigantic. Time and reflection will shrink that stature.[5]

In March 1791 the Pope had at last made known his opinion on the Civil Constitution of the Clergy, condemning it in strong terms and decreeing that all priests who had sworn the oath must recant in order to remain within the Catholic Church. A furious mob burned the Pope in effigy in the gardens of the Palais Royal, and fishwives broke into a convent and beat the nuns.

The king was now in a position that caused him great personal anguish because his Catholic faith was one of the most important things in his life. He had to decide at once whether to attend masses celebrated by priests no longer recognized by the Pope or to infuriate the revolutionaries by relying upon nonjuring priests. As Holy Week approached, the issue became crucial. Louis XVI finally decided to handle the problem by leaving early for his annual summer sojourn at St. Cloud, where he could receive Easter communion from a nonjuring priest. Word of his imminent departure reached the Parisian agitators, however, and a crowd gathered outside the Tuileries. As soon as the royal family got into their carriage and started to leave, they were stopped by some members of the National Guard. Mme. Tourzel described the "horrible scene":

> The grenadiers of the National Guard ... placed themselves at the horses' heads and declared that they would not permit the king to depart. MM. Bailly and LaFayette in vain endeavored to overcome their resistance by pointing out to them that, besides its being very reprehensible in itself, it was moreover unconstitutional. "It would be an astonishing thing," said the king to them, putting his head out of the window, "if, after having given liberty to the nation, I should myself not be free." The people who thronged the Carrousel upheld them in their determination, and nothing could stir them.... They grossly insulted those who surrounded the carriage of the king, compelled them to stand aside, and used such violence towards M. de Duras, the first Gentleman of the Bedchamber, that his majesty was obliged to order two loyal grenadiers to extricate him, telling them that he would be responsible.
>
> The dauphin, who up to this point had not displayed the slightest alarm, began to cry when he saw M. de Duras so ill-treated and shouted at the top of his voice, "Save him, save him!" ... After renewed efforts, as futile as their predecessors, M. LaFayette went to the king and informed him that his departure would be attended with danger. "Then I must go back," said his majesty, and he

got out of his carriage to reenter his apartments, alone, without any of his suite, profoundly affected by what had taken place and the small benefit he was deriving from all his concessions.[6]

The next day Lafayette resigned in protest against the insubordination of his troops. He was immediately besieged by requests to return to his command, and after a few days he resumed his post on the condition that the rebellious troops be dismissed.

15

Flight to Varennes

It was now abundantly clear that the king was a prisoner in Paris. He thus began to take more seriously the various escape plans that his advisers had been proposing. Finally he decided to attempt an escape on the evening of June 20, 1791, which ironically enough was the shortest night of the year. Detailed information about this crucial attempt comes from Mme. Tourzel, who was a member of the party.

Shortly after 10 P.M. on the appointed night, Marie Antoinette entered the bedroom where the six-year-old dauphin was sleeping. Awakening him, she told him they were going to travel to a place where he would see some of his own soldiers. At that news he jumped up and eagerly asked for his sword and boots, but to allay suspicion his mother dressed him as a girl.[1] Mme. Tourzel then took the dauphin and his ten-year-old sister, Madame Royale, out through a door of an unused apartment that happened not to be guarded. It seems curious that there should have been such a door; some historians have suggested that Lafayette purposely left it unguarded. According to their theory, this door was to provide easy access for a man reputed to be Marie Antoinette's lover — Count Axel Fersen. Even assuming this theory to be correct, it remains unclear whether Lafayette was merely being obliging or was trying to place the queen in a compromising position. Because Marie Antoinette was so unpopular with the people, Lafayette and other authorities believed it would strengthen the monarchy if they could persuade the king to separate from her.

At any rate, Fersen played a key role in what history has dubbed the Flight to Varennes. King Gustavus III of Sweden was very eager to help the French royal family escape from Paris and used Fersen as his agent, providing him with the financial and diplomatic resources necessary to organize the complex escape attempt. It was Count Fersen who was waiting in a fiacre outside the palace to drive the royal family to the outskirts of Paris, where a large carriage awaited them. Mme. Tourzel got into the coach with the children to wait for the other family members, who were to arrive in stages. They then drove around the quays for a while, ending up on the Rue St. Honoré. There Mme. Tourzel waited nervously for three-quarters of an hour while Count Fersen admirably acted the part of a public coachman, chatting in dialect with other cabmen waiting in the area for fares from deputies leaving the National Assembly. Once Madame Royale exclaimed, "There's M. Lafayette."[2] He was indeed passing down the street with Mayor Bailly to attend upon the king as he retired for the evening, but luckily he took no note of the coach. Rumors had been flying in the city concerning a possible flight of the king, so Lafayette was probably eager to reassure himself that all was in order at the palace that evening.

Madame Elisabeth, the king's younger sister, was the next to leave the palace, slipping out the same unguarded door. The king had to use another exit that was guarded, so a careful plan had been worked out to enable him to pass without being stopped. A courtier who was the same size and height as the king had for the past fortnight purposely gone out this doorway late every evening, wearing a gray outfit. By dressing in a similar gray suit and wearing an appropriate wig, Louis XVI was able to slip out this exit without the guards recognizing him.[3] When he reached the fiacre, he explained that Lafayette and Bailly had wanted to talk with him, and he had not dared to hurry the conversation for fear of arousing their suspicions. This was the first in a series of unfortunate delays during the voyage. A few more valuable minutes were lost when the queen, leaving the palace shortly after the king, lost her way and wandered through the tiny streets of the neighborhood for a while before she found the fiacre. When she at last arrived, the king embraced her, saying, "How glad I am to see you here!"[4]

The escape plan was rather complicated. The royal family was to travel under the passport of a Baroness de Korff, who had recently made this journey in a similar carriage. Mme. Tourzel would impersonate the baroness, while the others pretended to be her children and servants. Fersen was to leave them all at the outskirts of Paris, where a large carriage awaited; a smaller carriage with two of the queen's attendants was also to join them at this point. Their ultimate destination was the town of Montmédy, near the German border. The duke of Choiseul, the nephew of Louis XV's famous foreign minister, had left Paris ten hours in advance and was to be waiting with forty Hussars at the town of Pont de Sommevel. Other detachments of soldiers were waiting in the towns beyond. All these soldiers would ostensibly be waiting to guard a shipment of gold that was to pass along the route.[5] Once the royal party arrived at Montmédy, they would be protected by General Bouillé, who commanded the troops there, which were considered fairly reliable.

Traveling with the royal carriage were to be three bodyguards. The selection of these three men was one of the most unfortunate mistakes in the plan. One of the king's closest advisers had urged him to use instead three hand-picked men who were not members of the bodyguards. One was a commandant of the Gendarmerie, a cautious and cool person who was used to handling dangerous situations. Another man he suggested had spent his life in the post-horse business, thereby becoming thoroughly acquainted with the roads of France.[6] This knowledge would have proved invaluable as events transpired.

Louis XVI, however, was a man of tradition and honor. He felt a great loyalty to the men of his bodyguards, who had protected him with such courage heretofore. Rather than offend his faithful bodyguards, he insisted that three men from their ranks be used. In order to keep their departure as secret as possible, the king simply asked the commander of the bodyguards to give him three men to carry letters to his brother abroad. Being unaware of the real mission of these men, the commander just picked three men from the roster, with no real evaluation of their abilities. One even happened to be rather nearsighted.[7]

The royal party was forty-five minutes late in leaving the palace, and another precious half hour was lost when Fersen decided to take the long route out of Paris to be certain he did not miss the rendezvous with the three bodyguards. As the king's party passed through the gates of Paris, they were further delayed by a wedding celebration.[8] At last Fersen arrived with his passengers at the place where the two carriages were waiting with the queen's attendants and the three bodyguards. Fersen later told General Bouillé's oldest son that he had begged the king to allow him to continue on with the party, but Louis XVI had declined his offer, thanking him warmly for his help thus far.[9] It is hardly surprising that he did not want to ask for further assistance from the man widely reputed to be his wife's lover, but it was unfortunate that Fersen did not remain with the group. He was a man of great shrewdness, energy, and courage, who might have supplied the bravado necessary to make such a daring escape succeed.

Once the members of the royal family were safely en route beyond Paris, they all began to relax, thinking they had eluded their captors. The king announced, "You may be quite sure that when I am once firmly seated in the saddle, I shall be very different."[10]

The long voyage from Paris almost to the German border required over twenty different changes of horses at post-houses. Since the royal party had to stop every hour or so for these changes, it was hard to move quickly. Speed was essential, however, because the king's escape would be discovered at seven o'clock the next morning when his servants came to awaken him. It would not be long then before the National Assembly sent horsemen racing after them, and men on horseback could clearly travel much faster than a large coach.

Another delay occurred when the post-horses of the king's carriage fell and broke their harnesses before the party had reached Châlons. It took over an hour to repair the harnesses so that the carriages could continue.[11] But the farther the carriages traveled from Paris, the more hopeful their occupants became. "When we have passed Châlons, we shall have nothing more to fear," said the king. "At Pont de Sommevel we shall find the first detachment of troops, and we shall be safe."[12] After they had indeed passed Châlons without incident, everyone began to rejoice, believing that their escape was almost complete. Their elation was premature, as Mme. Tourzel's record demonstrates:

> We passed Châlons without being recognized. We were then absolutely easy in our minds, and we were far from thinking that our good fortune had come to the end of its tether and was to be succeeded by a most frightful catastrophe.
>
> When we reached Pont de Sommevel, what was our grief and consternation when the couriers reported to us that they had not found any trace of troops, nor of anybody who could give information about them; that they dared not ask any questions, for fear of arousing suspicion, and that we could only hope that at Orbéval, which was the next post, we should be more fortunate! But our good fortune was at an end.
>
> We were no more fortunate at Orbéval.... There was the same silence, the same anxiety. We reached Sainte Ménehould in a state of violent agitation, which was increased to a still greater extent when M. Daudouins, a captain in M. Choiseul's regiment, rode up to the carriage for a moment and said to me in an undertone, — "The arrangements have been badly made; I am going away, in order not to arouse suspicion."[13]

Meanwhile, the duke of Choiseul had spent several hours in a state of extreme agitation. According to the plan, the king was supposed to arrive in Pont de Sommevel by midafternoon. Someone in a similar carriage had been sent on the same route a week earlier to determine the length of time necessary for the trip. With the twenty stops en route to change horses, however, it was not hard for the royal party to lose enough time at each stop to cause a substantial delay in their projected schedule. These small delays together with the more major ones described by Mme. Tourzel, made the royal family about four hours behind schedule in reaching Pont de Sommevel, where Choiseul and his Hussars had been waiting since noontime.

By a fatal coincidence, there had recently been a dispute in the village between a landowner and some peasants who refused to pay various fees to her. When the Hussars suddenly appeared for no apparent reason in the village, the peasants were convinced they had come to force them to pay the fees. Hence the tocsin was sounded and the inhabitants of the village and the surrounding countryside gathered to resist the Hussars.[14] As two o'clock, then three o'clock came and passed and the courier who was supposed to be riding an hour ahead of the king's party failed to appear, Choiseul became more and more alarmed. At four o'clock there was still no sign of the king. In his record of the day's events, Choiseul wrote: "I cannot describe the agony it caused me to have to master my emotion, to disguise my thoughts, and to assume a mask of indifference, while all the time I was consumed with anxiety."[15]

Meanwhile the mood of the peasants surrounding the troops was becoming ugly. No one seemed to believe the cover story that the soldiers were awaiting a shipment of gold. Rumors were even flying that the troops were waiting for the queen. The agitation had spread to the larger town of Châlons, which was threatening to send National Guard troops to aid the villagers.

Choiseul was faced with an agonizing dilemma: Should he stay in the village with his troops at the risk of precipitating trouble before the king's party even arrived or should he leave in the hopes of defusing the situation so that the king's carriage might pass unnoticed? He decided upon the latter course. When the village officials told him that a bullion shipment had in fact passed through the village that morning, he turned to his troops and announced in a loud voice: "No doubt that's the convoy we were waiting for.... There is no point in our being here and the best thing we can do is to move on."[16]

When Choiseul led his Hussars out of town at a quarter of six, he could see that their departure calmed the situation. A messenger had already galloped off to Châlons with the news of their decision to leave. Choiseul now had to decide what route to take back to Metz. He chose to avoid Sainte-Ménehould, where the king would in theory eventually pass, because his troops had excited animosity when they had passed through the town earlier that day. In a message to the captain of the Dragoons stationed in Sainte-Ménehould as part of the king's escort, Choiseul explained that even though the king had not yet appeared he had decided to leave Pont de Sommevel to avoid inciting a violent conflict.

Choiseul took a shortcut to Varennes, skirting the Sainte-Ménehould area by bushwhacking through deep woods, where his men had to cross such difficult terrain that they lost a few hours. When night fell, they were obliged to dismount and lead their horses in order to avoid falling into the deep holes that happened to dot the area. One of the Hussars did fall into one of these holes and was seriously injured. Instead of leaving only a couple of men to aid him, Choiseul held back his entire contingent, thereby losing a crucial forty-five minutes.[17] It was an ironic episode, coming at the end of a day when Choiseul had found it difficult to imagine how the king could possibly be delayed by four hours in his long journey from Paris. By the time Choiseul reached Varennes, it was past midnight, and he was too late to save the king.

Louis XVI's carriage arrived in Pont de Sommevel about 6:15 P.M., just a half hour after Choiseul had left the village. The short interval by which they missed each other would be crucial to the history of France. The king was concerned that the troops that were supposed to be meeting him there were nowhere in evidence, but his party changed horses and passed through the village without incident. When the royal family passed through Clermont, the officer in charge of the troops awaiting the supposed shipment of gold tried to march his men after the carriage as an escort, but the inhabitants of the town urged them to disobey their officer's orders and they did so. He decided he could not tell them that it was the royal family they were to escort for fear they would still refuse to go and the king would be immediately arrested. Unable to aid the king, the captain sent off a message to Varennes, where a few officers and forty soldiers were also waiting. All circumstances seemed against the king that day. The messenger never reached Varennes with the message because he mistakenly took the road to Verdun.[18]

The town of Sainte-Ménehould proved a fatal spot for the royal family. An hour or so after they passed through this town the postmaster, Jean-Baptiste Drouet, rode after the king in hot pursuit. Drouet became a great Revolutionary hero for his crucial role in stopping the king, but the exact reasons for his pursuit remain unclear. He later testified to the National Assembly that he had recognized the king from his portrait on the paper money the Assembly had just printed.[19] The likeness was not a good one, however, so Drouet's claim must be viewed with skepticism.

The representative of the National Assembly who rode all day from Paris to try to overtake the king got as far as a town only a few hours away from Sainte-Ménehould but was too exhausted to go any further. He sent someone else on to Sainte-Ménehould with the dramatic news that the king had just passed through the countryside in disguise. Everyone at once began asking Drouet if he had asked to see the passports of the travelers who had passed through the town over an hour earlier. Since Drouet had neglected to ask for the passports, he knew he was in a difficult position and galloped off with a friend to try by means of a shortcut to catch up with the king at Varennes.[20]

When the royal party reached the outskirts of Varennes, they looked all over for the relay of horses that General Bouillé had agreed to have waiting for them on the edge of town because there was no post-house in the small village. There was no sign of the horses, however, and it was about 11 o'clock at night, so almost all the villagers had gone to bed. Their drivers, who were employees of the last post-house where they had changed horses, refused to continue the trip without letting their horses rest but finally agreed to take the party to the far side of town in search of the other horses.

In the meantime, Drouet and his companion had arrived in Varennes and had headed for a bridge over which the king's carriages would have to pass in their route through the village. There, as luck would have it, they saw a wagon full of furniture, which they overturned to block the bridge.[21] As the royal family approached the barricaded bridge, Drouet ran up with some armed men and demanded to see their passports. It was clear by now that they had been recognized. The bodyguards offered to try to fight their way across the bridge, and another officer offered to lead the party through a nearby ford. By this time, however, an angry crowd was gathering. Fearing that his forces were insufficient to enable his family to escape and that many would die if any fighting took place, the king did not order the use of force. He did, however, send the officer to carry an urgent request for help to General Bouillé, who was waiting in a town a few hours away.

The crowd now insisted that the travelers leave the carriages and enter the house belonging to the chief official of the town. They were taken to an upstairs room where there was one bed upon which the exhausted children immediately fell asleep. A man from the region who had seen the king at Versailles appeared and confirmed his identity. Seeing that all further dissimulation was useless, Louis XVI gave up and admitted that he was indeed the king. Within an hour the townspeople had gathered four thousand men of the National Guard to prevent his escape.

It was shortly after 11 o'clock in the evening when the king was arrested. Soon after midnight, Captain Damas, who was in charge of the Clermont Dragoons, came without his rebellious men to be at the king's side, and Choiseul and another officer arrived with their forty Hussars. These men offered to try to rescue the king, but the leaders of the angry citizens thronging the streets below said they would kill the king and his family if a rescue was attempted. In the face of these threats, Louis XVI refused to order an escape attempt. Everyone in his party was hoping that General Bouillé would arrive with sufficient forces to intimidate the villagers, but the hours passed with no sign of his troops. Meanwhile, the mob outside was shouting for the king's departure for Paris because they feared that General Bouillé would indeed arrive and attack the town in order to rescue the king.

In the years following these events, the military commanders in charge each wrote their own account of the affair, trying to clear themselves of blame and implicate someone else. General Bouillé, for example, criticized Choiseul for giving up too soon and stated that he should have at least left a courier behind to bring word in case the king did arrive. The escape plans had stipulated that if the king was not coming after all, he would send a messenger from Paris to notify the waiting troops. Because such a messenger never arrived, Choiseul should have at least remained close at hand for a few more hours, even if he believed it prudent to leave the village of Pont de Sommevel. Unfortunately, Choiseul also sent a message to the commanders who had been stationed with troops in other villages to protect the final part of the king's voyage, when there would be a danger of pursuit from Paris. This message stated that it appeared that the shipment the soldiers were awaiting would not pass that day after all, so these forces were not ready to help the king when he did arrive.

All might yet have been saved if the commander of the soldiers stationed at Varennes had acted properly because the king did in fact arrive there shortly ahead of Drouet. As fate would have it, General Bouillé had given this important post to his youngest son, an inexperienced young man only twenty-one years old, who apparently was ambitious to share in this important mission but only proved himself an incompetent. For reasons that remain unclear, this young man had sent away part of the horses for the relay and had not placed the remaining four horses at the entrance to the village, as had been agreed. At any rate, the royal carriage required six horses and the other small carriage needed two, so these four horses would not have sufficed even for the king's carriage. The king's party lost a crucial half hour searching throughout the dark village for these horses. The younger Bouillé had let his men retire for the night before the king even arrived. When he did hear of the king's arrest, instead of rushing to his aid with the forty soldiers he commanded, he rode off with his second-in-command to give the news to his father, thus leaving no one behind who was in a strong position of authority to direct the troops. Even then he seems to have spent far too long reaching the general. In his book *Enquête sur l'échec de Varennes* (Inquiry into the Failure of Varennes), Michel de Lombares has uncovered evidence suggesting that young Bouillé stopped in a tavern along the way to get up his courage to face his father with the bad news of the king's arrest.[22] This delay made it impossible for General Bouillé to arrive with reinforcements in time to rescue the king.

In the meantime, two emissaries from the National Assembly in Paris arrived in Varennes between three and four in the morning, bearing a decree that the king's party should be protected and brought back to Paris as soon as possible. The king and queen wished, however, to delay their departure as long as possible in the hope of relief arriving from General Bouillé. They kept insisting that the children needed to sleep before starting the long journey back to Paris, but finally the cries from the crowd below the windows became so vociferous that the king had no choice but to depart.

Just as the procession was leaving the village at 7 A.M., General Bouillé arrived with his troops on a hill above the town. To his dismay, he looked down and saw the king's carriage surrounded by a hostile crowd. Realizing that he could not be sure of the loyalties of his own men in this period when open revolt was common among soldiers, he concluded that any action on his part was likely to result in the deaths of the king and his family. With great reluctance he therefore turned and rode away. He escaped immediately across the frontier, being more fortunate than Choiseul and the other officers who had rushed to the king's side when they heard of his capture, only to find themselves imprisoned as soon as he left Varennes.[23]

Once again as on the fateful day of October 6, 1789, members of the royal family were captives in a carriage surrounded by an angry mob conveying them to Paris. The trip along the hot and dusty road took several days because many of the escorting troops were on foot. The family was exhausted before they even departed because they had been subject to almost unbearable tension during the last day and a half and no one except the children had slept for two nights. As they drove along, the king suddenly heard gunshots and saw some of the National Guard soldiers running through a field. When he asked what was the matter, he was told, "Nothing, they are only killing a lunatic."[24] He soon learned that the mob had cut the man's throat. As it turned out, he was not a lunatic, but a nobleman of the area who wanted to reach the king to tell him that he, at least, remained loyal to him. It was a bad omen for the return trip to Paris that served to remind the occupants of the carriage of the extreme danger of their situation.

As if Marie Antoinette needed any reminder of the great change that had occurred in her position, the cortege stopped for the night at Châlons, where the royal family slept in the Intendance, the very building in which she had been officially welcomed to France when she arrived to marry the future king. Many people in Châlons were still sympathetic to Louis XVI, and that night some of them showed him a secret staircase leading from one of the bedrooms, by means of which they offered to help him escape.[25] It would only be possible for him to go alone, however, and he refused to leave his wife and children, fearing that the mob might vent its fury on them were he to escape.

The original plan of escape from Paris had been jeopardized by the decision that the royal family would all travel together. On the night they left Paris, the king's brother Provence left the city on horseback with his wife and rode north, crossing safely over the border into Belgium. Both Louis XVI and Marie Antoinette were excellent riders and could have done the same, had there not been the problem of the children. By now, however, both parents were so thoroughly aware of the violent tendencies of the Parisian citizenry that they would not have dreamed of abandoning their children to an uncertain fate.

On the second night, the party halted at the town of Dormans, where the crowd was so noisy all through the night that it was difficult for the travelers to sleep. The dauphin awoke sobbing in terror because he had dreamed that he was surrounded by wolves in a forest and his mother was in danger. When he saw that she was safe, he went back to sleep, not even realizing that the situation in which they found themselves was as fraught with peril as that of his nightmare.[26]

Three commissioners from the National Assembly in Paris—the count of Latour-Maubourg, Antoine Barnave, and Jérôme Pétion—met the royal party before they arrived at Dormans. Maubourg, who was sympathetic to the king, told Mme. Tourzel he would ride in the second carriage with the queen's attendants so that Barnave and Pétion would have a chance to become better acquainted with the royal family. It was a shrewd move, as Barnave did in fact become more supportive of the king's position after the trip.

Pétion became mayor of Paris a few months later. In contrast to the other two commissioners, he was a crude and vulgar man, full of self-importance. His record of the fateful journey back to Paris, which is remarkable for its lack of taste, offers a startling contrast to the account written by Mme. Tourzel. Pétion first described the people awaiting the king's arrival in Dormans:

> The zeal that animated these good people was truly admirable. They came running from everywhere, old men, women, and children, some with spears, some with scythes, others with sticks, swords, or old guns. They came as if they were attending a wedding. The husbands embraced their wives, saying, "If need be, we will go to the frontier to kill this scoundrel, this bastard." They ran alongside our carriage, applauding and crying, "Long live the Nation! I was amazed and touched by this sublime spectacle.
>
> More and more couriers hurried toward us to tell us, "The king is coming." About a league or so from Epernay, on a beautiful road, we saw a cloud of dust in the distance, and we heard a great deal of noise. Several people came up to our carriage and cried, "There is the king." Slowing our horses down, we saw that we were approaching a huge group of people. We got out of our carriage. The king's carriage stopped and we approached it.... As soon as we were noticed, everyone cried, "Here are the deputies from the National Assembly!" Everyone was eager to make room for us, and an order for silence was given. The cortege was superb. National Guards on horses and on foot, some in uniform, some not, bearing all sorts of weapons. As the sun was setting, it illuminated this beautiful ensemble in the middle of the peaceful countryside.... It is hard for me to describe the respect that surrounded us.[27]

To Mme. Tourzel this agonizing journey with those she had sworn an oath to protect presented an entirely different aspect:

It is impossible to give any idea of the sufferings of the royal family during this unfortunate journey — sufferings both moral and physical.... The mayors of the towns, in presenting the keys to his majesty, allowed themselves to reproach him bitterly about his departure from Paris; and the manner in which they paid their homage was a fresh insult....

The people who surrounded the carriage of the king made remarks to their majesties with insolent familiarity whenever it pleased them and replied to their questions with revolting vulgarity.... The heat was excessive. The king, the royal family, and everybody in the carriage were covered with perspiration and dust.... Burnt by the sun and covered with dust, they bore on their faces the impress of all their sufferings.... They were not allowed to pull down the blinds of the carriage, so that the mob, which was renewed every moment, might be allowed the pleasure of feasting its eyes on the spectacle of the king and his unfortunate family in the power of his subjects....

The dust raised by the people who surrounded the carriage on horseback and on foot was as thick as the densest fog, and every breath of air was intercepted by the horse and foot soldiers, and by the crowd of inquisitive beings who pressed round the carriage.[28]

To make it possible for Barnave and Pétion to ride in his carriage, the king suggested that they could all crowd together and hold the children on their laps. Of course this only increased everyone's extreme discomfort from the heat. As soon as the two commissioners took their places, everyone in the coach frantically begged them to save the lives of the three bodyguards seated on the driver's box. Madame Elisabeth then started a long conversation with Barnave, speaking eloquently for an hour and a half about the difficulties her brother faced in trying to act like a king when the National Assembly had virtually reduced him to a puppet.[29]

Madame Elisabeth was completely devoted to her brother and had rejected many chances to emigrate to safety, preferring to remain by his side while he was in danger. It is one of the many ironies of the period that Louis XVI and Madame Elisabeth, who were both deeply devout, modest in their personal lives and expenditures, and sincerely concerned for the welfare of the lower classes of France, were destined to be victims of the Revolution. By contrast, their extravagant, worldly, and haughty brothers escaped beyond the frontiers and lived to return to rule France. Deluded by his vanity, Pétion completely misread Madame Elisabeth's character, leaving an account of his impressions that is at once amusing and revolting:

Madame Elisabeth looked at me intently with tender eyes and with the languid air that misfortune imparts, which aroused a strong interest in me. Our eyes met at times with a kind of communication and attraction. Night was falling, and the moon was beginning to spread its sweet light. Madame Elisabeth was holding Madame [Royale], who was sitting partly on her knees and partly on mine. We were both holding up her head as she fell asleep. I stretched out my arm and Madame Elisabeth extended hers on mine. Our arms were interlaced; mine touched her armpit. I felt some quick movement, and a warmth spread through her garments. Madame Elisabeth glance toward me seemed to become more touching. I detected a certain abandon in her bearing; there were tears in her eyes. Her glance combined both melancholy and a sort of voluptuousness. I could be mistaken; one can easily confuse the feeling of sadness with that of pleasure, but I think that if we had been alone, if all the world had magically disappeared, she would have thrown herself into my arms and abandoned herself to her natural instincts.[30]

Pétion's comments on the king are equally insensitive. Before leaving Paris, he had remarked to the other commissioners, "The fat pig has become a serious embarrassment.[31] When he later described the journey with the king, he wrote:

I said to him from time to time, "Look how beautiful the countryside is." We were indeed passing through some beautiful hills where the view was varied and extensive. The Marne was flowing beneath us. I said: "What a beautiful country France is! No other country in the world can compare to it." I purposely threw out these comments so that I could watch him to see what impression they would make on him, but his face remained cold.... This mass of flesh is unfeeling."[32]

But only a few pages earlier in his account, Pétion had noted, "The king talked about an accident that had just happened to a nobleman whose throat had been cut, and he seemed very affected by this."[33] Pétion's implication that the nobleman's throat had been cut in an accident seems a chilling bit of black humor. At this point he could afford to be casual about the violence of the Revolution, but it would later claim him as a victim.

When the procession was close to Paris, some detachments of Parisian National Guardsmen arrived to take charge, and trouble broke out among the different military factions. Pétion vividly described the turmoil:

The dispute was becoming heated. People were swearing and about to come to blows. Bayonets were waving around the carriage, whose windows were down. During this tumult, some hostile people could have struck blows at the queen. I noticed that some of the soldiers seemed very angry and looked at her in a threatening way. Soon some excited men were calling her a bitch and yelling, "It's no use her showing us her child; we know it isn't his." The king heard these comments very clearly. The young prince was frightened by the noise and the clanking of the weapons and began to cry in fright. The queen held him with tears running down her face. Seeing that matters were becoming serious, Barnave and I put our heads out the windows to address the crowd, which showed its confidence in us. The grenadiers told us, "Don't be afraid, we assure you that nothing bad will happen, but the post of honor belongs to us." This was, in fact, a quarrel about who should have the position of honor. But it could have become venomous and resulted in excess. When the posts were at last assumed by the grenadiers, there were no more disputes.[34]

Virtually the entire citizenry of Paris was lining the route through the city to the Tuileries Palace. In what was probably a very astute effort to maintain control of a highly volatile situation, Lafayette had given orders that the king should be greeted by total silence and that everyone should keep on their hats. Even those too poor to own a hat put handkerchiefs on their heads. Lafayette also had the National Guard soldiers stand with their muskets butt upward as a sign of disrespect. His famous order to all Parisians was: "Anyone who applauds the king will be beaten: anyone who insults him will be hanged."[35]

Pétion exulted, "Never was a more imposing sight presented to human eyes,"[36] but Mme. de Staël viewed the situation differently:

> The king and his family made a funereal entrance into Paris. The queen's and king's clothing was covered with dust. The two royal children looked with astonishment at an entire people showing itself master before its conquered rulers. In the middle of this illustrious family, Madame Elisabeth appeared to be a being already sanctified, who had nothing further in common with this earth. Thus it was that the king returned to the palace of his ancestors. Alas, what a sad foreshadowing of the future and how it would play out.[37]

Not all writers have been as relatively objective as Mme. de Staël. One of the most extreme examples of the distorted view of Louis XVI that has been presented by many writers in the last two centuries comes from Bernard Fäy's biography of Louis XVI. Fäy ended his chapter on the flight to Varennes with these incredible words: "At the sound of his son and his daughter crying, Louis XVI smiled with an unbelievable joy. Until this time he had never been anything more than a king; but now he was suffering a God-like agony."[38]

16

Final Steps Toward a Constitutional Monarchy

Now the great question in Paris was what to do with the king. To complicate matters, when he escaped he had left behind him a letter enumerating his grievances against the revolutionaries and disavowing various decrees to which he had been forced to acquiesce, such as the Civil Constitution of the Clergy. The National Assembly at last decided to suspend him temporarily and empowered its committees and the king's ministers to run the government while the deputies decided the future of the king. After two years of intensive labor, the National Assembly was about to complete its constitution creating a constitutional monarchy for France and would obviously be in an awkward situation if the country no longer had a monarch. Some deputies were already insisting that the king should be deposed and a republic set up. To add to the fear and uncertainty of the period, no one could predict what the response of the other European leaders would be to the capture and forcible return of the king. Many people feared that an invasion was now imminent. Moderate members of the Assembly insisted that it was important to keep the king as part of the government to ward off a possible attempt by the European powers to rescue him and reinstate the ancien régime.

The immediate problem of the king was handled by a curious maneuver — the National Assembly took the position that Louis XVI had not left Paris of his own free will but had instead been kidnapped. It was a useful fiction for all concerned. In order to prevent any further escape attempts, however, Lafayette stationed personal guards with the members of the royal family, who remained under constant surveillance. Realizing that many people thought he had connived in the original escape plan, Lafayette even went so far as to have chimney sweeps inspect the palace chimneys to be sure that the royal family could not exit by that route.

After Mirabeau's death, leadership in the National Assembly had passed to the hands of a moderate trio known as the Triumvirate that was composed of Barnave, the young lawyer who had accompanied the royal family back to Paris after their attempted escape, and Duport and Lameth, two liberal nobles. On July 15, 1791, the committee appointed by the Assembly to investigate the flight to Varennes reported back that the king was innocent, while General Bouillé and the three bodyguards were guilty of having tried to carry him off to the frontier. In a speech to the Assembly, Barnave argued: "Are we going to end the Revolution? Are we going to begin another one? You have made all men equal before the law, you have consecrated civil and political liberty, you have assumed for the State all powers that had been taken away from the people. One step more would be disastrous; one step further toward equality will mean the destruction of private property."[1]

At the same time that the National Assembly was moving toward a decision on the king, republican elements in the capital were actively trying to prevent his return to even a semblance of power. As soon as word had spread through Paris of his escape, many revolutionaries had gone through the city removing the fleur-de-lis and the words "king" and "queen" from public buildings and monuments. On July 15 the Cordeliers Club and the Jacobin Club drew up a petition calling for the king to be deposed and replaced by "constitutional means," but many members of the Jacobin Club resigned in protest to the petition. On July 16 the National Assembly passed a resolution saying that the king would be reinstated as soon as the constitution was finished and he had approved it. The Cordelier and Jacobin petition was clearly at variance with this decree of the Assembly, so many more Jacobins resigned from their club at this point. The defecting Jacobins formed a new club called the Feuillants, which included the Triumvirate among its members.

The opposing factions were clearly moving toward a confrontation. The republicans were planning a mass demonstration at the Champ de Mars on July 17, where thousands of protesters were expected to sign the republican petition on the Altar of the Country that had been erected for the Festival of the Federation. After the defection of the Jacobins, the Cordeliers had made their petition even more radical, calling for a new constituent assembly to try the king and establish yet another form of government for France. Meanwhile, the municipal government under Mayor Bailly and the National Guard under Lafayette were preparing to move against the republican faction.

On the morning of July 17, 1791, the petitioners discovered two men hiding under the platform of the large Altar of the Country. In his account of the day, Ferrières noted that one of these men was a crippled invalid and the other a young wig-maker who lived nearby. He related that some observers conjectured that the two men had hidden there so that they could look beneath the dresses of the women who would be passing up and down the steps under which they crouched. The republican protesters immediately accused the two men of being part of an aristocratic plot to blow up the altar when it was thronged with petitioners, although no materials were found with the men to support this theory. A furious mob surrounded them, refused to listen to their protestations of innocence, and hanged them from a nearby lamppost.[2]

This act of violence prompted the already nervous municipal government to declare martial law; the red flag announcing this decision was flown from the Hôtel de Ville. The National Assembly also passed a resolution urging the municipal government to control the situation. Although public assemblies were at that point illegal because martial law had been declared, five thousand people gathered at the Champ de Mars, where Danton, a leader of the Cordeliers, read their petition and Desmoulins made a speech to rouse the people. For the next few hours, the assembled people filed up to the altar to sign the petition asking for the king to be deposed and tried and for a new form of government to be created for France. In the early evening, however, Mayor Bailly and Lafayette arrived with twelve hundred National Guardsmen to disperse the crowd in accordance with the declaration of martial law.

At first the crowd was not alarmed because the National Guard had previously never really asserted itself against the people. Many of the demonstrators called out, "Down with the red flag!" and started to throw stones at the soldiers. Suddenly someone fired a shot, and the soldiers of the Guard responded with a volley at the crowd that killed fifty demonstrators and wounded many others. Two National Guardsmen were also killed that day.[3] The event marked a dramatic turning point in the Revolution because it was the first time the security forces had actually fired on the people. Although the action restored a temporary peace to the streets of Paris, it embittered the republican forces. Two years later they revenged themselves upon Mayor Bailly by guillotining him on the Champ de Mars with a red flag burning before his eyes.

After the confrontation at the Champs de Mars, the National Assembly took further steps against various radicals in the city. Desmoulins and Marat, two of the most extreme journalists, went into hiding to avoid arrest, and Danton fled to England. The Cordeliers Club was temporarily closed. In the ensuing period of relative quiet, the Assembly finished the constitution, which specified that new elections for a Legislative Assembly were to be held in the fall of 1791. Robespierre pushed through a disastrous law prohibiting any of the present deputies from running for election to the new assembly. The right-wing royalists supported this move in order to eliminate the men in the Assembly who had so often opposed them, little realizing that they would only be replaced by deputies who were more radical. As Ferrières wrote, "The great aristocrats and the wild men combined to pass the decree."[4] Thus by one rash action all the current leaders of France, many of whom possessed great talents and experience, were eliminated from the government.

The constitution was presented to the king for his consideration in early September 1791. The royalists urged him to reject it, as did his brothers through letters from abroad. Mme. Tourzel described the intense pressure Louis XVI was under to sign the constitution:

> Meanwhile the ministers redoubled their efforts to alarm the king and make him look upon the loss of those who were in prison on account of the Varennes journey as absolutely certain.... I thought it my duty to beg him, in my own name and in those of all who had helped him on his journey, to put out of his thoughts the idea that he would cause them to incur any danger by his refusal and that I could answer for it that there was not one of us who would not willingly expose himself to any danger in order to see him adopt the most honorable course and that which would be most useful to his present and future safety.
>
> "I am deeply touched," said his majesty to me, "by your very generous action; but I know what I owe to those who have sacrificed themselves for me." From that moment I had no longer any doubt about the acceptance of the constitution, and I had to content myself with prayers that it might not land his majesty in the misfortunes which were prophesied by those who advised him to refuse....
>
> Ministers represented to the king that the princes were not in a position to know the situation of his majesty; he alone could estimate the danger which he would cause France to incur if he refused the constitution. The king, tired of their importunities and his own position, alarmed as to that in which he might be placed, and above all, fearing to bring about a civil war in France, determined to follow their advice and to accept the constitution, the results of which were destined to be so disastrous to them and to himself.[5]

Once again the king was placed in a position that was to recur all too frequently as long as he retained even a semblance of power. Trusted advisers assured him that if he refused to follow their direction, his action would lead to bloodshed or perhaps even civil war. As a man who abhorred violence, Louis XVI could not bring himself to take action that might precipitate an armed conflict. Unfortunately, he was in a moral position that had no easy solution, and many observers have been quick to say that his reluctance to shed blood ultimately led to far greater violence and suffering.

Since the National Assembly wanted the king's acceptance of the constitution to appear to be a free act, they removed the guards from the Tuileries while he was deliberating. No one was really deceived by this maneuver, however, and a cartoon circulated around Paris picturing the king seated in a cage, signing the constitution. Finally, on September 13, 1791, Louis XVI sent a letter to be read to the National Assembly stating his acquiescence in the constitution. The Assembly then immediately passed on Lafayette's instigation a general amnesty freeing all those who had taken part in the flight to Varennes, as well as many other prisoners. Restrictions on emigration were also removed.

On September 14 the king went to give his formal consent to the Assembly, accompanied by the queen, his children, and Mme. Tourzel. The latter was shocked by the manner in which he was treated:

> The Assembly decided that he should be saluted on his arrival and that then every member should resume his seat; that there should be ... two armchairs ... exactly alike — one for the king and the other for the president. M. Malouet having observed that but little respect would be shown to the king by such conduct, he was greeted with a shout of, "Go on your knees if you like."
>
> The Right, in order to manifest its opposition to such a constitution, withdrew before the arrival of the king....
>
> The king, standing without a hat on his head, pronounced the oath prescribed by the Assembly. Then perceiving that he alone was standing, he seated himself by the side of Thouret, the president of the Assembly ... and expressed to him his ardent desire to secure, as the result of the step he had just taken, the return of peace and concord and to look upon it as a pledge of the happiness of the people and the tranquility of the empire.
>
> Thouret, with his legs crossed and his arms resting on those of his arm-chair in order to assume an air of complete freedom, replied to the king in a very insolent tone, eulogizing the Assembly and its courage in the destruction of abuses....
>
> The king, who still flattered himself that he should be able, under the shadow of the constitution and by dint of prudence and industry, to take advantage of every circumstance to open eventually the eyes of the nation to its real interests, declared to the queen that he was going to do all in his power to secure the progress of the constitution. He asked her and all about him to refrain from any reflections in regard to the proceedings which circumstances had just wrung from him, to abstain from anything opposed to the constitution, and, in conformity with one of its clauses, to call the dauphin for the future the Prince Royal.[6]

Mme. Tourzel's comments about the king's injunction to the queen and his other associates to avoid attacking the constitution are important to the historical record because he has often been accused of being hypocritical in his acceptance of the constitution.

Celebrations took place all over Paris after the king's acceptance of the constitution, and the principal streets and squares were illuminated to mark the occasion. Mme. de Staël's description of the festivities is particularly perceptive:

> The king and queen were asked to go to the opera, where their entrance was celebrated by universal and sincere applause. The program being presented was the

ballet of Psyché. At the moment when the furies dance around waving their torches when the light of the burning torches illuminated the hall, I watched the faces of the king and queen by the pale light of this portrayal of hell, and sinister presentments of the future gripped me. The queen tried to be pleasant, but a profound sadness was visible behind her obliging smile. The king, as usual, seemed more absorbed in what he was watching, rather than what he was feeling. He looked around calmly, almost nonchalantly. He was accustomed, like most sovereigns, to conceal his emotions, and perhaps as a result they had been diminished. After the opera, they went for a ride in the Champs Elysées, which were superbly illuminated. The Tuileries Palace and the gardens were separated only by that fatal square of the Revolution and the illumination of the palace and its gardens was admirably linked with that of the long alleys of the Champs Elysées, which were linked by garlands of light.

The king and queen drove slowly in their carriage in the middle of the crowd, and each time people saw their carriage, they cried, "Long live the king!" But these were the same people who had insulted the king when he returned from Varennes, and they gave no more thought to their applause than they had to their insults.

As I was walking along, I met some of the members of the Constituent Assembly. They resembled dethroned monarchs who are very worried about their successors.... There was a deafening noise everywhere. People were singing and paperboys were shouting, "The grand acceptance by the king," "a constitutional monarchy," etc. It seemed as if the revolution was over and liberty established, but everyone was looking at each other, as if to see in their neighbor the confidence that they themselves lacked.[7]

17

Acceptance of the Constitution

Everyone in the government was exhausted after these last few months of turmoil, and a period of relative calm followed the completion of the constitution. Lafayette retired for a brief time to his country estate before returning to Paris, where he lost an election to Pétion to succeed Bailly as mayor. Robespierre and other deputies of the disbanded National Assembly returned to their native towns because they had no part in the new Legislative Assembly.

This new body was moderate in its composition, comprising 264 Feuillant delegates, 350 delegates who listed no club affiliation, and only 136 Jacobin and Cordelier delegates representing the far left.[1] These latter men, however, succeeded through their energy and zeal in grasping much of the power within the new body. Effective control soon passed to a group known as the Brissotins, after their leader, Jacques-Pierre Brissot, whose father was the proprietor of a restaurant in Chartres. Brissot had studied law for a while but then became a journalist and involved himself in various intrigues. He eventually served the duke of Orléans in his behind-the-scenes struggles to displace his cousin the king.

Several talented lawyers from Bordeaux in the department of Gironde, including the great revolutionary orator Vergniaud, allied themselves with Brissot. This political grouping of Brissotins was also sometimes referred to as the Girondists because of the geographical origin of its principal leaders. One highly influential member of the group was Mme. Roland, a brilliant woman with a keen sense of political acumen. Her entrée into the world of government was through her husband, Jean Roland, a lackluster civil servant twenty years her elder, who eventually became minister of the interior in the king's council. Mme. Roland was a staunch republican, having never forgiven the social snub she suffered early in life when she was asked to eat with the servants at the estate of a nobleman.[2] In her salon she gathered around her a group of bright and idealistic young men who would briefly direct the course of the Revolution.

The chief thrust of the Brissotin policy was to advocate a preemptive war against the other European powers. The revolutionaries had long feared that the Austrian emperor, Leopold II, who had succeeded his brother Joseph II in 1790, would come to the rescue of his sister Marie Antoinette and that other European monarchs might wish to defend Louis XVI's rights in order to discourage popular uprisings in their own countries. The other European powers, however, were well aware of the advantages of leaving France in a weakened state. Austria and Prussia were at the moment far more concerned with the possibility that Catherine the Great of Russia might annex part of Poland, especially if their attention was focused on France. In August 1791, shortly after the flight to Varennes, Leopold II of Austria and Frederick William of Prussia had issued the Declaration of Pillnitz, in which they stated their willingness to take joint action against the French revolutionaries if other European rulers would join them. They knew full well that this was a highly unlikely possibility. So did Marie Antoinette, who said, "The emperor has betrayed us."[3] But most Frenchmen took the declaration at face value, and it contributed to a state of almost paranoid fear about the intentions of the European powers and the armies of émigrés, the size of which were constantly exaggerated in rumor.

After the general amnesty associated with the promulgation of the new constitution abolished the law against emigration, large numbers of noblemen took advantage of the new opportunity to leave France and flocked to join the king's brothers in Coblenz. Most probably expected that they would soon be returning to France after their side had prevailed, but as it turned out, it was many years before it was safe for them to return to their homeland. Some in fact died abroad before that day arrived. Many French observers have condemned these early waves of emigration, as did Mme. de Staël, who asserted that the presence of another ten thousand noblemen in France might have prevented the fall of the monarchy.[4] She believed that emigration became justified only during the Reign of Terror, the period when she herself escaped from Paris. Since she barely succeeded in escaping because she waited so long, her judgment on timing was dubious.

In October 1791, Brissot made a strong speech denouncing the émigré forces that had gathered at Coblenz under the protection of the elector of Trier. By late November he and other leading Jacobin deputies had persuaded the king to issue an ultimatum demanding that the elector and other rulers who supported the émigrés expel them.

Brissot hoped to provoke a war by this aggressive policy because he believed that the Revolution would benefit from a war. This was a sharp reversal of policy on the part of the revolutionaries, who had only two years earlier renounced all wars of aggression as being unworthy of a democratic state.

Now Brissot asserted: "War is actually a national benefit.... A people which has won its freedom after centuries of slavery needs war; it needs war to purge away the vices of despotism, it needs war to banish from its bosom the men who might corrupt its liberty."[5]

Brissot believed, as did most of his fellow countrymen, that as French armies advanced into other nations, the people would rise up to overthrow their aristocratic rulers. Robespierre was one of the few Jacobins to denounce this idea and the whole war movement, stating, "No one loves an armed missionary."[6] Robespierre believed that there was more danger from counterrevolutionary forces within the country than without and feared that a war effort would concentrate more power in the hands of the king and the generals.

This was in fact the very reason that Lafayette and Narbonne, the king's new minister of war (who happened also to be Mme. de Staël's lover), were so eager to see France attack the German states. They were convinced they could achieve a victory that would enable them to strengthen the throne and constitutional government. Lafayette himself was to command one of the three armies that would march to the northern frontier.

Although at the Brissotins' insistence, Louis XVI publicly demanded that the elector of Trier disperse the émigrés, he privately wrote to the Austrian emperor to tell him to ignore this demand. Marie Antoinette was secretly hoping for an Austrian victory that would liberate the royal family, and she eventually sent information about the French military plans to the Austrians, probably without the king's knowledge. Her brother Leopold II of Austria had responded to the French ultimatum by asking the elector of Trier to disperse the émigré armies, but at the same time he had asserted that Austria would send troops to protect the elector. It soon became clear that he would like to avoid a war with France but would not withdraw in the face of French advances.

During the fall and winter of 1791–92, the king's council was composed of a rather weak group of Feuillant ministers. By March 1792, Brissot and his followers were demanding that these men be replaced by others more to their liking. By this time Louis XVI had been worn down by the constant revolutionary pressure to the point that it seemed useless to him to resist the desires of the leaders of the Legislative Assembly, so long as the issues under discussion did not involve any major questions of conscience. He agreed to appoint a council from among Brissot's followers, but his real feelings are all too clear in the unusual statement he made to the Assembly on March 24, 1792:

> I had previously chosen as my ministers men whose integrity and opinions recommended them. These men have now left the ministry. I have decided that I should replace them at this point by men whose opinions are favored by the citizens of Paris. Because you have told me so many times that men of the party of

the people can alone reestablish order and administer the laws, I have decided I must cede to you so that there will no longer be any pretext for hostile people to doubt my sincere desire to cooperate in achieving the prosperity and happiness of my country.[7]

The new appointees, who included Jean Roland, were not men of any great ability, with the exception of the new minister of foreign affairs, Charles Dumouriez, who had been a capable military officer. Dumouriez felt a basic sympathy for the king, but Roland and two of the other ministers were quite contemptuous toward him. Roland underscored this attitude by coming to the palace in republican dress. Ferrières described the resulting situation in this way: "Roland looked like a Quaker in his Sunday best, with flat white hair, with very little powder, wearing a black suit, and shoes with laces. The first time that Roland appeared at the king's council in this dress, the master of ceremonies, who was upset by this breech of etiquette, approached Dumouriez with an uneasy air and raised eyebrows. Glancing at Roland, he said in a low, constrained voice, "Look, sir, no buckles on his shoes!" "Oh, sir," replied Dumouriez with great sangfroid, "all is lost."[8]

According to Ferrières, the king felt so much at odds with his new council that he often read the newspaper during council sessions or tried to deflect the discussion from divisive issues.[9] Ferrières further related that Louis XVI encouraged Dumouriez to entertain all of them with his witty anecdotes, but he asserts that this was not the real king:

> Louis XVI wasn't at all the man that he was said to be in a flood of pamphlets subsidized by his enemies, who never ceased to represent him to the people as an imbecile unworthy of the throne. He had an excellent memory and was very active and never lazy. He had read profitably and understood very well France's interests and all the treaties she had signed with foreign powers. He had a good knowledge of history and was the best geographer in his kingdom. He remembered the names of most of the people who had some potential relationship to him and connected their names and faces. He knew all the stories about them. This knowledge extended to everyone connected to the Revolution. Whenever anyone was suggested for a government post, he had already formed an opinion of him that was based on prior information.[10]

Louis XVI had little respect for several of the patriot ministers, but he felt some rapport with Dumouriez. Dumouriez was a strong supporter of the war movement, and together with the republican members of the council, he persuaded the king to go to the Legislative Assembly on April 20, 1792, to ask it to declare war. Mme. de Staël witnessed the historic moment:

> I attended the session during which Louis XVI was forced to take a step that would have such negative consequences for him. His expression did not betray

his thoughts, but it was not because of duplicity that he did not reveal his feelings. A combination of resignation and dignity had repressed in him all outward signs of what he was feeling.... He proposed war in the same tone of voice he would have used to ask for the most routine decree possible. The president replied to him in that arrogant and laconic tone that had been adopted by this Assembly, as if the pride of a free people consisted in mistreating the king it had chosen for its constitutional leader.

After Louis XVI and his ministers had left, the Assembly voted for war by acclamation. A few members did not participate in the deliberations, but the spectators in the galleries applauded wildly. The deputies threw their hats in the air, and this day, which began the bloody struggle that tore apart Europe during twenty-three years, did not arouse the slightest concern among most of these people. Among the deputies who voted to declare war, however, a great number would die in a violent way, and those who rejoiced the most had unwittingly pronounced their own death sentence.[11]

The first battles were disastrous for France. In one case the retreating troops even murdered their own general, wrongfully blaming him for the debacle. The French armies were not yet ready to fight because two-thirds of the officers had emigrated and revolutionary sentiments caused substantial disobedience in the ranks. Mutinies had been a constant problem for the past two years. Austria and Prussia made the mistake, however, of assuming that the French armies were in such disarray that they posed no threat to their own disciplined troops. They moved too slowly to take advantage of their initial rout of the French forces, a decision they must have bitterly regretted during the next two decades of almost constant European warfare.

As the war effort met with reverses, the mood in the country turned sour, and widespread food shortages intensified the discontent. In a food riot in Etamps, the mayor was killed. Many deputies of the Legislative Assembly organized a memorial in his honor, but men like Robespierre pointedly refused to join in the occasion and instead honored a group of soldiers who had just been freed after having been condemned to the galleys because they had mutinied.

Robespierre was moving steadily into a controlling position within the Revolution, but he was a man who appealed to his followers because of his policies, not his personal qualities, which tended to repel those coming in contact with him. He seems to have been a man driven by a deep frustration and insecurity who found in the Revolution his own raison d'être. A thin man who carried himself rigidly, he dressed impeccably and wore a wig even after it was no longer the Revolutionary style to do so. More than one observer has compared him to a cat, as did one nobleman who recounted an unforgettable anecdote about a dinner party: "He said not a word, and ... looked like a cat lapping vinegar, and when Pétion, who was also there, chided him for being so taciturn and farouche and said they must find him a wife to make him sociable, he opened his mouth for the first and last time with a kind of scream, 'I will never marry!'"[12]

Meanwhile, the king was faced not only with the great discontent over the performance of the French army but was once again in a position of open conflict with the Legislative Assembly. At issue were two laws awaiting his signature. The first law proposed to set up a camp of twenty thousand armed Federates on the outskirts of Paris, a force that Louis XVI knew could be used to dethrone him. But he was even more concerned about a new version of the previous edicts against priests who refused to take the oath to the Civil Constitution of the Clergy. This new law stated that any nonjuring priest who was denounced by twenty active citizens was to be deported. By now the king knew that the Pope was unalterably opposed to the Civil Constitution of the Clergy, so he resolved to stand firm against the new law. For three years he had continually given ground to the revolutionaries and let himself be persuaded to endorse policies to which he objected. At last, however, Louis XVI and the Assembly had arrived at the one issue upon which his conscience would not let him be moved.

Roland and his supporters in the council exacerbated the situation by proposing that all six ministers present a letter to the king demanding that he replace his nonjuring priest by a priest who had taken the oath. Foreign minister Dumouriez and two other ministers denounced this move and prevented the letter from being presented. When the king learned of the matter, he expressed his gratitude to Dumouriez, saying that he would accept many things, but he would die before he acted against his conscience.

Although Dumouriez did not believe that the king should be forced to change his confessor, he strongly urged him to sign the edicts establishing the Federates camp and deporting nonjuring priests. In the long arguments that the king and he had upon the subject of the camp, Dumouriez agreed that this many armed men assembled on the outskirts of Paris would indeed be a threat to the king and to the moderate deputies of the Assembly, but he insisted that Louis XVI had no choice but to acquiesce. Dumouriez was convinced that the republican forces demanding the camp were so strong that they would overthrow the king, the Legislative Assembly, and the constitution if he resisted. With regard to the decree ordering the deportation of priests, Dumouriez first argued that the king had taken the initial step in this direction when he sanctioned the Civil Constitution of the Clergy. Louis XVI replied that he had been wrong at the time and that he deeply regretted that action. Dumouriez then said that if the king did not sign the law, he would in effect be putting the knife to the throats of the priests, apparently arguing that only deportation would save them from the fury of the mob. Dumouriez's assertion distressed Louis XVI, but he held firm and refused to accept this specious reasoning.[13]

Dumouriez seems to have argued his viewpoint sincerely and to have been concerned for the king's personal safety. This was not the case, however, with Roland, Clavière, and Servan, the three more radical members of the council. They became increasingly insulting in their attitude toward the king, and Roland finally presented to him a highly critical and patronizing letter written by Mme. Roland that asserted: "The revolution has been decided upon in men's minds; it will be achieved and cemented by bloodshed if wisdom does not prevent the misfortunes it is still possible to avoid.... I know that the austere language of truth is rarely welcomed near the throne; I also know that because it can so rarely make itself heard, revolutions become necessary."[14]

In early June, the king dismissed these three ministers, who immediately appealed to the Assembly, accusing him of trying to destroy the Revolution. Dumouriez tried to counter their charges by addressing the Assembly and detailing the deplorable condition of the army. Together with Duranton and Lacoste, the other two members of the council who were more sympathetic to the king, Dumouriez then tried once more to persuade the king to sign the decrees for the Federates camp and the deportation of priests, saying that public opinion was already so aroused because of the king's dismissal of the three patriot ministers that it would be dangerous to further infuriate the republican elements. Ferrières considered these events to be a turning point for Louis XVI:

> The ministers told him with a respectful firmness that he was destroying himself. "My mind is made up," replied the king. "Tomorrow I will give you a letter for the president. One of you must countersign it, and then together you should take it to the Assembly." This decisive tone, to which the ministers were not accustomed, surprised them, but the king, as he had said, had made a firm decision. Deciding to brave all future consequences and to follow only his conscience in a matter that he considered to be the most sacred of his duties, he no longer showed either fear or hesitation. He displayed a strength and a reasoned submission to the will of God that his enemies did not believe him capable of sustaining. His character as a man and king, which had been previously worn down by the people who surrounded him, now regained its original energy. Rejecting all that was abhorrent to his soul, he no longer showed the slightest sign of weakness and marched with a firm and strong step along the difficult path he had chosen."[15]

Louis XVI had resolved on a course of action but so had his three remaining ministers, who all submitted their resignations because he had refused to sign the decrees. This left the king more than ever isolated in a hostile city. Several months later Dumouriez himself reached a point when he could no longer accept the excesses of the Revolution. After the king was guillotined in early 1793, he abandoned his command and left the country.

In his memoirs Bertrand de Molleville, who replaced Dumouriez as minister of war, recorded a conversation in which Louis XVI told him that he believed that he would soon be assassinated, saying that he did not fear death but worried about his family. "If I did not have my family with me, everyone would see that I am not as weak as they believe; but what would become of my wife and my children if I didn't succeed?"[16]

Louis XVI's statement makes it clear that he was all too aware that most people considered him to be a weak man. He had attempted to answer this charge in a conversation with Count Fersen, who had made a daring visit to Paris incognito in February 1792 for a last visit with the king and queen. On that occasion the king had said to Fersen: "I know that I am charged with weakness and irresolution, but no one has ever been in a position like mine. There was one opportunity that I missed, I know — July 14 [the fall of the Bastille in 1789]: then I ought to have got away. There has never been another since."[17]

Louis XVI blamed himself for not having left while there was still an opportunity, but countless others also misjudged the situation. All through the early stages of the Revolution, most French liberals believed that a constitutional monarchy could be successfully achieved with Louis XVI as king. He was not the only person who did not foresee the crucible of terrible violence through which France would soon pass. Although he frequently became impatient with the king, Ferrières was moved by his refusal to sign the decree for the deportation of the nonjuring priests:

> Thus this unfortunate monarch, acting out of the purest and most disinterested motives, could not bring himself to sanction a decree that he believed to be unjust, despite the certainty of the fate that awaited him. Surrounded by immoral men without religion, he sacrificed himself for them, believing that he should remain true to his religion. He alone, in the middle of a corrupt court, received with faith the church dogmas and carefully followed a sublime morality.[18]

With the king's refusal to sign either the decree for the camp of Federates or the decree for the deportation of nonjuring priests, the battle lines were clearly drawn, and the capital nervously awaited the approaching denouement. On June 17, 1792, Morris stated in a letter to Thomas Jefferson: "We stand on a vast volcano. We feel it tremble, we hear it roar; but how and when and where it will burst, or who may be destroyed by its eruptions, it is beyond the ken of mortal sight to discover."[19]

18

Invasion of the Tuileries Palace

It was Lafayette who made the move that precipitated the final stages of the developing drama. In a letter read for him in the Legislative Assembly on June 18, 1792, he denounced the domination of the French political scene by the Jacobin Club. Asserting that through their thousands of affiliated clubs throughout France, the Jacobins were becoming stronger than the official government, Lafayette called for their suppression. But it was too late for such action. The Jacobins enjoyed so much support in the Legislative Assembly that his plea went unheeded. Worse yet, it inflamed the already dangerous situation even further, convincing many of the republicans that Lafayette was about to lead a military coup to reestablish royal authority.

On June 19, the day after Lafayette's letter was read in the Legislative Assembly, the king sent to the Assembly a formal statement refusing to sanction the decree to deport nonjuring priests and the decree to establish a camp of Federate soldiers on the outskirts of Paris. His announcement had been anticipated by the republican forces of the city, who had already been busy organizing a mass protest in anticipation of his vetoes. Ever since the dismissal of the patriot ministers, the Faubourgs Saint-Antoine and Saint-Marcel had been in a state of perpetual agitation. As at other critical junctures of the Revolution when violence suddenly erupted, the populace of Paris was suffering from shortages of essential foodstuffs and was hence in an especially volatile state. Leaders of these republican quarters now asked the municipality and the Department of Paris for permission to have a march of armed citizens on June 20, the anniversary of the Tennis Court Oath. Count Pierre Louis Roederer, the attorney general for the Department of Paris, which included Paris and some of the surrounding areas, pointed out that such an armed march would be illegal. He unsuccessfully urged the municipality of Paris, under Mayor Pétion, to takes steps to prevent the march. One of the most important records of the turbulent events of the summer of 1792 is Roederer's fascinating account titled *Chronique des cinquante jours du 20 juin au 10 août 1792.*

At dawn on June 20, 1792, thousands of marchers set out from the faubourgs, armed with pikes, stakes, scythes, and axes. At this point in the Revolution, power was shifting from the bourgeois to the lower classes of laborers, who became known as the "sansculottes" because they wore long trousers instead of the short breeches called culottes worn by gentlemen. On this day the marchers carried a pair of old culottes on a pike to indicate their scorn for the upper classes; they also carried a calf's heart labeled "aristocrat's heart." Although these marchers were in general also suspicious of the bourgeois, one of their principal leaders was a man named Santerre, a wealthy brewer of the Faubourg Saint-Antoine, who soon rose to a top position of power in this group.

The first destination of the protesters that day was the Legislative Assembly because they wanted to march through the hall carrying their weapons. After this demonstration they planned to plant a tree of liberty near the Tuileries Palace and to present a petition to the king demanding that he sign the deportation and camp decrees.

Shortly after the Assembly opened its session at noontime, the deputies were informed that the demonstrators were waiting outside for permission to file through the hall. The crowd numbered twenty thousand demonstrators according to Roederer. The Assembly was in an awkward position because after the declaration of war in late April it had granted permission to many companies of volunteers to march through the hall bearing their arms. When Roederer addressed the Assembly, he pointed out that their present difficult position was a result of their previous failure to enforce the law against armed demonstrations. Vergniaud then spoke, urging the deputies to make an exception again in this case, but he at least suggested that a delegation of sixty deputies be sent to the adjacent palace to ensure the king's safety. The deputies undoubtedly felt pressured by the ever-increasing noise from the huge crowd pushing against the doors of the Assembly; at any rate they voted to admit the marchers with their arms.

At two o'clock the marchers began filing through the hall, carrying banners reading: "Down with the veto!" "Warning to Louis XVI: the people are tired of suffering — liberty or death!" "Long live the sansculottes!" One of their leaders named Huguenin made a speech in which he complained of the dismissal of the patriot ministers, the failure of the war effort, and the king's veto of the two important decrees, asserting:

> The blood of patriots must not flow to satisfy the pride and ambition of the treacherous Tuileries Palace....
>
> The people have risen to the circumstances, and they are ready to use extreme means to avenge their outraged majesty. How unfortunate it is that free men who have transferred to you their powers see themselves reduced to the cruel

necessity of dipping their hands in the blood of conspirators! There is no longer time to dissimulate. The plot has been uncovered, and the hour has come. Blood will flow and the tree of liberty that we are going to plant will flower in peace.[1]

As the crowd outside the Legislative Assembly kept pushing forward and could only move slowly into the hall, hundreds of people were pushed up against the gates of the gardens of the adjacent Tuileries Palace. These people, who were in danger of being crushed, became ever more insistent in their demands that the gates be opened to allow them into the gardens. Finally they forced their way through the gates, and large numbers of protesters rushed into the gardens and toward the palace. Now the point of confrontation moved to the Porte Royale leading into the palace courtyard. The demonstrators milled around in this area for an hour or so. Then, under the leadership of Santerre, they brought forward a cannon that they had pulled along with them on their march and placed it in position to fire at the huge door. The National Guard battalions that were supposed to be defending the palace were in a state of disarray, with many soldiers voicing support for the protesters. After a while two officials from the municipality ordered the guards at the door to open it. They complied, allowing thousands of demonstrators to pour through the entrance. The crowd immediately filled the courtyard and rushed into the palace. They dragged along one of the cannons, pulling it up the grand staircase. One group of rioters broke down the doors leading into the queen's bedroom and tore apart the beds as they looked for her, howling curses and shouting that they wanted her dead or alive.[2]

The king, surrounded by his family and a handful of followers and servants, was waiting in his bedroom. When he heard the sounds of axes chopping down the doors of the intervening rooms, he ordered that the doors be opened and went to meet the rioters. Romainvilliers, the current commander of the National Guard, was nowhere to be seen, but a battalion commander named Acloque rushed to the king's side with a few men. The soldiers drew their weapons, but Acloque shouted to them to put them away to avoid risking the king's life. A deputy from the Legislative Assembly who was present in the palace that day later commented that the king maintained an "unbelievable sangfroid." He witnessed the famous incident in which in response to someone urging him not to be afraid, Louis XVI replied by placing the hand of a National Guardsman on his heart and saying, "You can see that it's not beating any faster than usual."[3]

In order to make it easier to protect the king, the soldiers surrounding him urged him to move into a window embrasure, where he mounted on the window seat. The bodies of only a few men stood between him and the hostile crowd. While the mob was approaching the king's suite, several of his supporters had virtually dragged the queen and her children away to a safer location. Madame Elisabeth insisted, however, upon staying with her brother and placed herself in the adjacent window embrasure. In his record of those fateful days, Roederer described the dramatic encounter that ensued:

> Soon the crowd filled the room. A frightful noise was heard that consisted of cries and confused shouts, among which could be distinguished outrageous words and menacing threats: "Down with the veto! Recall the ministers! Sinister and atrocious faces were scattered through this audacious and malevolent crowd.
>
> A butcher named Legendre, who became famous in the National Convention, approached the monarch. The noise stopped and one could hear the words he addressed to the king: "Sir [not Sire],..." At this word the king made a movement of surprise. "Yes, sir," Legendre continued forcefully, "listen to us; it is your place to listen to us.... You are a traitor. You have always deceived us, and you are still deceiving us. We have taken as much as we can and are tired of being your plaything." Then Legendre read something that was supposedly a petition but was nothing but a tissue of reproaches, insults, threats, and injunctions that expressed the will of the sovereign people for whom Legendre declared himself to be the orator and authorized agent. The king listened to this lecture without showing any emotion and replied: "I will do what the constitution and the laws order me to do."
>
> After this scene, there were more cries and more tumult. People kept streaming into the room, but no one could get out, so everyone was crowded together. Then it became apparent that the most furious of these people had evil intentions. One of them, who had a pole to which was fastened a sword blade with a very sharp point, attempted to charge the king. The grenadiers placed in front of the king parried the blow with their bayonets. Another man, who was armed with a saber, forced his way through the crowd and advanced toward the king in a very menacing attitude. He too was kept away by the volunteer grenadiers. A strong man from the market who was holding a saber in his raised arm also tried hard to get to the king. Almost everyone who succeeded in getting close to him reprimanded him outrageously. He replied, "I am your king. I have never deviated from the constitution." Several times he attempted to speak, but his voice was lost in the tumult.[4]

Several rioters rushed at Madame Elisabeth, shouting that she was the queen. She whispered to the ministers beside her that she preferred to let them think she was the queen in order to deflect their anger from her sister-in-law. According to Mme. Tourzel, one of the men even placed his pike against Madame Elisabeth's throat but removed it when she said gently, "You would not do me any harm, put aside your weapon."[5]

Mme. Tourzel described the members of the crowd as "careless, furious, and gay at one and the same time."[6] Roederer mentioned the disparity of motives that day, with many having come only to satisfy their curiosity or to indicate their displeasure with the king, while a handful were motivated by "violent passions and ferocious goals."[7] He also commented upon the evident embarrassment that many experienced as they realized that they had invaded the king's private quarters. Roederer believed that although there was no carefully organized conspiracy to kill the king that day, several of the more radical leaders of the march hoped that his death would be the inevitable result of the turmoil. According to Roederer, Legendre later told a friend that the object had indeed been to kill the king. Roederer further quoted three prominent citizens of the Faubourg Saint-Antoine who in the subsequent investigations asserted that one of the mob leaders had urged the protesters to assassinate the king.[8]

Louis XVI's calm courage in facing all these violent people shouting at him to sanction the two decrees was clearly a factor in preventing his death that day. He did what he could to placate the crowd in small ways, even donning a red bonnet the demonstrators passed to him. (This type of hat had become a sanscullottes symbol.) When someone handed him a bottle of wine, he drank to the nation. For hours he stood in the suffocating heat surrounded by hostile demonstrators demanding that he withdraw his vetoes, but he refused to take this step.

The day of June 20, 1792, marks a crucial epoch in the king's life when he took a strong stand on an issue paramount to his conscience and refused to capitulate, despite the grave personal danger in which his decision placed him. He had previously let himself be pushed into decisions with which he was uncomfortable, thinking that others perhaps understood the situation better or fearing that violence would result from his maintaining a strong position. Now he had reached a point where the issues were so clear that he had no doubt about his proper course. If he sanctioned the decree establishing a large camp of soldiers, it was obvious that it would be manned by radical troops working for the downfall of the monarchy. Far more important to the king, however, was his opposition to the deportation of nonjuring priests. This was an issue of conscience that Louis XVI, as a deeply religious man and a devout Catholic, could meet in only one way. It was a particularly courageous decision because he no longer had any illusions about the future course of events. When he faced the crowd that day, he knew that sooner or later the Revolution would demand his death.

After the king had been trapped in the hostile crowd for over an hour, two deputies from the Assembly, Isnard and Vergniaud, arrived. They tried to convince the crowd that a sanction of the decrees won by force would be meaningless, but their words were ignored. At six o'clock, after the confrontation had already lasted two hours, Mayor Pétion finally arrived. According to Roederer, Pétion said, "Sire, I just this moment learned about your situation." With evident sarcasm Louis XVI replied, "That's certainly surprising because it's been going on for two hours."[9] Pétion made a speech and tried to persuade the crowd to disperse, but no one moved. Roederer recorded the subsequent events:

A tall blond young man about twenty or twenty-five succeeded in pushing through the crowd to the armchair on which Pétion was standing. He kept shouting: "Sire, sire, I demand in the name of the hundred thousand souls who surround me that you recall the patriot ministers whom you have dismissed. I demand that you approve the decrees on the priests and the camp of twenty thousand men and that you execute the laws, or you will perish." The king replied to him: "You are placing yourself outside the law; address yourself to the officials of the people." This miserable person kept acting in a furious way, but Pétion, who was near him, never told him to be quiet. Another municipal officer, M. Champion, who was standing beside the mayor, thought he showed no proper concern, while he himself judged the peril to be constantly increasing. He thought it was imperative to evacuate the room, but the mayor said nothing and gave no such order. At last he said to the mayor, "Order the people in the name of the law to leave." The mayor, who was by nature indolent and indecisive, did not reply. Then M. Champion said to him sharply: "Sir, your conduct in this event will be judged. Beware." The mayor then spoke, saying, "Citizens, you can achieve nothing further here. Go home if you don't want your officials to be compromised and unjustly accused. Leave, I repeat, go home. By staying longer, you will enable the enemies of the public welfare to cast aspersions on your respectable intentions."[10]

A discussion then took place about what doors should be opened to allow the crowd to exit if it could be persuaded to do so. At this point, the king gave permission for the people to pass through the royal apartments on their way out of the palace. Once more Pétion spoke: "You have done what you had to do. You have acted with the pride and dignity of free men. But that is enough; you should now leave."[11] Pétion's injunction, coupled with the king's invitation to view the royal apartments, at last persuaded the crowd to start moving slowly out of the room.

On their route out of the palace, the demonstrators passed through the room where the queen had taken refuge with her two children and had eventually been joined by Madame Elisabeth. Loyal guards had placed the family behind a huge table and then ranged themselves in front for protection. By the time the crowd started filing through this room, Santerre had arrived and taken charge of the situation, acting partly as the protector of the royal family and partly as a master of ceremonies showing them off to the people of Paris. One passerby gave the queen a red wool bonnet to put on the dauphin, which she did. In the stifling heat of the close-packed room, the little boy was obviously suffering from the heavy cap, and Santerre at last told the queen she could take it off his head.

About eight o'clock in the evening, the king's supporters were at last able to lead him to safety, but it was ten o'clock before the last of the marchers had left the palace and its grounds. It had been an incredibly grueling experience for the royal family and one that left them with little hope for the future. Many members of the mob had said they would be back if the king did not sanction the two controversial decrees, and they clearly meant what they said. A lawyer named Lavaux has left a memorable account of a conversation he had that day:

This June 20th I was walking aimlessly in the Tuileries Gardens amidst the din of the armed mob invading the palace, when I was accosted by M. Perronet, the engineer of roads and bridges. We were both deploring such an outrage to the royal dignity, when we were interrupted by a young man, whom I should have distrusted, but for M. Perronet's reception of him. He looked like a soldier: his eyes were piercing, his complexion pale; he had an uneducated accent and a foreign name. He spoke his mind freely about the disorderly scene before us and said that if he were king such things would not be tolerated. I paid little attention to this remark at the time, but later events recalled it to my mind, for the speaker was Bonaparte.[12]

19

Attacks by Austrian and Prussian Forces

The royal family was once again safe for the moment, but it was clear that their very lives were now threatened by the Parisian mobs. The invasion of the palace by men who insulted the king to his face and tried to assault him with deadly weapons was an event of far-reaching consequences. That evening Gouverneur Morris wrote in his diary, "The constitution has this day, I believe, given its last groan."[1] Never again would the throne be surrounded with the same respect and aura of inviolability. Immediately after the June 20 attack caricatures appeared on the walls of Paris depicting the king wearing a red bonnet and drinking to the health of the nation. Beneath the engravings were written the derisive words "The Executive Power."

On the other hand, the king's great courage on June 20 brought him the respect and admiration of large numbers of people who were deeply shocked that their sovereign could have been so mistreated. Twenty thousand people signed a petition asking that the perpetrators of the events of June 20 be punished. It was an act of courage to sign this document in the volatile atmosphere permeating the country; many who signed the petition were imprisoned or guillotined during the Reign of Terror because of their signatures.

The Department of Paris, the larger political unit that contained the city and its surrounding areas, was more conservative than the Commune and voted to suspend Mayor Pétion and Attorney General Manuel from their functions because they had failed to take sufficient action to stop the invasion of the palace. Roederer argued against this act, believing that it would only increase Pétion's popularity by making him a martyr. That was indeed the case, as Pétion and Manuel were reinstalled by the Assembly in mid–July with enhanced prestige.

On June 28 Lafayette returned to the capital to protest against the events of June 20. In his speech to the Assembly, he asked the deputies to punish the leaders of the mob that had invaded the Tuileries Palace, to suppress the Jacobins, and to implement measures to ensure respect for the established authorities, especially the king and the Assembly. He told the deputies that it was important to take these actions so that French soldiers shedding their blood in battle on the northeast frontier could be sure that the constitution was not being undermined in their absence.[2]

Lafayette was unsuccessful in this plea and also in his efforts to rally the National Guard, which he had formerly commanded, to back him in maintaining the constitutional monarchy. His abortive effort to reinstate moderate control of the Revolution accomplished nothing and only further infuriated the sansculottes and the Jacobins, who at once initiated a movement in the Assembly to have him impeached.

In the midst of all these movements and reactions, a strange event took place that has come to be known as "Lamourette's Kiss." On July 7, Bishop Lamourette from Lyon rose in the Assembly to appeal to the deputies to forget their partisan differences and unite in their support of the constitution. In a great wave of emotion, all the deputies rushed onto the floor, embraced each other, and swore their allegiance to the constitution. A delegation was at once sent to the king to tell him of the event, and he immediately went to the Assembly to express his pleasure at their act of reconciliation. But the days that followed showed how meaningless this emotional outburst had been.

After having been violently attacked in the Assembly by Brissot, the king's ministers all submitted their resignations on July 10, leaving the government even more paralyzed. Louis XVI succeeded only with great difficulty in replacing them because it was increasingly apparent that a position in the king's council would expose one to the fury of the mob.

A letter written by Gouverneur Morris to Madame Royale, the king's daughter, in 1796 sheds additional light upon the ministers' resignations. With this letter he returned to her the balance of a large sum of money that the king had entrusted to him during his last days in power in order to facilitate various escape and defense plans. The information Morris sent to Madame Royale when she was the only surviving member of her immediate family must have given her reason to regret that her father had not pursued the escape attempt that Morris described: "Among the different steps which suggested themselves the one that seemed to them most essential was to get the royal family away from Paris. Measures were so well taken for this that success was almost assured, but the king (for reasons it is useless to detail here) renounced the project on the very morning fixed for his departure, when the Swiss Guards had already left Courbevoie to cover his retreat. His ministers, who found themselves seriously compromised, all resigned."[3] Success may not have been as certain as Morris believed. According to Mme.

Tourzel, the king had received negative intelligence about the support he might receive from the inhabitants of Rouen, which was one of the principal places under consideration as a possible refuge.[4]

On July 14, 1792, the usual Bastille Day celebration was planned at the Champs de Mars. Pétion was the hero of the day, and his name was written on hats and banners. The members of the crowd repeatedly acclaimed him with cries of "Vive Pétion" and also shouted, "Down with the veto!" "Hang Lafayette," "The aristocrats to the lamppost." Mme. de Staël was once again a witness that day:

> Only a few faint voices were heard shouting "Long live the king!" like a last good-bye, like a last prayer.
>
> The expression on the queen's face will remain in my memory forever. Her eyes were full of tears. Her splendid apparel and the dignity of her bearing contrasted with the cortege that surrounded her. Only a few National Guards separated her from the crowd of armed men, who seemed to have assembled more for a riot than for a festival. The king made his way on foot from his assigned pavilion to the altar that had been erected at the far end of the Champs de Mars. There it was that he swore for the second time to uphold the constitution whose debris would crush his throne.... Only the character of Louis XVI, this character of a martyr that he never denied, was able to support him in such a situation. The way he walked and his expression were striking. On other occasions, one had often wished that he would carry himself with more grandeur, but at this moment it sufficed for him just to be himself to appear sublime. I watched from a distance his powdered head surrounded by heads with dark hair. His garments, which were embroidered as previously, stood out against the clothing of the crowd of people who surrounded him. When he ascended the steps of the altar, one had the impression of seeing a holy victim voluntarily offering himself as a sacrifice. He descended the steps and making his way back through the disordered crowd, he returned to the queen and his children. After that day, the people saw him again only on the scaffold.[5]

In early July, Vergniaud had attacked the king, but as the last days of July approached, he and other Girondists became alarmed at the turn of events and opened secret negotiations with the king, urging him to make various moves to placate the Parisian populace. Louis XVI refused to agree to their suggestions, which included the appointment of a democratic tutor for his son, the dismissal of Lafayette from his command, and the replacement of the chief officers of the National Guard, whom the radicals considered moderate.

The war fever was accelerating at the same time that the political unrest in Paris was growing. On July 22, 1792, a solemn declaration that the country was in danger was made throughout Paris, and recruiting centers were set up to encourage men to volunteer to go to the front. During this state of emergency, the forty-eight sections of Paris were given the right to meet permanently. Many sections opened their assemblies to the "passive" citizens, those paying little or no taxes, and some sections formally demanded the deposition of the king.

On July 30 over five hundred soldiers chosen for their revolutionary zeal arrived in the capital from Marseille. These troops were summoned to Paris by those who wished to dethrone the king. As these soldiers entered the city, they sang a rousing new song that soon became known as the "Marseillaise." Other Federate troops from Brest also joined them in Paris, and the republican leaders arranged to have all these men billeted near the Cordeliers Club, where they would be under the direct influence of the more radical Paris elements. The Marseillais troops clashed almost immediately with soldiers of the National Guard, and several were killed in the fighting. Some of the wounded men from the National Guard returned to the Tuileries, where Madame Elisabeth herself helped bind their wounds, a service her judges denounced when she was later tried for her life.[6]

As the situation became increasingly dangerous, one of the king's supporters brought him vests made of twelve layers of taffeta, supposedly impenetrable by bullet or sword, to protect him and the other members of his family. Marie Antoinette at once tried one on, and handing a dagger to Mme. Tourzel, she asked her to strike her with it. Mme. Tourzel instead donned one of the vests and struck herself; the dagger was indeed deflected. Henceforth the king and queen both wore these vests whenever they believed their lives to be threatened.[7]

Paris was already experiencing an almost unbearable tension when there arrived on August 1 a manifesto from the duke of Brunswick, commander of the allied armies of the Austrians and Prussians. This document that further enraged the population had originally had some basis in suggestions from the king and queen, but the émigré who drew up the manifesto had cast their ideas in a much more extreme and provocative form. The duke first announced his desire to end the unrest in France and restore Louis XVI to a position of power. He then asserted that any National Guard troops or civilians who opposed his advance into France would be killed, and he threatened to carry out "an exemplary and unforgettable vengeance" if any harm was done to the king or queen.[8]

This manifesto not only failed to protect Louis XVI and Marie Antoinette, it was in fact one of the major factors leading to their downfall, despite the king's immediate disavowal of it. The people of Paris were furious when they heard the arrogant language of the manifesto and sought to arm themselves. Workshops began manufacturing pikes as quickly as possible in order to put rudimentary weapons into the hands of all citizens. Even the iron grilles of churches were converted into pikes.

Rumors spread throughout Paris that an arsenal of eighteen thousand muskets was hidden in the Tuileries. The king finally insisted that Pétion come to the palace to assure himself that there were no weapons secreted there. Many orators railed against the "Austrian committee" of the court, asserting that Marie Antoinette and her advisers were engaging in treasonous activity. Vitriolic personal attacks upon the king increased from the pens of radical journalists such as Marat. Gouverneur Morris even heard someone say that the king used to amuse himself at Versailles by roasting cats alive on a spit.[9] During the first week of August, Morris began one of his journal entries with this striking comment: "Go to court this morning. Nothing remarkable, only that they were up all night expecting to be murdered."[10]

Robespierre now abandoned his support of legal measures and the constitution and demanded the election of a National Convention by universal male suffrage to give France a new form of government. Behind the scenes he was working with a secret committee drawn from the ranks of the Federates from Marseilles and Brest. One member of this committee shared lodgings with Robespierre. These men were working with others like Santerre to organize an armed uprising of the citizenry of Paris in order to depose the king.

To facilitate their approach to the palace, the republican forces of Paris demanded that the Feuillant terrace, that part of the Tuileries Gardens bordering the Manège, where the Legislative Assembly met, should be open to the public. After the Assembly acquiesced in this demand, only tricolored ribbons prevented the populace from entering the rest of the Tuileries Gardens.

The Feuillant terrace was the scene of a violent encounter between a group of Parisians and one of the original revolutionary leaders named d'Eprémenil, who was walking there to judge the temper of the crowd when someone recognized him and accused him of being a spy for the émigrés. Several Federates on the terrace struck him with their swords, and only the intervention of a group of National Guardsmen saved him from being hanged from a lamppost. They took him to a nearby building, where Pétion hastened to visit him as he lay on an old mattress, covered with blood from his wounds. As Pétion started to offer him words of sympathy, d'Eprémenil exclaimed: "I too, Pétion, I too was once beloved by the people, who gave me their crowns. I was the strongest supporter of their rights, and look how they treat me now."[11] His words were prophetic. Within two years Pétion lay dead of poison in a country field, his body half-eaten by wolves. He apparently took his own life to escape arrest and execution by those in power during the Reign of Terror.[12]

On August 3 Pétion made a speech to the Assembly on behalf of almost all the Parisian sections, demanding the deposition of the king and accusing him of fomenting bloody projects. The Assembly agreed to consider the issue on August 9. In the meantime, on August 8 a final vote was taken on the earlier proposal to impeach Lafayette. The deputies exonerated Lafayette by a vote of 406 to 224, numbers that indicate that most deputies in the Assembly were much less radical than men like Pétion, Robespierre, Danton, Santerre, and their followers from the streets of Paris. This vote infuriated the Jacobins and their followers because one of Lafayette's main suggestions had been to disband their club. Early on the morning of August 9 protesters began to gather in the cafes and on the streets of the city. The final act of the drama that had been developing throughout the summer months of 1792 was about to be begin.

20

Insurrectional Commune Seizes Power in Paris

On August 9, 1792, Roederer, the attorney general of the Department of Paris, was trying to stay ahead of a situation fraught with imminent danger. A man dedicated to an exact interpretation of the law, he occupied a political middle ground between the far left, which wanted to depose the king and set up a republic, and the far right, which wanted to return to the ancien régime. Only the day before, he had written to Mayor Pétion to ask what measures the city was taking to prevent a recurrence of the violence of June 20. He received a casual reply from Pétion saying that he had authorized the marquis of Mandat, who had succeeded Lafayette as the commander of the National Guard, to call up more troops. When Roederer received this letter, Mandat was at the headquarters of the Department of Paris and denied having received any such order. Roederer cleverly used Pétion's letter as an authorization for Mandat to call up extra men, adding to this authority that of the Department of Paris itself.[1] Further evidence of Pétion's duplicity was forthcoming when Roederer learned that the Parisian police headquarters had just distributed five thousand cartridges to the Marseillais Federates, despite a ruling by the Department of Paris that it must authorize any distribution of ammunition.

All information reaching the Department of Paris on August 9 confirmed that an insurrection would begin that night, signaled by the ringing of the tocsin in all the sections of Paris. Shortly before 11 P.M. the king called Roederer to the palace to seek his advice about the current situation in the city. In a few minutes Pétion also arrived to report to the king. When Commander Mandat complained to Pétion that the police headquarters had refused to give him powder for his troops, the mayor said that he was not authorized to have more and that he should have some left over from previous supplies. Mandat rejoined that most of his troops had only three rounds of ammunition left and some had only one round and were complaining.[2] Pétion's Commune

142

had just a few days earlier handed out ammunition to the Marseillais soldiers, so his refusal to provide supplies to the National Guard indicated only too clearly where the sympathies of the Paris Commune lay. Many of the National Guard troops defending the palace thought that Pétion should be held there as a hostage against an attack, but realizing their intentions, he arranged to have the Legislative Assembly summon him and hence made his escape before it was too late.

Just after midnight on August 10, Roederer received a report that there was a great deal of agitation in the Faubourg Saint-Antoine, but protesters had not yet begun to assemble. The king and queen were eager to read this report, whose information was confirmed by one of their agents returning from the streets of the city. No one had any thought of going to bed that night, and the palace rooms were full of servants, together with a few hundred noblemen who had come to help defend the king. One of the noblemen was a marshal of France who was eighty-four years old. Despite his advanced age, he was one of the handful of men appointed by the king to be in charge of defending his apartments. Some of the National Guard officers complained about the presence of these noblemen, but Marie Antoinette assured the officers that the noblemen would follow the orders of the National Guard and help reinforce their ranks.

About 12:45 A.M. the tocsins began to ring all over the city, a sound that must have heightened the feeling of overwhelming dread experienced by all those in the palace. Everyone rushed to the windows, trying to distinguish by the distinctive peals of the various church bells which Parisian sections were marching. Shortly thereafter, Roederer received further information saying that 1,500–2,000 men had assembled with cannons in the Faubourg Saint-Antoine. But by 2:30 A.M. reassuring news arrived to the effect that the demonstrators were tiring and it appeared that there might be no march that night. It was only a brief respite in the tension that gripped the Tuileries, for soon word was received that Manuel, the attorney general of the Paris Commune, had sent orders to have the cannons on the Pont Neuf removed. This was a crucial move in the drama because Mandat, the National Guard commander, had placed the cannons there to prevent marchers from the Faubourg Saint-Antoine from joining forces with the men of the Faubourg Saint-Marcel and the Marseillais and Breton Federates who were billeted on the Left Bank. With the cannons gone the palace was dangerously exposed to its enemies.

The court was unaware of the fact that during the night radical forces had asked each of the forty-eight Paris sections to send three men to the Hôtel de Ville to form a new insurrectional Commune to govern the city. During the early hours of August 10, these men met and forced the members of the official Commune to disband, keeping only Pétion and Manuel in their posts.

One of the first acts of the new Commune was to send a message to the Tuileries asking Mandat, the commander of the National Guard, to come to the Hôtel de Ville to discuss the situation. The insurrectionists were particularly eager to retrieve from him Pétion's order authorizing him to repel force with force. Mandat was most reluctant to leave his command at the palace, but Roederer persuaded him to go. The latter once again took the legal point of view despite the fact that the mobs in the street and their leaders had thrown legality to the winds. He believed Mandat to be subject to the mayor's orders and thought it was possible that Pétion wished to discuss action to restrain the marchers.[3] Roederer's advice turned out to be disastrous. Mandat was hated by the radical leaders of Paris, who considered him to be too sympathetic to the king. He was arrested upon his arrival at the Hôtel de Ville and was killed as he was being taken to prison. The mob decapitated him and threw his body into the Seine, despite the protests of his son, who wished to give his father a proper burial.

The insurrectional Commune had gained much by removing Mandat from the Tuileries Palace because his absence demoralized everyone and resulted in a disorganized defense. When Jean-Baptiste Cléry, the dauphin's valet, left the palace at 6 A.M. to reconnoiter the neighborhood, he encountered the following scene:

> I again went out and walked along the quays as far as the Pont-Neuf, everywhere meeting bands of armed men, whose evil intentions were very evident; some had pikes, others had pitch-forks, hatchets or iron bars. The battalion of the Marseillais were marching in the greatest order, with their cannons and lighted matches, inviting the people to follow them, and "assist," as they said, "in dislodging the tyrant, and proclaiming his deposition to the National Assembly." I was but too well convinced of what was approaching, yet impelled by a sense of duty, I hastened before this battalion, and made immediately for the Tuilleries, where I saw a large body of National Guards, pouring out in disorder through the garden gate opposite to the Pont-Royal. Sorrow was visible on the countenances of most of them; and several were heard to say, "We swore this morning to defend the king, and in the moment of his greatest danger we are deserting him." Others, in the interest of the conspirators, were abusing and threatening their fellow-soldiers, whom they forced away. Thus did the well disposed suffer themselves to be overawed by the seditious, and that culpable weakness, which had all along been productive of the evils of the Revolution, gave birth to the calamities of this day.[4]

During the early morning hours, the queen summoned Roederer to a private conference. When she asked his opinion of their situation, he said that the royal family should seek refuge in the Legislative Assembly. "But, sir," she replied emphatically," we have forces here. The time has come to find out whether the king and the constitution or the factions will prevail."[5] In his account of this climactic night that he wrote only a few days later, Roederer recorded his reaction to her words: "Under the circumstances, the queen's words made me think that there was a strong resolution in the palace to fight and that the queen had been promised a victory. I suspected that this victory was desired partly to impress the Assembly. These circumstances produced in me vague fears of either a resistance both useless and bloody or of an attempt upon the Assembly after the retreat or defeat of the mob. These apprehensions added an unbearable weight to my responsibility."[6]

During the interview between Roederer and the queen, it was at least decided that two ministers would be sent to the Legislative Assembly to report the state of affairs in the palace and to request that the deputies send representatives to assess the situation. While Roederer was still waiting with Marie Antoinette and the ministers, they suddenly heard cries and boos from the gardens below the windows. To their dismay, the ministers saw that the king had gone down to survey the situation and was being booed by the demonstrators. They at once went down to seek him. Roederer described the ensuing scene: "The queen was crying without saying a single word.... When she went into the king's bedroom to wait for him there, I followed her. Her eyes were red to the middle of her cheeks. A few minutes later two ministers brought the king back. He returned all out of breath and very hot from his exertion, but did not seem particularly upset by what had just happened."[7] Roederer's further comments upon the queen's demeanor on that terrifying night show how much maturity and strength of character she had developed under the pressure of the perilous situations she repeatedly found herself facing:

I do not know on what basis almost all historians have attributed to the queen on the night of August 10 speeches and resolutions of an extreme and exalted heroism. For example, she was said to have announced that she would rather be nailed to the walls of the palace than to be forced to leave. According to another story, she gave the king pistols and suggested that he commit suicide. I have no idea at what time and to whom she could have said and done such things. As for me, I saw nothing of this sort. What I did see was in fact incompatible with these strange stories. During that fateful night, I observed in the queen no effort to be virile or heroic or to act in an affected or romantic way. I saw in her neither anger, nor despair, nor a spirit of vengeance. She was a woman, a mother, a wife in danger. She feared, she hoped, she worried, and she reassured herself. She was both queen and Maria Theresa's daughter; she wept without moaning, without sighing, and without speaking. Her concern and her grief were contained and concealed by respect for her rank, for her dignity, for her name. When she reappeared in the middle of the courtiers in the council room, after having been dissolved in tears in Thierry's room, her eyes and cheeks were no longer red. She appeared somber but calm, even disengaged. The courtiers said to each other, "What serenity, what courage!" Her bearing did show courage, but I want to repeat that she gave no sign of bravura, as has been suggested, or of exaltation, anger, or despair.[8]

Realizing that the court intended to wait out the crisis at the palace, Roederer decided to go to the Legislative Assembly with his fellow officials from the Department of Paris to discuss matters further. As they were crossing the gardens, they met the two ministers who had preceded them to the Assembly. They reported that only sixty or eighty members were there, far below a quorum that could take action. At this point Roederer and his colleagues saw a large crowd of protesters approaching and decided to return to the palace before they could be cut off from the entrance. There they were accosted by the soldiers in charge of the cannons, who asked, "Are we going to be forced to fire upon our brothers?" Roederer replied: "You are here only to guard this door and to keep anyone from entering; you will fire only if you are fired upon. If they fire on you, they are not your brothers."[9] Roederer's companions then suggested that he should make the same statement to the National Guardsmen in the courtyard, who were also tormented by the thought that they might be asked to attack the marchers. Accordingly, he went to the courtyard to tell the soldiers there that their purpose was only to repel force by force. The gunners were obviously disaffected, however, and for an answer, one pulled the charge out of his cannon and stepped on his match fuse to extinguish it.

After speaking with members of the crowd in the Carrousel area in front of the palace who were about to force the Porte-Royale, Roederer decided that not a moment was to be lost, so he quickly ran with his companions back to the palace, where they raced up the grand staircase. Hurrying through the apartments crowded with people, he at last arrived at the king's room. In his *Chronique*, Roederer recorded his speech to the king:

> "Sire," I said in an urgent tone, "your majesty does not have five minutes to spare; you will be safe only at the Assembly. The Department of Paris is of the opinion that you must go there without delay. You do not have sufficient soldiers to defend the palace and their loyalty is in question. The cannoneers unloaded their cannons when it was suggested that they use them to defend the palace." "But," said the king, "I didn't see that large a crowd at the Carrousel." "Sire," I replied, "they have twelve cannons, and a huge crowd is arriving from the faubourgs."...
>
> "But sir," the queen said to me, "we have forces." "Madame, all Paris is marching," I replied, and I immediately restated even more emphatically what I had just been saying to the king: "Sire, time is running out; this is no longer a

prayer that we are addressing to you, it is no longer advice that we are taking the liberty of offering to you. We have only one option at this point, and that is to ask your permission to take you away."

The king raised his head, looked intently at me for a moment, and then, turning toward the queen, said, "Let's go," and got up. Madame Elisabeth ... said to me, "Monsieur Roederer, will you take responsibility for the life of the king?" "Yes, Madame," I replied, "I will answer for his life with my own. I will walk right in front of him."[10]

Mme. Tourzel later wrote her own version of this dramatic departure from the Tuileries Palace: "The queen, who was standing by the king, remarked that it was impossible to abandon all the brave men who had come to the palace solely to defend the king. 'If you oppose this step,' said Roederer to her, in a severe tone of voice, 'you will be responsible, Madame, for the lives of the king and your children.' The poor unhappy queen was silent, but she experienced such a revulsion of feeling that her face and neck in a moment became suffused with blotches."[11]

Arrangements were hastily made for a detachment of National Guardsmen to escort the royal family, the ministers, and the Department of Paris officials, together with Mme. Tourzel and Princess Lamballe, to the Legislative Assembly. Roederer insisted that all the others in the palace stay behind. In order to fulfill her vow of office never to leave the dauphin, Mme. Tourzel was forced to leave her seventeen-year-old daughter Pauline behind in a position of terrible danger. There was no time, however, to discuss any of these matters because every minute was crucial to the king's safety.

As the king was passing through the apartments with his cortege, he suddenly, in an oddly whimsical and perhaps symbolic gesture, took the hat of the soldier who was marching beside him and placed his own white-plumed hat upon the man's head. Was it an effort to relieve the almost unbearable tension of the departure, or was Louis XVI in this way indicating the burden his office placed upon him, in effect saying he wished he were not the king?[12]

Continuing his account of the night's events, Roederer wrote: "When we reached the peristyle at the bottom of the grand staircase, the king, who was right behind me, said, 'What will happen to all the people who remain behind?' 'Sire,' I replied, 'it appeared to me that they were in ordinary clothing. Those with swords can discard them and follow you, leaving through the gardens.' 'That's true,' said the king."[13]

One of the most unfortunate aspects of the day of August 10 was that Roederer rushed the king out of the Tuileries in such haste that no clear decision was made about what those remaining in the palace should do, and they were left to a terrible fate. In Roederer's defense, however, one must say that he achieved the paramount objective of keeping the king alive. Even a fifteen-minute delay might well have meant his immediate death. Roederer had no way of knowing that same fate awaited Louis XVI a few months hence.

As the procession wound through the gardens, with Roederer keeping his promise to walk right in front of the king, everyone had to wade through deep piles of leaves that had fallen very early that year because of the extreme heat. It seemed an evil omen, for Manuel had only a few days earlier written in a newspaper article that the king would not last until the leaves fell.[14]

When the royal family arrived at the Feuillant terrace just outside the Manège, where the Assembly was in session, their progress was stopped by a large and angry mob. Roederer described the tense situation in this way:

> One of these men was carrying a pole that was eight or ten feet long. He was furious against the king. Beside him was a citizen who was even more worked up. "No," they cried, "they aren't going to enter the Assembly; they are the cause of all our misfortunes. This must end! Down with them! Down with them! Very menacing gestures accompanied these words. I went forward and ... said: "Citizens, I request your silence in the name of the law.... You seem to want to prevent the king and his family from entering the Assembly. You are not justified in putting an obstacle in their path. The king has a right to be there in light of the constitution, and although his family doesn't have a constitutional right to be there, a decree that has just been passed authorizes them to be there. Here are the deputies that the Assembly has sent to accompany the king; they can verify the existence of this decree. The general opposition seemed to cease, but the man with the long pole waved it around while he kept yelling, "Down with them! Down with them!" I went up on the terrace, grabbed the pole out of his hands, and threw it in the garden. He was so astonished that he stopped yelling and vanished in the crowd.[15]

At last the royal family arrived safely within the doors of the Assembly, where they were welcomed by the current president, who happened to be Vergniaud. The king made a short statement, saying, "I have come here to avoid a great crime, and I believe that I could not be safer anywhere else but among you."[16] Louis XVI in effect was saying not that he feared death, but that he did not want to see French citizens take the odious step of murdering their monarch. On many other occasions he manifested this same curious tendency to view himself with great detachment, discussing his role as king almost as if he were talking about someone else.

Vergniaud replied to the king: "You may count upon the firmness of the Assembly. Its members have sworn to die upholding the rights of the people and the constituted authorities."[17] They were brave words, only too soon to be forgotten under the threat of mob violence.

21

Battle at the Tuileries Palace

A few minutes after the royal family took refuge in the Legislative Assembly, someone pointed out that the deputies could not constitutionally debate in the presence of the king. It was yet another example of the bizarre contrast between those members of the government who insisted on a punctilious application of the laws and the mobs in the street who were trampling the law beneath their feet as they marched. Fortunately, someone suggested that the royal family could be put in the press box, which was technically separated from the main room but opened into it through a barred window space. The king and some of his guards pulled out the bars to give more ready access to the box in this tense situation. The king, the queen, their two children, Madame Elisabeth, Mme. Tourzel, and Princess Lamballe were all crowded into the twelve-foot-square room for more than three days in the sweltering August heat.

The king's sudden departure from the palace left everyone there in a chaotic state, with none of the defensive units sure what its role should be. The Swiss Guards fell back from their forward emplacements, leaving the Marseillais and Breton Federates free to enter the main courtyard. There they began to fraternize with the National Guardsmen and some of the Swiss Guards. Suddenly a shot was fired. In the ensuing panic, both sides began to fire wildly. Within a few minutes many of the Federates and a few of their opponents lay dead. It has never been known who fired the first shot, but at any rate the violence that had been only strongly potential up to that point now erupted with brutal force. The Marseillais and Bretons fell back initially, but they soon returned with reinforcements. The protesters were now furious because they believed they had been ambushed. They surged forward to avenge their dead comrades, firing their cannons at the Tuileries Palace.

At the Manège, where the Legislative Assembly was in session, everyone suddenly heard the frightening sound of cannon fire and screams from the battle. The king hastily wrote out an order and sent it to the Swiss Guards, stating, "The king orders the Swiss to lay down their arms at once and to retire to their barracks." Of course, it was difficult for the king to judge the chaotic situation from inside the Manège, where he could only hear the ominous sounds of battle. As always, he was motivated by a desire to minimize bloodshed, but in this case it was too late for the Swiss Guards to save themselves. Some abandoned their weapons and attempted to flee, but the mob pursued them with a brutal vengeance, setting fire to their barracks to force out those who had retreated there. In his memoirs Ferriéres described the ensuing carnage:

> The people, who were now masters of the palace, spread through it like a devastating torrent. The vestibule, the grand staircase, the chapel, the hallways, the antichambers, the throne room, and the council room were all flowing with blood. No one was spared. The mob searched the cellars and every small nook and cranny. They pitilessly cut the throats of defenseless people who were in the palace only as servants and had taken no part in that fatal day. The invaders destroyed the furniture, the mirrors, and the paintings and forced open armoires and desks. The Swiss Guards were pursued with special ferocity, all the more so because they could no longer defend themselves. They were killed with pikes in the gardens and in the streets, and they were dragged out of houses where they had sought refuge. Sixty of these unfortunate men were taken to the Hôtel de Ville, where they were put to death on the Place de la Grève.[1]

By the end of the day, 600 Swiss Guards lay dead, together with 200 other supporters of the king. The attackers lost 100 men and many of their numbers were wounded. Most of the National Guardsmen had vanished as the fighting began or had joined the insurgents. Cléry had the misfortune to be inside the palace when the attack upon it began. In his journal he described the horror of that morning:

> Compelled to remain in the apartments, I awaited with terror the consequences of the step the king had taken, and went to a window that looked upon the garden. In about half an hour after the royal family had gone to the Assembly, I saw four heads carried on pikes along the terrace of the Feuillans [sic], towards the building where the legislative body was sitting; which was, I believe, the signal for attacking the palace, for at the same instant there began a dreadful firing of cannon and musketry. The palace was everywhere pierced with balls and bullets; and as the king was gone, each endeavoured to take care of himself, but every passage was blocked up, and certain death seemed to await us all. I ran from place to place, and finding the apartments and staircases already strewed with dead bodies, took the resolution of leaping from one of the windows in the queen's room down upon the terrace, whence I made across the parterre with the utmost speed to reach the Pont-Tournant [Revolving Bridge], but a body of Swiss, who had gone before me, were rallying under the trees. Finding myself between the two fires, I ran back in order to gain the new flight of steps leading

up to the terrace on the water-side, intending to throw myself over the wall upon the quay, but was prevented by the constant fire that was kept up on the Pont-Royale. I continued my way on the same side till I came to the dauphin's garden gate, where some Marseilleois, who had just butchered several of the Swiss, were stripping them. One of them came to me with a bloody sword in his hand, saying: "How, citizen! Without arms? Take this sword and help us to kill." However, another Marseillois seized it. I was, as he observed, without arms and fortunately in a plain frock, for if anything had betrayed my situation in the palace, I should not have escaped.

Some of the Swiss who were pursued took refuge in an adjoining stable; I concealed myself in the same place. They were soon cut to pieces close to me. On hearing the cries of these wretched victims, M. le Dreux, the master of the house, ran up, and I seized that opportunity of going in, where, without knowing me, M. le Dreux and his wife invited me to stay till the danger was over. In my pocket were letters and newspapers directed to the prince royal, and a card of admission to the Thuilleries [*sic*], on which my name and the nature of my employment were written; papers that could not have failed to betray me, and which I had just time to throw away before a body of armed men came into the house, to see if any of the Swiss were concealed in it. I pretended, by the advice of M. le Dreux, to be working at some drawings that were lying on a large table. After a fruitless search, these fellows, their hands tinged with blood, stopped and coolly related the murders of which they had been guilty. I remained at this asylum from ten o'clock in the morning till four in the afternoon, having before my eyes a view of the horrors that were committed at the Place de Louis Quinze. Of the men, some were continuing the slaughter, and others cutting off the heads of those who were already slain, while the women, lost to all sense of shame, were committing the most indecent mutilations on the dead bodies, from which they tore pieces of flesh, and carried them in triumph.[2]

While the battle was raging at the palace, the deputies at the Legislative Assembly continued their debates in an atmosphere of almost unbearable tension. At the beginning of the day, many of them had feared an attack by the Swiss Guards or the noblemen at the Tuileries. It was quickly apparent, however, that the Paris marchers were the victors, and the Assembly passed a decree asking them to respect person and property. But the slaughter was so wholesale by this point that no suggestion coming from the Assembly was going to have the least effect upon the mob. The invaders of the palace were, however, surprisingly careful to avoid any appearance of looting and put to death on the spot anyone in the crowd who tried to steal something. All jewelry, gold, and other valuables seized were brought to the Assembly. Throughout the long, hot day protesters entered the Manège to denounce the king and demand his deposition. To add to the ordeal of the royal family, various prisoners taken by the people were brought before the bar of the Assembly. Among them was a nobleman covered with blood, his clothes torn, who had stayed at the king's side to defend him until he left the palace. He was taken away from the Assembly to the Abbaye prison, where he was among those massacred on September 2.

Word also reached the royal party that many of their personal servants had been killed, including several attending upon Mme. Tourzel. Her son, who was one of the king's attendants, brought the welcome news that his younger sister, Pauline, had escaped from the palace. Pauline's account of her horrifying experience, like that written by Cléry, has the immediacy only those who have lived through such an episode can impart:

A bombardment of the palace commenced shortly after the departure of the king. We heard the shot whistle past in a frightful way. The noise of the breaking glass and windows was awful. To get under shelter and away from the side where the bombardment was going on, we retired into the apartments of the queen on the ground floor. There the idea occurred to us of closing the shutters and light-ing all the candles in the candelabras. We hoped that if the brigands forced the door, their astonishment at the sight of so many lights would save us from a sud-den onset and would give us time to parley.

Scarcely had we made this arrangement when we heard fearful shouts in the next room. The rattle of weapons told us only too plainly that the palace was forced and we should have need of all our courage. It was the affair of a moment; the doors were burst open, and men with swords in their hands and their eyes starting out of their heads rushed into the room. They halted for a moment, astonished at what they saw and at only finding a dozen women in the room. The lights reflected in the mirrors, contrasting with the daylight, had such an effect on these brigands that they remained stupefied. Several ladies were completely upset, among others Madame de Genestoux, who lost her head so completely that she fell on her knees and begged for pardon.... Good Madame de Tarente begged a young Marseillais to have pity on this woman's weakness and take her under his protection. The man consented ... and evidently struck by the display of such courage under such circumstances, he said to her, "I will save that lady, and you too, and your companion [Pauline Tourzel]." ...As we left we were obliged to pass over the bodies of Diert, an attendant to the queen, and Pierre, one of her footmen, who would not leave their mistress's room and had fallen victims to their attachment. This sight cut us to the quick, and Madame de Tar-ente and I looked at each other, thinking that we might perhaps speedily meet with the same fate. After a great deal of trouble the man succeeded in getting us out of the palace.... We were walking quietly on ... when we heard frightful shouts behind us. When we turned around we saw a crowd of brigands rushing on us sword in hand. Others at the same time appeared in front of us on the quay and over the parapet. These latter aimed at us, shouting that we had escaped from the Tuileries.... This manner of being massacred appeared frightful to me. Madame de Tarente spoke to the crowd and succeeded in arranging that we should be taken under escort to the district headquarters.

We had to cross the length of the Place Louis XV in the midst of the dead and dying, for many of the Swiss and unfortunate gentlemen had been massacred there. We were followed by an immense mob, who overwhelmed us with insults as they escorted us to the district headquarters.[3]

Fortunately for these women, the district judge was sympathetic to them. To protect them from the wrath of the mob, he announced in a loud voice that they should be sent to prison. But after their captors had departed, he sent them out the back door with an escort to help them to safety.

While the crowds were still roaming through the palace seeking further victims, the Legislative Assembly was reacting quickly to the pressure of the inflamed populace. Vergniaud addressed the deputies to demand the king's immediate suspension and the election of a National Convention to give France a new form of government. His motion quickly passed, although only two days earlier the deputies had refused to follow the will of the crowd when they voted against indicting Lafayette by an almost two-to-one majority. At this point, however, it would have been hard for any deputy to have voted against the mob when it was brutally murdering anyone it considered an enemy at the very door of the Assembly. Decrees followed rapidly, one after another, implementing the desires of the Parisian insurgents. Suffrage for the upcoming elections for the Convention was extended to any employed male over twenty-five. The new Commune's appointment of Santerre as the commander-in-chief of the National Guard was also confirmed by the deputies. The former patriot ministers— Roland, Servan, and Clavière — were reinstated, and Danton was appointed minister of justice. The latter's great ability to move a crowd with his extemporaneous oratory had advanced him to a position of leadership in the Cordeliers Club, and together with Robespierre and Marat, he is credited with instigating the uprising of August 10. Pétion, Manuel, and Danton were the only three former Commune officials kept on in their offices by the new insurrectional Commune, so Danton was clearly on the side of the populace in this episode. Mme. Tourzel recorded her impression of the Legislative Assembly's proceedings:

> As soon as the ministers heard the reproaches heaped upon the king, on which the Assembly based its motion for the suspension of royalty, they wanted to appear at the bar of the Assembly to take upon themselves the responsibility for the conduct of the king, but he absolutely forbade them to do so. "You will increase the number of victims without being able to be of any use to me, and there will be one sorrow more for me. Withdraw, I order you, and do not return here." The misfortunes that were overwhelming this excellent prince did not prevent him from watching over all those who were attached to him.[4]

After listening to twelve hours of denunciations against him in the Assembly, the king was allowed to retire for the night with his family to rooms in the former Feuillant monastery, which was now part of the Assembly complex. The deputies had decided to lodge the royal family in the Luxembourg Palace henceforth, but it would take a few days to prepare rooms for them there.

When they awakened the next morning, the king and queen learned that several of the king's closest friends and supporters would no longer be allowed to remain near them. In her memoirs, Mme. Tourzel related the dismay of the king and queen at this news:

> "I am then in prison," said the king, "and less fortunate than Charles I, who kept all his friends with him to the scaffold!" Then, turning to these gentlemen, he expressed his regret at having to part from them and ordered them to withdraw. The queen said to them with tears in her eyes, "Only now do we feel all the horror of our position; you would mitigate it by your presence and your devotion, and they are depriving us of this last consolation." As the royal family were without money and clothes, they all of them laid at the feet of the king the gold they had upon them, but the king would not accept it. "Keep your purses, gentlemen, you will need them more than we shall, as you will have longer to live, I hope."[5]

After spending three days in the press box at the Manège, the royal family learned that Manuel had insisted that the new Commune take full charge of them, housing them in the Temple instead of the Luxembourg Palace. According to Mme. Tourzel: "The queen shuddered when she heard the Temple mentioned and said to me in an undertone, 'You will see, they will put us in the tower, and they will make it a regular prison for us. I always had such a horror of that tower that I over and over again begged the Count of Artois to have it pulled down; that must certainly have been a presentiment of all we shall have to suffer there.'"[6] There was a residence in a wing attached to the Temple that would have provided fairly comfortable quarters for the royal family, but as Marie Antoinette guessed, the Commune intended to house them in the forbidding tower.

Manuel carefully orchestrated the king's departure for the Temple on August 13, lining the streets with supporters of the new insurrectional Commune. As the family rode for the last time in the royal carriage, they passed slowly through streets filled with people shouting, "Vive la nation" and "Vive la liberté," as well as vulgar insults. Manuel, who was riding in the royal carriage along with Pétion, gave orders to the coachman to stop in the Place Vendome next to the giant statue of Louis XIV that had been pulled down by the crowds during the recent disorders. "You see," he said insolently to Louis XVI, "how the people treat their kings." Louis XVI turned red for a moment but then calmly said, "May it please God that its fury only be vented on inanimate objects."[7] Mme. Tourzel related the rest of the journey:

> The king was two hours and a half in reaching the Temple by way of the boulevards. His terrible escort, not content with making the carriage proceed at a

walk, also brought it to a standstill from time to time. Many of them came up to it with their eyes gleaming with rage, and there were moments when we saw anxiety depicted on the faces of Pétion and Manuel. At such times they put their heads out of the windows, harangued the mob and entreated it, in the name of the law, to allow the carriage to proceed.

Dreadful as was the entry into the Temple to the royal family, they were driven to desire it, in order to bring to an end a scene as atrocious as it was prolonged.[8]

22

The Royal Family in Prison

The members of the insurrectional Commune had festooned the entire Temple, even to its garden walls, with hundreds of lights, and its holiday atmosphere contrasted strangely with the somber mood of the royal family. After a dinner in the elegant residence adjoining the tower, the king and queen were taken with their children and attendants into the stark tower, where they were assigned hastily prepared rooms. The king's sister, Madame Elisabeth, and Pauline Tourzel, who had just been reunited with her mother, had nowhere to sleep but a filthy kitchen. Municipal officials, or "municipals," representing the new Commune alternated guard duty over the family while they were imprisoned in the Temple, and they were never left alone during their waking hours. At night the municipals on duty slept just outside their rooms.

After the royal family had been imprisoned for several days, municipal officers came to the tower late in the evening of August 18 to arrest the Princess Lamballe, Mme. Tourzel, her daughter Pauline, the queen's three attendants, and the king's valets, Hué and Chamilly. The queen tried to insist that Princess Lamballe was part of the royal family because her deceased husband had been a great-grandson of Louis XIV, but her plea was to no avail. Madame Royale recalled in her memoirs of their captivity that it was only with great difficulty that her mother could tear herself from the arms of the princess, who had been one of her closest friends since her arrival in France.

The group was taken to the Hôtel de Ville for immediate questioning, where according to Mme. Tourzel's memoirs they succeeded in answering their inquisitors carefully enough that the spectators seemed to favor letting them return to the Temple. Manuel had other ideas, however. By making a joke about women always getting their way in France, he persuaded those assembled to send them to prison, except for Hué, who was allowed to return to the Temple for a few days before he was again arrested.

Even in the midst of the scenes of greatest terror and ruthlessness during the Revolution, there were always some in positions of power who tried to mitigate the suffering they saw around them. Mme. Tourzel wrote of such a man:

> After our examination we were taken into Tallien's office, hovering between hope and fear. One of the secretaries, moved with pity at our situation, went to see what was going on at the meeting of the Commune, and he gave us some hope of returning to the Temple. But half an hour later, after having paid another visit to the meeting, he returned without saying a word. Then looking at us he said, "No, I cannot bear it any longer." He left the room, and we saw no more of him. We could no longer doubt that our fate was decided.[1]

Shortly after the arrest of their attendants, the royal family learned that Lafayette had fled across the northern border of France in protest against the extreme course the Revolution was now taking. While attempting to reach England and then continue on to America, he was arrested by the Austrians, who imprisoned him for several years in dungeon-like conditions, to the dismay of his American friends.

After hearing of the arrests of the attendants who had been taken to the Temple with the royal family, the dauphin's former valet, Cléry, asked permission to serve the family. On August 26 he entered the Temple, where he acted as valet initially for the dauphin and later for the king. He remained in the Temple until March 1, 1793, and managed to keep a secret record of the life of the royal family there, which he later published. His journal is an invaluable document for those interested in understanding the character of Louis XVI, for through Cléry's words we see the king as he appears in relief, no longer surrounded by courtiers and advisers.

According to Cléry, the king arose every morning at six, knelt to pray for several minutes, and then read until nine o'clock, when his family came up from the floor below to join him in the dining room for breakfast. After breakfast they all went downstairs to spend the day in the queen's room. The king now took charge of his son's education, hearing him recite passages from Corneille and Racine and helping him with his own favorite subject, geography. Cléry noted that the seven-year-old boy was so precocious that he could write on a blank map of France the names of the eighty-three new departments and the principal cities and rivers. Marie Antoinette taught Madame Royale. The suspicious guards hampered attempts to teach the children mathematics, however, because they believed a multiplication table was some sort of a code. When these lessons were done at eleven o'clock, the women spent the next hour doing needlework, but to their disappointment, they were not allowed to send the chair seats they made to friends outside the tower because their guards thought the designs might contain secret messages.

Shortly after noon the family went for a walk in the garden. The king and queen were eager for the children to have fresh air, although they suffered from the insults they received from those on guard duty in the passages leading out of the Temple and from workmen within the garden. The man in charge of unlocking the main entrance to the garden was particularly unpleasant. His horrible face with its distinctive long mustaches made him easily recognized whenever a Parisian mob gathered. A large saber that he always carried added to his frightening appearance. He was the man who on June 20 had broken open the door to the king's room in the Tuileries with blows from an axe. Whenever the royal family descended to the garden, he subjected them to a humiliating ritual. First he would make them wait at the door while he fumbled through all his keys to find the right one. Then after he had opened the door, he would stand beside it and blow puffs of pipe smoke into the face of each one as they passed by. The National Guardsmen in the passage would laugh uproariously at this spectacle and purposely remain seated in the passage with their hats on their heads to show their disdain for the royal family.[2] Madame Royale later recorded that her father's attitude toward this mistreatment was one of calm forgiveness, while her mother responded with a heightened air of dignity.[3]

While the family walked in the garden and the dauphin played games with Cléry, the guards and the gardeners sang revolutionary or obscene songs. One of the first days that the family went to the garden, a workman told the king that he would like to cut off the queen's head with his garden tool. Even Pétion found this behavior excessive and had the man arrested. Twelve-year-old Madame Royale was so distressed by this incident that she included it in her memoirs years later.[4] Sometimes there was no peace for the family even when they returned to their rooms, where they might find that there had appeared in their absence the kind of graffiti Cléry described:

> The walls were frequently covered with the most indecent scrawls, in large letters, that they might not escape notice. Among others were: "Madame Véto shall swing." "We shall find a way of bringing down the great hog's fat." "Down with the red ribbon." "The little wolves must be strangled." Under a gallows with a figure hanging were these words: "Louis taking an air bath." And under a guillotine: "Louis spitting in the bag."[5]

After their daily walk in the garden, the family had their main meal of the day together at 2 o'clock. They ate reasonably well because one of the royal cooks continued to manage the kitchen that provided for them. The kitchen was at such a distance, however, that the food could not have been very hot when it arrived in the tower. Cléry served the meal, and as always, a municipal watching over them inhibited the conversation. Every day at this time Santerre, the new commander-in-chief of the National Guard, came to the tower to inspect the premises and assure himself that the royal family was still there. After dinner the family returned to the queen's room, where the king and queen usually played a game of tric trac or piquet, mainly in order to exchange a few words in a low tone of voice that could not be heard by the municipal standing guard in the room. Madame Elisabeth often took the children to her room to play, where Cléry accompanied them. The two adults would ostensibly read, but by prearrangement the children would periodically make sufficient noise to cover the low voices of Madame Elisabeth and Cléry as they exchanged information. At four o'clock the king took a nap in an armchair while the others read or the children played. Then Cléry would give the dauphin his daily lesson in penmanship, after which the two of them played a game of ball.

From six to eight o'clock, the queen and Madame Elisabeth read aloud to the family from plays or other works. Then it was time for the dauphin to have his early supper and go to bed. While the child was eating, his father amused him and his sister by asking them riddles because he had found a ready supply in a collection of magazines in the Temple library. After the rest of the family ate supper at nine, the women retired for the evening and the king read until midnight, not wishing to retire until he saw who the new guards appearing at that hour would be.

The king was always an inveterate reader. He had available during the five months of his captivity 250 books in Latin, French, English, and Italian and looked through or read a great many of them, according to Cléry.[6] In late November he sent to the Commune a list of thirty-three books that he wished to read that included works by Bossuet, Virgil, Ovid, and various Roman historians. After some debate, the committee in charge sent the books, although at least one member observed that the king would not live long enough to read them all.[7] During this period religious works such as Thomas à Kempis's *Imitation of Christ* were more important than ever to the king.

One striking example of the myths about Louis XVI that have been propagated for over two centuries comes from one of the first entries one obtains when googling "Louis XVI." The short biography on the website of the Notable Names Database (NNDB) states, "Louis XVI was weak in character and mentally dull." Unfortunately, this kind of statement about Louis XVI appears with far more frequency than do accurate evaluations of him. Another remarkable example is *Newsweek*'s statement during in its coverage for the 1989 Bicentennial of the French Revolution, in which it referred to "stout and stupid Louis XVI."

The image of Louis XVI, who was hardly "stupid" or "mentally dull," sitting quietly reading dozens of books in his tower prison while the violent events of the French Revolution swirled about him is a memorable one. While some of the politicians were becoming so wild that a new term was coined to describe them — the enragés, or the madmen — Louis XVI calmly faced the insults and ignominious treatment to which many of his captors subjected him. At this point in his life he had no doubts about his proper course. Viewing existence from a broader religious context in which the current political upheavals were only transitory, he was able to sustain his courage by an unshakable faith in God. He would soon have need of all of this fortitude, as the Revolution suddenly took an even grimmer turn.

23

The September Prison Massacres

The September prison massacres are one of the darkest events in the French Revolution. In early September 1792, the prisons of Paris were filled not only with ordinary criminals, but also with many political prisoners arrested on August 10 or rounded up in the following days in house-to-house searches. Hundreds of priests were also incarcerated during this volatile period.

In the weeks following the August 10 attack on the Tuileries Palace there had been a running battle between the new Commune and the Legislative Assembly for control of France. One of the issues that particularly inflamed the Parisian radicals was the question of punishment for those who had opposed them on August 10. Robespierre demanded on behalf of the Commune that a special court be set up to punish those who had defended the Tuileries or were suspected of opposing the elimination of the king from the government. The Assembly was reluctant to take this step, but on August 17 members of the Commune threatened to stage yet another armed revolt if the deputies did not at once authorize a special tribunal, whose members were to be elected by the Paris sections. At this time fewer than three hundred of the more than seven hundred members of the Assembly remained in Paris because after the upheaval of August 10 many deputies retired to the security of their homes in the provinces. They no longer felt safe from the Paris crowds, which in particular had threatened those deputies who had voted to acquit Lafayette. Now many deputies protested that the Commune was trying to coerce them into doing its bidding, but their voices were unavailing, for the Commune was fast becoming an irresistible power. The Assembly quickly set up the special tribunal that the Commune was demanding.

When this tribunal met for the first time on August 21, it condemned to death a man named Louis d'Angremont for his part in the defense of the Tuileries. That evening he was guillotined on the Place du Carrousel, which was adjacent to the Tuileries Palace, because the Commune thought it fitting that he die on the spot where his crime had been committed. He was the first political prisoner to die by the guillotine, a form of execution the Assembly had introduced only a few months earlier as a more humane way to take the life of a condemned person. Despite the desires of the Parisian republicans for a swift and terrible vengeance for their losses on August 10, the tribunal moved relatively slowly, condemning only a handful of men during the latter part of August.

In their fury the Parisian radicals began to hint that perhaps the best solution was for their forces to enter the prisons and kill the prisoners without waiting for the special tribunal to act. On August 19, Marat suggested such a massacre. This was not surprising because he frequently incited the Parisian crowds to wholesale slaughter. As early as January 1791, he had written an inflammatory article in his newspaper asserting: "Ten months ago you could have cut off 500 heads to assure your happiness; now to avoid perishing, you will perhaps be forced to cut off 100,000 after you have seen your brothers, your wives, and your children massacred."[1] It seems incredible that the author of these words could declare in August 1792, "No one abhors bloodshed more than I, but to prevent rivers of blood from flowing, I urge you to shed a few drops."[2]

Unfortunately for the prisoners, France at this point suffered a series of military defeats that both frightened and infuriated the populace. On August 26 the fortress at Longwy fell to the duke of Brunswick and his Prussian and Austrian troops. Rumors began to spread throughout Paris that as the enemy forces approached the city, there would be an uprising in the prisons and all the counterrevolutionaries would escape from their cells and murder the wives and children of those soldiers who had departed for the front. As fear grew in the city, the Assembly passed a new law saying that any nonjuring priests who had not left France within two weeks would be deported to New Guinea, a colony whose unhealthful climate would leave them prey to yellow fever and other tropical diseases.[3] To add to the harshness of this law, Paris refused to issue passports to its priests. In addition, the Assembly passed a law requested by Danton, the new minister of justice, which authorized house-to-house searches for weapons and suspects. These searches, which began on August 30, resulted in the arrest of three thousand people, many of them nonjuring priests, who were incarcerated in the already overcrowded Parisian prisons.

Terror seized all those in the city who could be suspected of royalist sympathies, and many tried to go into hiding. Gouverneur Morris's house, viewed as a haven because of his theoretical diplomatic immunity, was full of friends and acquaintances trying to escape the wrath of the populace. Mme. de Staël barely succeeded in using her husband's position as the Swedish ambassador to keep the patrols from searching her house, where she was hiding her lover, Narbonne, the former minister of war.

While this roundup of suspects was taking place, a bitter battle was being waged between the Brissotin-Girondist majority of the Legislative Assembly and the new Commune, which many members of the Assembly believed was far too radical. On August 30 the Assembly voted to ask the Paris sections to elect another Commune. The members of the Commune were of course infuriated, and Robespierre accused Roland, Brissot, and others in their group of being agents of the duke of Brunswick. Acting upon Robespierre's instigation, a committee of the Commune issued arrest warrants for these men. Danton, however, refused to have these warrants served, and thus these leaders narrowly escaped finding themselves in prison when the massacres broke out. From this time on, the Girondists hated Robespierre because they believed he had tried to kill them through this maneuver.

On September 2 news reached Paris that Verdun, the last major fortress on the route to the capital, was about to fall. In a state of panic, the Commune proclaimed that the enemy was at the gates, and the tocsin rang throughout the city. While Roland, Servan, and their associates were considering moving the government out of the city to the Loire Valley, Danton assured his place in history by rallying the populace with the words: "For victory we must dare, and dare, and dare again. So France will be saved."[4]That morning a new municipal named Mathieu burst in upon the royal family and arrested Hué, the king's valet, leaving only Cléry to serve the family. Mathieu was furious about the news of the fall of Verdun. In her memoirs the king's daughter, Madame Royale, described the tense scene:

> Mathieu then turned to my father, saying everything that the most indignant rage could suggest. Among other things, he said: "The call to arms has been sounded, the tocsin has rung, the alarm cannon has been fired, and the émigrés are at Verdun. If they arrive, all of us will perish, but you will be the first to die." My father listened to these insults and a thousand similar ones with the calm that hope provides. My brother burst into tears and ran into the next room. I had great difficulty comforting him because he could already imagine his father dead.[5]

That same morning of September 2 a newly appointed Vigilance Committee of the Commune, which included Marat as a member, met at the mayor's home. Marat arrived accompanied by a group of armed citizens from his section. It was probably under his instigation that the committee decided to send an unprotected convoy of twenty priests through the city streets to the Abbey of St. Germain des Prés, which was being used as a prison. The abbey was located in Marat's section, where he had been fomenting hatred against all the prisoners. It is not surprising that as the priests arrived, they were set upon by a crowd that murdered them. Then the assailants proceeded to kill many of the prisoners inside the abbey.

Not far away was the former Carmelite convent, where priests were also being held as prisoners. The mob went there next and massacred a hundred and fifty priests. After the first few murders, rudimentary courts were set up in the prisons, where the attackers meted out a very crude and hasty justice, based primarily upon the will of the assembled crowd. Those the court ruled against were simply sent out the door of the prison into the arms of a crowd waiting to slaughter them.

It was two hours before the massacre spread to other prisons, a crucial period during which the Commune or Assembly could have at least attempted to stop the killing. The only security force available was the National Guard, under control of its new commander, Santerre, and Mayor Pétion, but neither man tried to stop the slaughter. Mme. de Staël related in her memoirs that when she tried to escape Paris at the height of the massacres, she was temporarily detained at the Hôtel de Ville, where Santerre spent several hours sitting in her empty carriage. He was supposedly protecting it from the crowd, while all about him were running men whose arms were soaked with the blood of their victims.[6] While the killing was still going on, Pétion had nothing better to do than to send a representative to the Temple to settle some minor financial arrangements with the king.

Although various apologists for the September massacres have tried to say that the people of Paris had a legitimate fear that the prisoners were going to escape and kill them if the Parisians did not murder them first, it is hard to see any rational motive for the generalized slaughter that engulfed the nine prisons of Paris. Between 1,100 and 1,400 prisoners were killed, but only one quarter of them were priests and other political prisoners. The others were common criminals, many of them in jail for minor offenses. Prostitutes were murdered at the Salpêtrière prison, and boys and girls were clubbed to death at the Bicêtre reformatory. The manner in which the murders were carried out was brutal and sadistic; those participating seem to have degenerated into an incredible sort of blood-lust. Instead of setting up a firing squad or another relatively humane form of execution, those manning the mock tribunals simply sent their condemned victims out of the prison doors to a waiting crowd of enraged people who felled them with blows from swords, clubs, pikes, or whatever weapons they had at hand. Gouverneur Morris was among the many shocked foreign observers still remaining in France. He recorded a grisly aftermath of the event:

> Some days ago a man applied to the Convention for damages to his quarry. The quarries here are deep pits dug through several feet of earth ... and then extended along the bed of stone under the surface. The damage done to him was

by the number of dead bodies thrown into his pit and which choked it up so that he could not get men to work at it. Think of the destruction of hundreds who had long been the first people of a country, without form of trial, and their bodies thrown like dead dogs into the first hole that offered.[7]

Just before the massacres began, a lawyer named Varenne had been imprisoned because of a dispute with an acquaintance who had denounced him to the authorities. His description of the horror of the day the killers reached his prison makes grim reading:

> I saw two men who were also in uniform; the arm and jacket sleeve of one of these men was covered in blood to his shoulder, as was his sword. He announced: "For two hours I've been chopping off limbs right and left. I'm more exhausted than a mason who has been applying plaster for two days."[8]

Varenne was one of the lucky prisoners who was released by the mock court, but his departure was in itself an ordeal:

> It was at this moment that I realized more sharply than at any other time the magnitude of the danger that I had just escaped, and the pallor that spread over my face indicated that I was close to fainting. I was taken away immediately and led outside the gate by men who held me up under my armpits, assuring me that I had nothing to fear because I was under the protection of the people.
>
> In this manner I went down the Rue des Ballets, which was filled on both sides by a triple row of men and women of all ages. When we got to the end of the street, I recoiled in horror upon seeing in the gutter a heap of nude bodies covered with mud and blood. I was forced to swear an oath of allegiance on these bodies.[9]

After having rested in his parents' home for an hour, Varenne decided he should go into hiding, lest he be rearrested. While passing the Conciergerie prison, he witnessed the following horrible sight:

> At about two o'clock, some of those who had been slaughtering the prisoners became overcome by fatigue and were no longer able to raise their arms.... They were trying to catch their breath as they sat in a circle around the bodies that were lying there near the prison. When a woman who was carrying a basket of rolls passed by, they asked her for the rolls and dipped each one in the wounds of their victims, a few of whom were still palpitating. Never were cannibals as ferocious and barbaric as this.[10]

In the prison of La Force, where they had been sent on August 19, Mme. Tourzel, her seventeen-year-old daughter Pauline, and Princess Lamballe were sharing a cell when the massacres broke out. In a letter to her sister written a few days after her escape, Pauline told a gripping story of terror, beginning with her entrance into the prison:

We entered this horrible prison by the wicket-gate opening on to the Rue des Ballets, and we had first of all to pass through the Council Hall, so that our names might be entered in the prison register.

I shall never forget one well-dressed man there who came to me when I was alone in the room and said, "Mademoiselle, your position interests me, and I advise you to leave off your courtly airs and be more familiar and more affable." Indignant at the impertinence of this man, I looked at him straight in the face and told him that such as I was I should always be; that nothing could change my disposition and that the expression he had noticed on my face was neither more nor less than the reflex of what was passing in my heart, indignant at the horrors we were witnessing. He made no reply, but withdrew by no means pleased.... We had been a fortnight in this sad place when, on the third of September at one o'clock in the morning, all three of us being in bed, ... we heard our door unlocked, and saw a man who said to me, "Mademoiselle de Tourzel, get up quickly and follow me." I trembled and neither spoke nor moved. "What are you going to do with my daughter?" said my mother to this man. "That is no business of yours," he replied, in a manner that seemed to me somewhat harsh, "she must get up." ... I got up slowly. The man still remained in the room, repeating, "Make haste." ... The man, seeing that I was up, came to me, took me by the arm, and dragged me away in spite of myself. "Adieu, Pauline, and may God protect you and bless you!" exclaimed my mother. I was no longer able to answer her; two huge doors were already between us, and the man was still dragging me on.

As we were going downstairs, he heard a noise and with an uneasy and agitated air he thrust me hurriedly into a small cell, locked the door, and disappeared. This cell had just been occupied and was still lighted by a little bit of the end of a candle. I saw it burn out in less than a quarter of an hour, and I cannot tell you what I felt or describe to you the sinister reflections inspired within me by this flickering light, now brilliant, now expiring. It represented to me the agony of death and inclined me, more than the most touching speeches could have done, to sacrifice my life.

I remained, therefore, in the most profound darkness, and in a short time I heard my door open softly. I was called, and by the light of a small lantern I saw a man come in whom I recognized as the same who had locked me in — the man who was in the Council Hall when we entered La Force and had given me the advice about which I was so indignant.

He made me walk quietly, and when we reached the bottom of the staircase, he ushered me into a room, showed me a parcel, and told me to dress myself in what I should find inside. He then shut the door, and I remained motionless, without doing anything and almost without the power of thought.

I do not know how long I remained in this state. I was only roused from it by the noise of the door opening, and I saw the same man. "What! Not dressed yet" he said, with an anxious air. "It will be all over with you if you are not quickly out of this." I then looked at the parcel and saw a peasant's dress. The things seemed to me to be large enough to go over my own, and I put them on in a moment.... When we were outside the door of the prison, I perceived in the clear moonlight a prodigious number of people, and at the same moment I was surrounded by armed men of ferocious aspect, who seemed to be awaiting some victim to sacrifice. "A prisoner being rescued!" they all shouted at once as they threatened me with their swords.

The same man who was leading me did all he could to thrust them aside and make himself heard. I saw then that he wore the badge which distinguished the members of the Commune of Paris. This badge made it possible for him to secure a hearing, and he was allowed to speak. He told them that I was not a prisoner, that I was in La Force by sheer accident, and that he had just extricated me by a superior order, it not being just to make the innocent perish with the guilty.

This sentence made me tremble for my mother, who remained in captivity; the speech of my liberator (for I saw clearly that this was the part being played by this man, whose manner had appeared so harsh to me), had an effect on the crowd, and I was being permitted to pass when a soldier in the uniform of the National Guard stepped forward and told the people that they were being deceived, that I was Mademoiselle de Tourzel ... and that my fate ought not to be different from that of the other prisoners.

The fury which had calmed down now redoubled against me and my protector to such an extent that I really thought my last moment had arrived and that the service which he had desired to render me would be to conduct me to my death, instead of leaving me to await it. He did not give way an inch, however. His tact, his eloquence, or perhaps my good luck extricated me from this danger also, and we found ourselves free to go on our way.[11]

Pauline was still in great danger of being rearrested, so Hardi, her protector, left her in a small courtyard while he reconnoitered the neighborhood. When he returned, he brought a pair of trousers and jacket for her to wear, but he had forgotten to bring a hat and replacements for her colored shoes, so she could not wear this disguise after all. She was much relieved, being unable to bear the thought of dying dressed as a boy.

To get out of the courtyard, they had either to pass once again through the crowd of assassins by the gate of the prison or to pass through a church where other members of the mob were holding a meeting. Choosing the latter, they slipped down a side aisle, and then Hardi left Pauline hiding behind an altar while he once again checked outside the church. After she had waited for a long time, all the while listening to the harrowing screams of more victims, Hardi at last returned and took her to his home. This time he left her for an hour and then returned in a state of great agitation, as Pauline noted in her record of her escape.

"You have been recognized," he said ... "and it is known that I have rescued you; they want to get possession of you again, and they believe that you are here; they might even come here to seize you; you must get away at once, but not with me, for that would be exposing yourself to certain danger. Take these," he continued, handing me a hat with a veil and a black mantle, "listen attentively to what I am going to say to you and do not forget the least detail."[12]

Hardi then gave Pauline careful instructions for passing through several streets to an alley where she should await him. At last he arrived in a carriage, accompanied by Billaud de Varennes, Danton's secretary, who had examined Pauline at her original trial. They took her to see Danton, who ruled that she could go free. It was still imperative, however, that she hide somewhere from the mob. She suggested the home of a seamstress who lived in a poor, out-of-the-way quarter of the city. In her account, Pauline recalled: "Billaud de Varennes ... asked me the name of the street in order to tell the coachman. I said the Rue du Sepulcre. This name, just at that time, made a great impression on him, and I saw on his face an expression of horror at this connection with all the current events.[13]

As they rode along in the carriage, Pauline begged Hardi to save her mother, and he promised that as soon as he left her, he would return to the prison, where he hoped to be in time to rescue her also. In her memoirs Mme. Tourzel described what had been happening at the prison in the meantime:

About eleven o'clock in the morning our door opened, and our room was filled with armed men who demanded Princess Lamballe. They did not mention me at first, but I would not abandon her....

In the clerks' office a court had been established for the trial of prisoners; each one was escorted there by two assassins belonging to the prison, who took them under their protection to massacre them or save them according to the judgment pronounced against them. In the courtyard where we were all assembled, there was a great crowd of these men of blood; they were badly clothed, half drunk and they looked at us with a barbarous and ferocious air. There were, nevertheless, among them some honest men who were only there in the hope of being of some use to the prisoners should any opportunity present itself, and two of these rendered me great service during this fatal day....

There was no disguising the danger we were all running, but the peril which I believed was surrounding Pauline absorbed all idea of any that confronted me. I saw the man who had so harshly taken away my daughter; the sight of him inspired me with horror, and I was trying to avoid him, when, passing close to me, he said in an undertone, "Your daughter is saved," and he went away from me at once.... During this time M. Hardi, my liberator, did not forget me.... In order to dispel from the minds of the people all idea of any connection between me and the unfortunate Princess Lamballe, he contrived to send to the tribunal before me a large number of malefactors who were to be tried by it, and all those who were convicted were massacred without mercy. One passed by me who made a frightful impression upon me. His terror was so great that death was already written on his face; with sobs he implored the mercy of his conductors. At that moment I was surrounded by men of ferocious mien, who made no secret of the fate in store for me. M. Hardi, who felt that I was lost if these men took me to the tribunal, conceived the idea of making them drunk. He succeeded in doing this.... The wretches who were made drunk, unable to stand upright, were obliged to lie down, and the others who remained behind became sensibly milder, especially two among them who were always by my side.

Several men of the National Guard began to show some interest in me and said to me, "You always treated us very well at the Tuileries.... You will have your reward." ... When the National Guard saw me ready to go before the tribunal they wanted to offer me an arm, but those about me opposed this, saying, "We have been by her side ever since she has been in the greatest danger, and we will not leave her now that she is on the eve of being saved." They endeavored to inspire me with confidence, and this feeling increased within me when I saw M. Hardi, for it was evident to me that he was only present for the purpose of protecting me.[14]

Mme. Tourzel answered the questions of the court with a calm courage and tact that preserved her life; she was one of the lucky ones set free. Describing her exit from the prison, she wrote:

I was conducted to the door of the prison, and just as I was passing through the little gate, these very men, who had been ready to massacre me, threw themselves upon me to embrace me and congratulate me on having escaped the impending danger. It made me shudder, but I was obliged to comply. I experienced a far greater thrill of horror when, on emerging from the Rue des Ballets into the Rue Saint Antoine, I saw, as it were, a mountain of the remains of the bodies of those who had been massacred, mingled with clothes torn and covered with mud, and surrounded by a furious mob who wanted me to get on this hideous heap to shout "Vive la Nation!" At this spectacle my strength gave way and I fainted. My conductors shouted for me, and I did not regain my consciousness until I got into a hired carriage.... This carriage was surrounded by the same men who were by my side in the courtyard of La Force. Three of these men got inside with me.... Throughout my journey they showed me every imaginable attention, recommending the driver to avoid the streets where anything terrifying might be encountered....

During the drive I noticed with astonishment the extreme desire they displayed to see me in a place of safety. They urged the coachman to drive more quickly, and each one seemed personally interested in my preservation.[15]

Mme. Tourzel and her daughter Pauline were extremely fortunate to escape death on a day on which their companion, Princess Lamballe, met a horrible fate. Princess Lamballe seems to have been marked out by the crowd for its special vengeance. Mme. Tourzel believed that this was because she had helped the duke of Orléan's wife, who was her sister-in-law, to obtain a legal separation from him. The duke was still a center of influence during this period and succeeded in being elected to the Convention under his new name of Philippe Egalité (Equality). This unscrupulous man might well have relished the chance to even the score with Princess Lamballe. Within a few months he was to vote for the death of his cousin the king.

It also seems highly likely that Princess Lamballe was so closely associated with Marie Antoinette that she had become a surrogate queen for the mob to destroy. Except for the prostitutes killed at the Salpêtrière prison, women prisoners were in general spared during the massacres. In the report of one of the officers of the Commune named Tallien, the special hatred directed toward the princess is apparent, a hatred whose motivation appears in the thinly veiled allusion to charges about her sexual relationship with the queen that circulated in the gutter press: "Her relationships with the fiercest enemy of the nation, Marie Antoinette, whose companion in debauchery she had always been, justified to a certain extent the excesses committed in her case."[16]

If the only motivation behind the prison killings was in fact self-defense, there seems little reason for the crowd to have killed Princess Lamballe, who could not have been much of a threat to anyone. At her perfunctory trial in the prison, she was asked to swear eternal hatred to the king and queen. This she would not do. So deep was her devotion to the queen that she had left a safe haven abroad to return to Marie Antoinette's side when it became apparent that the queen was in increasing danger from the revolutionaries. After she refused to swear the oath against the king and queen, she was condemned and sent out to face the murderous crowds awaiting her. She was brutally struck down as she emerged defenseless from the door of the prison, a small figure in white according to an eyewitness. Her assassins cut off her head and carried it through the streets on a pike, dragging her body along behind. The wild mob also paraded her heart, breasts, and genitals through Paris on pikes, an action that seems to suggest that some of her persecutors were motivated by a belief in the salacious rumors implying a lesbian relationship between the queen and Princess Lamballe. In the records of the ensuing judicial inquiries, there is a grisly case involving a charge that a member of the mob had grilled and eaten Princess Lamballe's heart.[17] Regardless of the truth of the charge, the very fact that a court was discussing such a matter shows the incredible level to which the assassins had descended during the September prison massacres. The mutilation of Princess Lamballe's body clearly seems to indicate that the murderers were wreaking their vengeance upon Marie Antoinette through her friend. The mob was not satisfied with simply murdering and mutilating the princess but headed in its fury to the Temple, intent on showing her bloody remains to the queen. Cléry described in his journal the horror of the resultant scene:

At one o'clock the king and the family expressed a desire to walk, but were refused. When they were dining, drums were heard, and soon after the cries of the populace. The royal family rose from table with great uneasiness, and assembled in the queen's chamber. I went down to dine with Tison and his wife, who were employed for the service of the tower.

We were scarcely seated, when a head on the point of a pike was held to the window. Tison's wife gave a violent scream, which the murderers supposed to have proceeded from the queen, and we heard the savages laughing immoderately. Imagining that her majesty was still at dinner, they placed their victim in such a manner that it could not escape her sight. The head was the Princess de Lamballe's, which, though bleeding, was not disfigured, and her fine light hair, still curling, waved round the pike.

I ran instantly to the king. My countenance was so altered by terror, that it was perceived by the queen, from whom it was necessary to hide the cause; and I wished to make it known to the king only, or to Madame Elisabeth, but two commissioners of the municipality were present. "Why don't you go and dine?" said the queen. I replied that I was not well; and at that moment another municipal officer, entering the tower, came and spoke to his associates with an air of mystery. On the king's asking if his family was in safety, they answered, "It has been reported that you and your family are gone from the tower, and the people are calling for you to appear at the window, but we shall not suffer it, for they ought to show more confidence in their magistrates."

In the meantime the clamour without increased, and insults addressed to the queen were distinctly heard, when another municipal officer came in, followed by four men, deputed by the populace to ascertain whether the royal family was, or was not in the tower. One of them accoutered in the uniform of the National Guards, with two epaulettes, and a huge sabre in his hand, insisted that the prisoners should show themselves at the windows, but the municipal officers would not allow it, upon which the fellow said to the queen, in the most indecent manner: "They want to keep you from seeing de Lamballe's head, which has been brought you that you may know how the people avenge themselves upon their tyrants. I advise you to show yourself, if you would not have them come up here." At this threat the queen fainted away. I flew to support her, and Madame Elisabeth assisted me in placing her upon a chair, while her children, melting into tears, endeavoured by their caresses to bring her to herself. The wretch kept looking on, and the king, with a firm voice, said to him: "We are prepared for everything, sir, but you might have dispensed with relating this horrible disaster to the queen."[18]

The crowd tried to force its way into the Temple prison with the naked and bloody body of Princess Lamballe. If they had succeeded in entering the tower, they would almost certainly have massacred the royal family. There were very few troops there to protect the royal family, and the Commune did not bother to send reinforcements, despite the obvious danger from the marauding crowds. Fortunately, a quick-thinking official on duty at the Temple persuaded the rioters to leave by telling them that Princess Lamballe's head belonged to all the people of France and it would be more fitting to display her head and body at the Palais Royal, the revolutionary center of the country. As a further defense, the municipals put up a tricolored ribbon across the entrance to the Temple. They later sent a bill for this ribbon to the king.

Once again the royal family had survived another tumultuous day, but fate was inexorably closing in upon the small group in the tower.

24

French Military Successes

The Prussian and Austrian troops were slow to take advantage of the momentum they had gained in capturing Longwy and Verdun. Dumouriez was now in command of the northern army, and he took up a bold position in the hills of the Argonne, backed by the troops under the command of General Kellermann. The duke of Brunswick attacked the French forces at Valmy on September 20, 1792, expecting an easy victory, but the French benefited from their superior artillery, which had been introduced in the latter part of Louis XVI's reign. The spirit of their troops was also better. Kellermann rode along the lines with his hat on the end of his sword shouting, "Vive la Nation." The battle became known as the "operetta combat" because the French soldiers all sang the "Marseillaise" and "Ça Ira." By contrast the duke of Brunswick's troops were in a weakened condition as the result of widespread dysentery brought on by the constant rain. Surprised at the good spirits of the French troops, the duke decided to withdraw from the field. Within two weeks his forces had left France.

Further south, battles were also going well for the French in the last days of September. Montesquiou had conquered Savoy, and the city of Nice had fallen to the French. Dumouriez now decided to turn his attention toward the Austrian Netherlands (which included Belgium), where he won the decisive battle of Jemmapes on November 6. Within a month France controlled Belgium.

The new legislature called the Convention was now ruling France. In theory its members were to be elected by universal suffrage, but in practice its deputies were elected by fewer than ten percent of the voters. Those in power automatically excluded from the franchise any of the twenty thousand people who had signed the petition of protest against the first invasion of the Tuileries on June 20, and throughout the country many royalists and former Feuillants felt too intimidated to cast their votes. Robespierre arranged to have the Paris voting take place at the Jacobin Club, with voters casting their votes publicly.[1] Needless to say, Paris elected the most radical list of deputies. The Girondists fared well in the provinces, but within Paris their opponents, who were led by Robespierre, gained most of the seats. These deputies became known as the Montagnards because they occupied the high seats, or the "Mountain," in the Convention.

The Convention met for the first time on September 20, the day of the French victory at Valmy. It immediately voted to depose the king and declare a republic. Troops were then sent to the Temple, where they assembled in the courtyard. After the call of trumpets produced silence in the neighborhood, one of the municipals with a very loud voice read an announcement of the king's deposition that was clearly audible to the royal family in the tower. Two of the municipals sat insolently smiling as they watched the king and queen, but the king, perfectly aware that they were hoping to see some sign of dismay, never raised his eyes from the book he was reading. At this point the announcement could hardly have surprised him.[2]

As news of French successes in battle reached Paris in late September, the mood of fear that had gripped the city in the early days of the month began to dissipate, and there was a revulsion of public opinion against the September massacres. The Girondists attempted to use this more moderate feeling to move against Robespierre, Danton, and Marat, but they did not succeed in dislodging them. They did achieve one of their goals, however, which was to have a new Commune elected to govern Paris.

One of the leaders in the new Commune was Jacques Hébert, who wrote a notorious newspaper full of foul language that was called "Le Père Duchesne." As a member of the former Commune, he had taken a turn as a guard at the Temple and was one of the men who tried to catch an expression of despair on Louis XVI's face as he listened to the proclamation of his deposition. In his newspaper, he described his tour of duty in the tower, giving posterity an indication of the kind of journalism that prepared the way for the execution of the king, a journalism so extreme as to seem its own parody:

My turn came, damn it, to go to guard the menagerie in the Temple as a municipal. I made it a kind of holiday to examine the ferocious beasts. Consider first the rhinoceros, foaming with rage to see himself in chains and panting with the thirst for blood that consumes him. Trait for trait this is the portrait of Louis the traitor, who snores at night like a hog on his manure pile and passes the day doing nothing but grunting. He is happy only when his sees his food arriving and devours a chicken in one bite while he says to himself, "I wish I could do the same to a Jacobin or a sansculotte!" As for the Austrian, she is no longer that tigress swimming in the torrents of blood that she caused to flow on the day of St. Lawrence. She now wears the treacherous face of a cat and meows sweetly. She pretends to have a velvet paw so that she can find a better time to scratch with her nails.... As soon as he [the king] noticed me near his bedside when he woke up, he made a friendly gesture and wanted to start a conversation about the rain and the weather. But, damn it, I made him hold his honeyed words and keep quiet.... We should conduct the trial of Louis the traitor promptly so that we don't keep a lot of people busy watching him and making such a show of guarding a stingy pig.[3]

Since their arrival at the Temple, members of the royal family had been lodged in the small tower while renovations were being carried out in the large tower to partition each floor into several smaller rooms. On September 29 a half-dozen municipals appeared before the royal family and announced that they had come to take the king to his new room in the large tower. He separated from his family in a state of anxiety, not knowing if he would ever see them again. Cléry followed him into his new quarters.

The next morning a servant brought a breakfast of bread and lemonade to the king, who immediately asked if he could eat breakfast with his family as usual. He was told, however, that the decision would have to be made by the Commune. After he had eaten part of his bread, Louis XVI realized that nothing had been brought for Cléry, who was sitting despondently wondering whether the Commune might now remove the dauphin from his parents as they had often threatened to do. The king immediately offered Cléry half his bread and within a few minutes both men were crying together over the uncertain future of the royal family.[4]

The king asked one of the municipals to bring him some of his books from his old room, and he asked Cléry to accompany him because the municipal could not read. Cléry found Marie Antoinette, Madame Elisabeth, and the children crying in anguish over the thought that the separation from the king might be permanent. The queen begged the municipals to let the family be reunited for mealtimes, and the officer in charge at last consented to let them eat together that day and to walk together in the garden. Fortunately, this policy was continued thereafter. When the two women and the children demonstrated their great joy at this permission, even the municipals present were moved to tears. Simon, a shoemaker who was one of their number, announced, "I believe these b — s would make me cry." But then he turned to the queen and said, "When you were assassinating the people on the 10th of August, you didn't cry at all."[5]

The royal family was fortunate that the municipal in charge that day took a sympathetic attitude because many of these men treated the family with insolence. The guards found themselves in a difficult position because they usually worked in pairs, and each of them was afraid of being denounced by his colleague if he appeared to be lenient with the prisoners. There was one man in particular that Cléry thought to be harsh toward the royal family, but to his surprise he later learned that this municipal was communicating secretly with Marie Antoinette. Subsequently, this guard was implicated in a plot to try to help the queen to escape. Another episode that occurred when the queen was later imprisoned in the Conciergerie also shows that an unbending official demeanor could sometimes mask an underlying sympathy. The chief jailer was present one day when Marie Antoinette asked a girl who worked in the jail to arrange her hair. The official immediately objected, saying he would do it himself, at which point Marie Antoinette gave up and fixed her own hair. As he was walking away from the cell, the jailer confided to the girl that he was sorry to distress "that poor woman," but he could not risk being thrown into a dungeon as had been his predecessors who had been too lenient with the queen.[6]

Most of the municipals who came to the Temple were there to guard the royal family. Tison and his wife were hired to clean their rooms and perform similar tasks. They were also supposed to spy upon the prisoners. Tison seems to have been a particularly unpleasant man who coerced his wife into participating in this espionage. She ultimately denounced the queen and several of the municipals but as a result suffered terrible nightmares in which her victims appeared. Being overcome by remorse, she knelt at the queen's feet to beg her forgiveness, a forgiveness that Marie Antoinette freely offered. Mme. Tison's mind was destroyed by her guilt, however, and she soon had to be confined in an insane asylum. Despite Mme. Tison's denunciation of her, Marie Antoinette pitied her and kept informed of her condition, even sending linen for her use when she learned that she had none.[7]

Although the royal family was not generally permitted to have newspapers, antagonistic municipals sometimes left in their rooms newspapers containing insulting articles. On one occasion the king picked up a newspaper he found lying in his room and read it, only to discover that it quoted a soldier who said he wished to load his cannon with the king's head. Another newspaper left for the royal family contained outrageous fabrications concerning the sexual conduct of Madame Elisabeth, whose character was beyond reproach.[8]

Even though they were almost never able to read any newspapers, the family remained relatively well informed about what was going on outside the Temple through a series of subterfuges. Cléry's wife hired a newspaper vendor to stand just outside the Temple walls every day to call out the headlines as he sold his papers, and his words were heard by the royal family. Every week Cléry's wife came to the Temple with a friend to bring him laundry, and they managed to exchange information by various means. One ruse they employed was for Cléry's wife to tell him something of no importance in a relatively loud voice while her companion whispered a crucial message.

By a remarkable oversight on the part of the authorities, three former kitchen helpers from the Tuileries boldly introduced themselves into the kitchen staff that now served the royal family by telling the municipal guards of the Commune that they had been sent by the Legislative Assembly.[9] One of these three was devoted to the king and acted as a liaison between the prisoners and the outside world by carrying notes back and forth, hiding them in stove vents or balls of yarn or wastebaskets when he brought meals to the tower. Despite his audacity he managed to escape detection.

It became increasingly difficult for members of the royal family to write notes, however, because in late September the Commune sent a deputation to search their rooms to remove all writing materials. Then in December, fearing the king might take his own life, the Commune decided to deprive the family of all knives, scissors, and other sharp instruments. Of course, it was unthinkable that Louis XVI, a devout Catholic, would ever contemplate this possibility, but the men of the Commune who had abandoned religion found it hard to believe that anyone else could be strongly motivated by it.

A couple of weeks after the king was moved to his new room in the large tower, the rest of the royal family was also moved to rooms in the large tower. At this time, the guards removed the dauphin's bed from his mother's room and placed it in the king's room. This seven-year-old boy had already had to face constant changes in his life. All who wrote about him cite his high spirits and charming personality, but he also had to learn at a very young age to dissemble his opinions and to be cautious in his conversation. Mme. Tourzel quoted him as saying even before he left the Tuileries, "You must admit that I have never compromised anyone."[10] In the tower prison he said a nightly prayer for the soul of Princess Lamballe and for the safety of Mme. Tourzel, but whenever municipals were within earshot, he lowered his voice to a whisper. Cléry remarked upon the fact that the child never referred to their former life at Versailles or the Tuileries, sensing that this would only give pain to his parents. Cléry also recorded one of the incidents when the child seemed overwhelmed by the circumstances of their imprisonment:

There was a stone-cutter employed in making holes at the antechamber door to admit enormous bolts; the prince, while the man was eating his breakfast, played with his tools. The king took the mallet and chisel out of his son's hands, and showed him how to handle them. He used them for some minutes. The workman, seeing the king so employed, said to his majesty, "When you go out of this tower, you will be able to say that you had worked yourself at your own prison."

"Ah," replied the king, "when and how shall I go out?" The dauphin burst into tears, and the king, letting fall the mallet and chisel, returned to his room, where he walked about hastily and in great agitation.[11]

25

Trial of the King

In the fall of 1792, the overriding question facing the newly elected Convention was the fate of the king. Should he be tried or should he simply be guillotined at once as some proposed? The whole issue became inextricably entwined with the struggle between the Girondists and the Jacobins, or Montagnards. The latter in general wanted the king executed without delay, while the Girondists covered a wider range of opinion, some believing that the king was inviolable under the constitution, others believing that the Convention should try him. The Girondists preferred to postpone the question as long as possible. To this end they tried various delaying tactics, including a proposal that the provincial assemblies should first be asked to ratify the new republic. Through their control of the Convention, they also appointed a committee to investigate the evidence against the king, a process that could be used to postpone an actual trial.

The case for the king's inviolability or immunity was stated in the Convention by a deputy named Morisson, who argued that the constitution clearly gave the king this immunity.[1] One of the Montagnards who presented the opposite point of view was a newcomer to the political scene, a young man only twenty-five named Saint-Just. His maiden speech on November 13 was a condemnation of kingship. He argued that Louis XVI was guilty simply by being a king and that he should thereby be punished, not judged. In a famous phrase, Saint-Just declared, "One cannot reign innocently." To drive home his point, he asserted that his colleagues should emulate the ancient Romans who had eliminated Julius Caesar "with no other formality than twenty-two dagger thrusts."[2]

Robespierre also presented a radical point of view, asserting that if the king was not guilty, then those who dethroned him were.[3] He insisted that the king should not be tried because by implication the whole Revolution would then be on trial. Many other Montagnards agreed that the people themselves had judged Louis XVI on August 10 when they attacked the Tui-

178

leries Palace and that nothing remained but for the Convention to punish him.

The issue was brought to a head on November 20 when Roland made a startling announcement to the Convention. The king's locksmith had led the minister to a secret iron cupboard in the Tuileries that he had helped the king construct for the purpose of hiding private papers. Roland had made the mistake of looking over the papers without witnesses before he alerted others to their existence. At this news, his Jacobin opponents erupted in angry protests, fearing that he had destroyed documents incriminating the Girondists, while preserving those damaging to themselves.

After the Jacobin and Girondist charges and countercharges had subsided, the fact remained that the iron cupboard contained many documents that the ardent revolutionists considered damaging to the king. In one letter Louis XVI promised to restore the Catholic Church to its former position of eminence if he returned to power. The Convention was also angry to discover a correspondence between the king and Lafayette. Many of the letters were part of the correspondence Louis XVI had carried on with Mirabeau when the latter was offering his services to the court. It was clear from the letters that Mirabeau had accepted large sums of money from the king. As a result of these disclosures, Mirabeau's reputation as a revolutionary leader suffered greatly; some deputies indignantly suggested removing his remains from their place of honor in the Pantheon. Even his bust in the Manège was defaced.

The cupboard also contained statements against the Revolution. In one letter Louis XVI had written, "It is clear to every person who walks on two feet that in my heart I cannot approve the Revolution and the absurd and detestable constitution that makes me less than the king of Poland."[4] To most of the deputies of the Convention, this was a damning statement, although one can put a less negative interpretation upon the king's words. Louis XVI was the kind of man who could at one and the same time disapprove of the Revolution and yet be willing to go along with it if that was what his countrymen wanted. He was certainly not alone in thinking that the constitution was a faulty document; by now most of the deputies of the Convention had rejected it.

Evidence was also found about payments that the king had made to some former members of the bodyguards who had emigrated; this infuriated many deputies. These payments are hardly surprising, however, given the king's character. On the day before his death, he expressed his hope that a way could be found to continue payments to all those people such as pensioners who had been dependent upon him for their livelihood.[5] During his trial he stated that as soon as he was told it was illegal for him to send such payments abroad, he had cut off the funds.

The discovery of the iron cupboard made it almost inevitable that the king would be tried. There was so much pressure from the Parisian sections for his death that the only real question at this point was whether he would be given a trial as the Girondists desired or summarily executed as the Commune and Jacobins demanded.

The Girondists tried one last delaying tactic by attacking the former duke of Orléans, who as a deputy to the Convention had taken on the new name of Philippe Egalité and sat with the Mountain. The Girondists proposed instituting the death penalty for anyone who tried to reestablish royalty in France. This maneuver would have prevented the Montagnards from ever putting Orléans on the throne, and if they had opposed it, they would have been accused of royalist tendencies. When it appeared that the issue would be a long and divisive one, however, pressure from the streets of Paris mounted for the Convention to return to the main issue of the king's fate. The deputies conceded and postponed the question until a later date.

Finally, Pétion, now a deputy to the Convention, made a motion on December 3 asking that Louis XVI be tried, a motion that carried immediately. A committee of twenty-one deputies was then appointed to draw up an indictment against the king and to decide on procedures for a trial. Many people were troubled, however, to see the Convention operating outside the Criminal Code of 1791, the Revolution's answer to arbitrary justice under the ancien régime. The code, for example, called for a grand jury to hand down an indictment and for another jury to try the defendant. The Convention assumed both roles in trying the king.

On December 10 the committee reported back to the Convention, and arrangements were made for the king to appear the next day to answer the charges against him. Fortunately, Cléry was alerted about these developments by his wife and was able to warn the king in advance, so that the news did not come as a sudden announcement from the authorities.

At five o'clock on the morning of December 11, the royal family could hear the call to arms being sounded throughout Paris, and calvary and cannons assembled in the Temple gardens. Pretending not to know the reason for all this activity, the prisoners questioned their guards, but they received no answer. At nine o'clock the king and the dauphin joined the rest of the family for breakfast. Because two municipals were present at the meal, the royal family had to endure the torment of being unable to express their anguish at the impending separation or even to let on that they knew it might well be their last meal together. According to Cléry, they separated after the meal with their looks expressing all they dared not say in words.[6]

The king returned to his room with the dauphin as usual. That day the boy begged his father to play a game called Siam with him, and the king acquiesced, despite the great tension he must have been experiencing. Cléry recorded the incident: "The dauphin lost every game, and twice he could get no farther than sixteen. 'Whenever,' cried he, in a little pet, 'I get to the point of sixteen, I am sure never to win the game.' The king said nothing, but he seemed to feel the coincidence of the words."[7]

After the game the king gave the dauphin a reading lesson as usual, but they were interrupted at eleven o'clock by two municipals who came to take the dauphin to his mother. The king embraced his son and then sent Cléry to accompany him to the queen. One of the municipals then told Louis XVI that Chambon, the new mayor of Paris, was in the conference room and would be coming to see him. After pacing up and down his room for a few minutes in great agitation, the king sat down in an armchair. The municipal in charge could not see him through the half-closed door and became uneasy after hearing no sound for a half hour. Cléry described the municipal's conversation with the king: "He went softly in; he found him leaning with his head upon his hand, apparently in deep thought. The king, on being disturbed, said, raising his voice, 'What do you want with me?' 'I was afraid,' answered the municipal, 'that you were ill.' 'I am obliged to you,' replied the king, in an accent replete with anguish, 'but the manner in which they have taken my son from me cuts me to the heart.'"[8] Louis XVI clearly feared that he might have seen his son for the last time.

The mayor did not show up until one o'clock that afternoon, when he entered with Santerre and other officials to announce to the king that they were taking him to the Convention to be judged. The king usually did not complain to his captors, but now he said: "I could have wished, Sir, that the commissioners had left my son with me during the two hours I have passed waiting for you, but this treatment is of a piece with the rest I have met with here for the last four months. I am ready to follow you, not in obedience to the Convention, but because my enemies have the power in their hands."[9]

The officials took Louis XVI down to the mayor's carriage, which was waiting outside the Temple. Extraordinary security measures had been taken to guard against any attempts by royalists to rescue the king. A large number of troops surrounded the carriage, and the streets were lined with armed men. No one was allowed to move without a special identification card issued by his or her local section.

While the deputies were awaiting the arrival of the king, the current president, Bertrand Barère, announced that the Convention was about to give "a great lesson to kings and a useful example for the emancipation of nations."[10] One of the Montagnards, the butcher named Legendre who had invaded the Tuileries Palace and harangued the king on June 20, now asked his fellow deputies to maintain "the silence of a tomb to terrify the guilty man."[11] This was only rhetoric from a man who had seen at close range how little the king could be frightened or intimidated. When Louis XVI was brought to the bar of the Convention, he appeared composed as always.

The king could have asserted that the Convention had no right to try him, as Charles I of England had done. He knew every detail of this historical precedent, but he chose instead to defend himself. It was consistent with his character that he refused to assert any kind of divine-right defense but instead attempted to refute the charges that he had not acted for the good of France. He later conveyed a further motive for his actions to the lawyers he obtained, stating that he wished to do everything within his power to keep his countrymen from committing a great crime.

President Barère first read the entire indictment to the king and then reread it, item by item, asking the king to reply separately to each charge. The king was also shown the various pieces of evidence supporting each charge. He had not yet been allowed legal counsel and was forced to answer immediately charges that he had not had time to study. Even under these difficult circumstances, Mme. de Staël was impressed by his bearing:

> Louis XVI did not refuse, as Charles 1 had done, to recognize the court before which he was brought, and he responded to all the questions he was asked with an unvarying gentleness. When the president asked him why he had gathered troops at the palace on August 10, Louis XVI replied: "The palace was threatened. All the constituted authorities were aware of that, and because I myself was a constituted authority, it was my duty to defend myself." What a modest and detached way of speaking of oneself, and what burst of eloquence could have been more moving![12]

For some reason Louis XVI denied knowledge of the iron cupboard in the Tuileries; this was perhaps an attempt to protect the other parties to the correspondence it contained. The king did deny emphatically the charge that he had wanted to shed French blood.[13] This was obviously a sensitive point with him, perhaps all the more so because he realized that he found himself in his present deplorable position in large part because of his reluctance to shed blood. Before he left the Convention, Louis XVI asked to be allowed to choose lawyers to aid him. After his departure a violent debate broke out over this question, with the Montagnards attempting to deny counsel to the king and asking for a roll call vote in order to intimidate the deputies. A motion giving the king the right to counsel was carried by a voice vote, however.

Louis XVI requested the services of two of the leading lawyers of France, Guy Target and François Tronchet. The former had defended Cardinal Rohan in the necklace scandal. He now declined to serve the king, pleading ill health.

Tronchet accepted, however, stating that he could not refuse to serve a fellowman whose head was under the blade of justice. He was sixty-six at this time and was joined within a few days by an even older colleague, Malesherbes. Hearing of the king's trial, Malesherbes wrote a letter offering his legal services: "I want Louis XVI to know that if he chooses me for this purpose, I am ready to devote myself to it.... I was twice appointed a member of the king's council at a time when everyone was ambitious to obtain that office. I owe him the same service now when everyone considers it dangerous to serve as one of his defenders."[14]

The Convention granted Malesherbes's request when it was learned that the king wished to have him serve. On December 14 he went to the Temple for his first conference with the king. As the seventy-two-year-old man was climbing the hundred steps leading to the king's tower apartment, he became so tired that he had to sit down on a step to keep from fainting.[15] When Malesherbes at last arrived at the king's room, he found him seated at his table reading Tacitus, a Roman historian who was interested in the psychological motivations involved in political power struggles and shared not only Louis XVI's compact style, but also his love of hunting. When Louis XVI saw his old friend, he hurried to embrace him. Malesherbes burst into tears at the sight of his former sovereign, now imprisoned and facing an uncertain fate. Louis XVI said to him, "Your sacrifice is especially generous because you are risking your life, and you will not be able to save mine." Malesherbes recorded his response in his journal: "I told him that I was in no danger and was in any case fulfilling the most sacred of duties while acting upon my heartfelt devotion. I assured him that by defending him vigorously we would save him."[16] As it turned out, Malesherbes was indeed to die on the scaffold together with several other members of his family during the Reign of Terror because of his role in defending the king.

In the former routine of the prison, the king had never been allowed to be alone with anyone, but the Convention now ruled that he could speak privately with his counsel whenever they wished to go to the Temple. His lawyers were frequently searched, however, because the municipals were always afraid that Louis XVI would obtain poison or a knife with which to kill himself.

The king and his lawyers immediately established a daily routine to prepare their case. From 5 o'clock to 9 o'clock every evening, the king conferred with Malesherbes, Tronchet, and De Sèze, a third lawyer whom the other two wanted to have join them. De Sèze was a brilliant lawyer much admired for his eloquence who had defended Marie Antoinette in the necklace case. Because he was younger than Malesherbes and Tronchet, they hoped he would assume an important share of the work. The king also asked Malesherbes to come to the tower alone each morning to talk to him. The two of them planned what would be discussed at each evening session, and Malesherbes brought with him newspaper articles containing the opinions of the various deputies concerning the fate of the king. Louis XVI was eager to read these, but they only served to confirm his impression that his case was a hopeless one. "I am sure," he said to Malesherbes, "that they will make me die. They have the power and the will to do so. But that makes no difference. Let us prepare my case as if I could win it, and I will in effect have won, because I will leave behind me an untainted memory."[17]

Since the beginning of his trial, Louis XVI had been totally separated from his family, and for this reason, he particularly appreciated having the company of Malesherbes every morning. In asking him to come, Louis XVI said: "I wish to be alone with you, reviewing our memories and our former conversations; we shall talk of the trial in the evening.... Here the pleasures shall be in the morning and business in the evening; it was exactly the contrary at Versailles."[18]

The evenings were busy ones, as the four men attempted to work their way through the 158 documents constituting the case against the king. His lawyers wrote to the Convention to say that it was impossible for them to cover so much material in the dozen days allotted to them. The deputies refused to give them any extension, however. The king's counsel had to work at a feverish pace, particularly because they knew that the radical Parisians were insisting that the Convention try the king without further delay. Louis XVI urged Malesherbes in particular to get more rest and not to exhaust himself on his behalf, but Malesherbes was working hard to try to recover missing pieces of evidence that the king's supporters now living in England had sent to the Convention. He never succeeded, however, in retrieving from the Convention these documents favorable to the king's position; he was told they had been lost.

The day set for Louis XVI's trial was December 26. De Sèze, who had been chosen to deliver the summation, reportedly went without sleep for the four days preceding this date. After he had prepared his speech, he read it to the king, Malesherbes, and Tronchet. Malesherbes recorded the scene in his journal: "I have never heard anything more touching than his peroration. We were moved to tears. But Louis objected, 'You must leave that out; I do not wish to appeal to their emotions.'"[19] It was not a surprising statement for the king to make. He was willing to suffer all sorts of indignities from his municipal guards without altering his usual affable manner, but his strong sense of personal dignity made him feel that it would be demeaning to beg for his life. His lawyers bowed to his wishes, but with great reluctance. One of the principal reasons Tronchet and Malesherbes had urged the appointment of De Sèze was that he possessed an unusual ability to move men with his oratory.

In their struggle to save the king, they could ill afford to abandon this opportunity to influence the deputies. On many occasions in the past few years, the deputies had been motivated by the emotional fervor of the moment into taking some unusual action. De Sèze's peroration might well have brought to the surface the undercurrent of personal sympathy many deputies felt for Louis XVI but were afraid to express. At any rate, it would appear that at this stage in the Revolution the furious and implacable Parisian mobs were going to settle for nothing short of the king's death, despite any temporary delays that might have been achieved.

In the midst of these final preparations for the trial, the king decided to write a new will. On Christmas Day, when the sense of separation from his family must have been particularly intense, he sat down alone in his prison room and wrote out a document eloquent in its simplicity, in which the strong points of his character are movingly apparent.

The Will of Louis XVI

In the name of the holy Trinity, of the Father, the Son, and the Holy Ghost; on the 25th day of December, 1792, I, Louis XVI, king of France, having been more than four months immured with my family in the tower of the Temple at Paris, by those who were my subjects, and deprived of all communication whatsoever, even with my family, since the 11th of this month, involved, moreover, in a trial the issue of which, from the passions of men, is impossible to foresee, and for which there is neither pretence nor foundation in any existing law, having God only as the witness of my thoughts, and to whom I can address myself, do hereby declare in his presence my last will and the feelings of my heart.

I render my soul to God, its creator, beseeching him to receive it in his mercy, and to not judge it according to its own merits, but according to the merits of our Lord Jesus Christ, who offered himself a sacrifice to God his Father, for us men, unworthy of it as we are, and I above all others.

I die in the union of our holy mother, the Catholic, apostolic, and Roman church, which holds its powers by an uninterrupted succession from Saint Peter, to whom they were confided by Jesus Christ.

I firmly believe and acknowledge all that is contained in the creed and the commandments, of God and of the church, the sacraments and mysteries, such as the Catholic Church teaches and has ever taught them. I have never pretended to render myself a judge in the different modes of explaining the dogmas that divide the church of Christ, but I have ever conformed, and ever will conform, if God grant me life, to the decisions which the superior ecclesiastics of the Holy Catholic Church have made, and shall make, according to the discipline of the church adopted from the time of Jesus Christ.

I grieve with all my heart for such of our brethren as may be in error, but I presume not to judge them, and do not the less love them all in Christ Jesus, as we are taught to do by Christian charity. I pray God to forgive me all my sins! I have endeavoured scrupulously to discover them, to detest them, and to humble myself in his presence. Not having it in my power to avail myself of the ministry of a Catholic priest, I pray to God to receive the confession I have made of them to him, and especially my deep repentance for having put my name (though against my will) to instruments that may be contrary to the discipline and belief of the Catholic Church, to which I have always remained from my heart sincerely attached. I pray to God to accept my firm resolution of taking the earliest opportunity, if he grant me life, to avail myself of the ministry of a Catholic priest, to confess all my sins and receive the sacrament of penitence.

I entreat all whom I may have offended through inadvertence (for I do not recollect having ever willingly given offence to any person) or to whom I may have given any bad example or scandal by my actions, to forgive the evil I may have done them. I entreat all charitable persons to unite their prayers with mine, that I may obtain pardon of God for my sins.

I forgive with all my heart those who have become my enemies without my having given them any reasons for so doing, and I pray God to forgive them, as well as those who, through a false or misconceived zeal, have done me much evil.

I recommend to God my wife and my children, my sister and my aunts, my brothers, and all who are related to me by ties of blood, or in any other manner whatsoever. I pray God more especially to look with mercy upon my wife, my children, and my sister, who have been suffering a long time with me, to support them by his grace, if they lose me, and as long as they remain in this perishable world.

I recommend my children to my wife. I have never doubted her maternal tenderness. I particularly recommend it to her to make them good Christians, and to give them virtuous minds, to make them look upon the pomps of this world, if they are condemned to experience them, as a dangerous and transitory inheritance, and to turn their thoughts to the only solid and durable glory of eternity. I entreat my sister to continue her tenderness to my children, and to be a mother to them should they have the misfortune to lose their own.

I entreat my wife to forgive me all the evils she suffers on my account, and whatever vexations I may have caused her in the course of our union, as she may be assured that I harbor nothing against her, should she suppose there was anything with which she might reproach herself. [This last phrase was a standard formula in wills and should not be taken as a reference to a possible affair between the queen and Count Fersen.]

I recommend most earnestly to my children, after their duty to God, which must always stand first, to continue united together, submissive and obedient to their mother, and grateful for all the cares and pains she takes for them, and in memory of me. I entreat them to look upon their aunt as a second mother.

I recommend to my son, if he should have the misfortune of becoming king, to reflect that he ought to devote himself entirely to the happiness of his fellow-citizens, that he ought to forget all hatred and resentment, and particularly in what relates to the misfortunes and vexations I have suffered, that he cannot promote the happiness of a nation but by reigning according to the laws, yet, at the same time, that a king cannot enforce those laws, and do the good which his heart prompts, unless he be possessed of the necessary authority, for that, otherwise, being fettered in his operations, and inspiring no respect, he is more hurtful than useful.

I recommend to my son to take care of all who were attached to me, as far as circumstances may put it in his power, to recollect that it is a sacred debt which I have contracted with the children or relations of those who have perished for me, and, lastly, of those who are themselves unfortunate on my account.

I know that there are several persons, formerly in my service, who have not conducted themselves towards me as they ought, and even shown ingratitude towards me, but I forgive them (in times of tumult and effervescence we are not always masters of ourselves) and I entreat my son, if he should ever have an opportunity, that he will think only of their misfortunes.

I wish I could here express my acknowledgments to those who have evinced a true and disinterested attachment for me. On the one hand, if I have been keenly wounded by the ingratitude and disloyalty of people who have experienced from me nothing but bounty, either themselves or in the persons of their relations or friends, on the other hand, I have had the consolation of seeing an attachment and concern manifested for me by many on whom I never bestowed a favour. I entreat them to accept my best thanks. In the situation in which things still remain, I should be afraid of endangering them if I were more explicit, but I recommend it particularly to my son to seek occasions of showing his acknowledgment.

I think, however, that I should do injustice to the sentiments of the nation if I hesitated openly to recommend to my son M. de Chamilly and M. Huë, whose sincere attachment to me prompted them to shut themselves up with me in this melancholy habitation and who looked to become the unhappy victims of that attachment. I also recommend Cléry to him, with whose services ever since he has been with me I have had every reason to be entirely satisfied. As it is he who has remained with me to the last, I entreat the gentlemen of the Commune to see that my clothes, books, watch, purse, and the other small articles that were lodged with the council of the Commune be delivered to him.

I also most freely forgive those who were guards over me for the ill treatment and constraint they thought it their duty to inflict upon me. Some there were whose souls were tender and compassionate; may their hearts enjoy that peace which should be the reward of such dispositions.

I request M. de Malesherbes, M. Tronchet, and M. de Sèze to receive here my best thanks for, and acknowledgments of, the sense I entertain of all the care and trouble they have taken upon themselves for me.

I conclude by declaring before God, in whose presence I am about to appear, that my conscience does not accuse me with any of the crimes which are imputed to me.

Written and signed by me, and a duplicate hereof made, at the tower of the Temple, on the 25th day of December, 1792.

Louis[20]

Only a few days earlier Gouverneur Morris had written a letter to Secretary of State Thomas Jefferson that contained this report about the king's trial:

> To a person less intimately acquainted than you are with the history of human affairs, it would seem strange that the mildest monarch who ever filled the French throne, one who is precipitated from it precisely because he would not adopt the harsh measures of his predecessors, a man whom none could charge with a criminal act, should be prosecuted as one of the most nefarious tyrants that ever disgraced the annals of human nature — that he, Louis the Sixteenth, should be prosecuted even to death.[21]

26

King Condemned to Death

On December 26, 1792, Louis XVI returned to the Convention for his trial. While he was conferring with his lawyers in an anteroom, one of the deputies present noticed that Malesherbes addressed the king as "Sire." When he asked Malesherbes what made him so bold as to use a term outlawed by the Convention, Malesherbes replied, "Contempt for life."[1]

The trial began in complete silence as the deputies listened attentively to De Sèzes's plea. In his introduction he stated: "Today, gentlemen, there is no power equal to yours, but there is one power that you do not have — you do not have the power to condemn unjustly."[2] He argued that the Convention might decide whether the king was guilty or innocent, but that it had only the right to dethrone or exile him, not to execute him. After refuting the forty-three accusations against the king, he closed by stating that in the future history would relate the following:

> Louis came to the throne at age twenty, and he set an example of morality, justice, and economy; he abolished serfdom in his personal domains. The people wanted liberty, and he gave it to them. Louis had the glory of always anticipating the desires of his people.... I stop here before history. It is important that you realize that she will judge your judgment.[3]

After De Sèze finished, Louis XVI faced the court for the last time when he stood up to make a final short statement:

> You have just heard the arguments in my defense.... In speaking to you for what may be the last time, I wish to declare that I have nothing for which to reproach myself and my defenders have spoken the truth. I have never been afraid to have my conduct examined publicly, but my heart is grieved to find in the indictments the charge that I wished to spill the blood of my people. I regret that the many proofs of my love for my people and my willingness to expose myself to danger to avoid shedding their blood have not sufficed to spare me such a charge.[4]

.is XVI's last effort to defend himself against the charge that he was
.rent to violence and bloodshed recalls the instructions quoted previ-
/ that he gave many years earlier to the explorer La Pérouse, enjoining
.. a to avoid attacking the native peoples he would encounter on his trip to
the South Seas, "His majesty considers one of the most desirable results of
the expedition to be its accomplishment without the loss of the life of a single
person."[5]

At noon the Convention sent Louis XVI back to the Temple. Tumult
then broke out in the Manège as the Mountain demanded an immediate vote
upon his guilt, while the Girondists tried to postpone the decision. Nothing
was resolved that day, but on December 27 one of the Girondist deputies proposed a vote on what became known as the "appeal to the people." According
to this proposal, the judgment that the Convention passed upon the king
would be submitted to the forty-four thousand primary assemblies of France
for their ratification. Much of the discussion in the ensuing few weeks revolved
around this highly controversial suggestion, with the Girondists backing it
and the Montagnards violently opposing it. Most political observers believed
that the local assemblies would be more conservative than the Convention or
the Parisians; hence the king's chances of receiving clemency from them would
be much greater. Those who were torn between their desire to find Louis XVI
guilty and their reluctance to execute him thus seized upon this measure as
a way of escaping their own personal dilemma.

As the debate dragged on into January, public opinion began to become
more favorable to the king. His calm and courageous bearing during his trial
had impressed even his enemies. Many now began to see him as a victim, not
a tyrant. In early January a play called *L'Ami des Loix* (Friend of the Laws)
was presented in Paris; it had clearly been hastily written to support the king's
cause. According to Cléry, "Every allusion to his majesty's trial was caught
and received the most unbounded applause." The Commune soon had to
suppress the play to prevent it from becoming a rallying point for royalist
sympathizers. Another play drew great applause with the line: "How can you
be accusers and judges at the same time?"[6]

Malesherbes took these plays to the Temple for the king to read. They
must have been a welcome diversion during the long period while he awaited
a verdict. When Malesherbes brought him anything to which the municipals
might object, Louis XVI always read these things during the evening and
burned them in his stove before retiring. During these weeks he also asked
Malesherbes if he had a copy of Hume's *History of England*. When Malesherbes
brought it to the tower, the king spent several days rereading the sections
concerning the long struggle of Charles I with Parliament, which ultimately
beheaded him.

Louis XVI was lonely without his family. He particularly regretted being unable to spend his daughter's fourteenth birthday with her but was able to have Cléry buy her an almanac that she wanted. The king did manage to keep up a correspondence with his family during this period, however, thanks to a clever ruse by Cléry. The latter had carefully saved the pieces of string with which the packages of candles he received were tied. When he had accumulated a sufficient amount, he suggested to the king that notes could be passed back and forth between the window in a small hallway off of Cléry's room and the window of Madame Elisabeth's room that was located directly above. The Commune had by now taken the precaution of putting up barriers outside the windows to prevent the royal family from seeing anyone outside or being seen. These barriers facilitated Cléry's scheme because no one could see the notes on the string that were passed in the space between the barriers and the windows. At the beginning of the trial, the king had been given pen, ink, and paper to use in preparing his case, and by means of the string, he was able to pass some of these materials to Madame Elisabeth. While the king was sending notes in this way, Cléry would engage the municipals in conversation in another room.[7]

This secret correspondence was the only contact with his family that Louis XVI was able to maintain. At the beginning of his trial, the Commune had offered to let him have his children with him during this period, but only on the condition that they never see their mother. The king thought it was out of the question to take charge of his daughter, however, and he did not feel that he should deprive the queen of the comfort she received from having the dauphin with her. Hence he reluctantly refused to accept this offer.

While Louis XVI remained sequestered in his tower awaiting a verdict, the Convention continued to debate furiously day after day. Because the Revolution had virtually suppressed religion, the legislators met on Sunday as well as all the other days of the week. Sessions were held early in the day and in the evening, with a short recess usually occurring in the afternoon. It was hard for the deputies to keep any sense of balance or perspective in their deliberations when the sessions went on day after day without respite. The tension in the Manège was mounting, as the fate of not only the king, but also the Girondists and the Jacobins hung in the balance. There were veiled threats from the streets of Paris that if the Convention refused to act soon to execute Louis XVI, the people would take matters into their own hands, as they had done on so many earlier occasions. Lord Gower, the English ambassador, sent home a dispatch stating, "There were some thousands of armed men parading in different parts of the city ready to commit any sort of riot, and threatening destruction should the king not be put to death."[8] The memory of the dreadful September massacres remained all too vivid in the minds of the deputies.

ppeal to the people also feared that this appeal might lead
n citizens throughout France took sides on the issue. There
established procedures for consulting the primary assemblies,
ess would indeed have been chaotic.

on January 14, 1793, the deputies began a crucial series of votes.
The   which the votes were to be taken was of paramount importance.
After much argument it was decided that there would be three separate votes.
The first vote would decide whether the king was guilty of treason, the second
whether this verdict should be appealed to the people, and the third the punishment if the king were found guilty. The decision was also made that day
that all questions concerning the king's fate would be decided by a roll call
vote. On January 15 the crucial vote on the question of the king's guilt took
place. The vote was overwhelmingly against him. Of the 719 deputes present,
693 pronounced the king guilty, while 26 made ambiguous statements, citing
their belief that as legislators they had no right to judge the king or offering
other reasons for their uncertainty. None of these 26, however, voted that the
king was innocent.

Once this vote found the king guilty of treason the Convention was in
a position of little flexibility because the criminal code stated that the penalty
for treason was death. A great many deputies, however, did not really want
to see the king die and hoped that a favorable vote on the appeal to the people
would circumvent the issue. They were disappointed by a vote of 424 against
the appeal to 283 in favor.

On the following day, January 16, the deputies assembled to take the crucial vote on whether to sentence the king to death. The session opened in
midmorning amidst rumors that demonstrators would attack those who voted
against the death penalty and that cannons were being moved toward the
Manège. On the other hand, Dumouriez had returned to Paris from the front
to try to rally support for the king's cause. During the opening hours of the
session, the Convention sent representatives to consult with the Commune
to be sure there was no disorder in the city. Reassured at last that all was calm
in Paris, the deputies moved toward the final vote in the late afternoon. Before
this vote could be taken, however, one of the deputies suggested that a vote
for death should be valid only if it were carried by a two-thirds majority.
After a few more hours of wrangling, this idea was rejected, and the Convention proceeded to the final vote starting at 8 o'clock in the evening.

With 720 deputies present, a simple majority was 361. No one knew
when the voting began what the outcome would be, so a sense of high drama
gripped the chamber as the roll call began. The first vote, recorded by a deputy
named Jean Mailhe, further confused the issue, as he stated: "I vote for
death.... If the majority rule for death, I believe it would be worthy of the

National Convention to examine if it might be useful to delay the time of execution."[9] This was yet another attempt to state that the king was guilty, to acknowledge that the penalty for treason was death, and at the same time to avoid executing him.

The voting dragged on for thirteen hours. Finally at ten o'clock on the morning of January 17 the results were tabulated. A total of 288 deputies voted for a penalty other than death, 46 favored a suspended death sentence, and 26 voted for death, but with further delays and consideration. A vote for immediate execution was cast by 361 deputies, or exactly the requisite number to obtain condemnation. With Louis XVI condemned by a single vote, it is particularly ironic that his cousin the duke of Orléans voted unequivocally for his death, shocking most of those present. As a man to whom the values of honor and loyalty were paramount, Louis XVI found his cousin's action incomprehensible. He told Cléry, "I grieve exceedingly to think that Monsieur d'Orléans, my relation, should have voted for my death."[10]

Later in the day the king's lawyers presented a statement asking for an appeal of the verdict to the people, but the Convention had in effect already voted on this issue, so nothing came of this maneuver. De Sèze and Tronchet argued that the king should not be sent to his death by a margin of only one vote. Malesherbes attempted to address the deputies to urge that a two-thirds vote be required for a death sentence, but he was so distraught that he could not speak coherently and had to sit down. He later described that painful moment, "My colleagues spoke well, but my performance was bad, because in place of reasons I could find only tears."[11]

Malesherbes was the one who carried the news of the verdict to the king. When Cléry admitted him to the apartment, he said, "All is lost; the king has been condemned."[12] As Louis XVI came to meet him, Malesherbes fell at his feet, choked by sobs that left no doubt as to the verdict. Louis XVI showed no surprise to learn of the sentence and attempted only to comfort his old friend, whose grief affected him strongly. Cléry related in his journal the moving scene that followed Malesherbes's departure:

From the arrival of M. de Malesherbes I had been seized with a trembling through my whole frame: however, I got everything ready for the king to shave. He put on the soap himself, standing up and facing me while I held his basin. Forced to stifle my feelings, I had not yet had [the] resolution to look at the face of my unfortunate master, but my eyes now catching his accidentally, my tears ran over in spite of me. I know not whether seeing me in that state put the king in mind of his own situation or not, but he suddenly turned very pale. At the sight, my knees trembled and my strength forsook me. The king, perceiving me ready to fall, caught me by both hands, and pressing them warmly, said, in a gentle voice, "Come, more courage." He was observed; the depth of my affliction was manifested by my silence, of which he seemed sensible. His countenance was re-animated, he shaved himself with composure, and I then dressed him.[13]

When Malesherbes spoke with Louis XVI for the last time, he told him that many men had approached him as he left the Convention, saying that they would try to rescue their king. Louis XVI was distressed by this news and later told Cléry: "I should be very sorry to have it take place, for then there would be new victims. I do not fear death, but I cannot without shuddering contemplate the cruel lot which I leave behind me to my family."[14] The king insisted that Malesherbes return to find these men and ask them to abandon any such projects.

On January 18 a municipal arrived to take an inventory of the contents of the king's apartment; he was accompanied by the warden, who was named Mathey. It soon became obvious that the object of the visit was to make certain that the king had no weapons he might use to take his own life. The Commune clearly wanted Louis XVI not just to die, but to die a symbolic death before the people of France. While this search was going on, the king, feeling the dank January chill of the stone tower, went into another room and tried to warm himself by the fire. Mathey was standing directly in front of the fireplace with his back to it and ignored the king's attempt to approach the fire. Finally the king spoke sharply to him, asking him to move over.[15]

At two o'clock in the afternoon on January 20, the door of the king's apartment opened and a dozen government officials entered. The minister of justice, Garat, announced that they had come to convey the decrees passed by the Convention during the last few days. The secretary then read the decrees to the king in a voice that Cléry reported was weak and trembling, which seems to indicate that sympathy for the king's plight could be found in unexpected places.[16]

Cléry noticed no change of expression on the king's face during the reading of his death sentence, to be carried out within twenty-four hours, except that when one article referred to the king's "conspiracy against the liberty of the nation," a smile of indignation crossed his face. After the reading was finished, the king took the paper and put it in his briefcase. Then he removed another paper and asked the officers to take it to the Convention. He first read it to them:

I request a delay of three days in order to prepare myself to appear before God; I ask for this purpose to be able to see freely the person whom I will indicate to the officers of the Commune, and I ask that this person need have no fear or anxiety because of the act of charity he performs for me.

I ask to be relieved of the perpetual surveillance that the council has established during the last few days.

I ask to be able to see my family when I wish and without witnesses during this period. I want the Convention to take up at once the question of the fate of my family and to permit them to leave freely for a place judged appropriate.

I commend to the beneficence of the nation all of those persons who were dependent upon me. There are many of them who have spent all of their fortune in their offices and having no further income, must be in want.... There are many old people, women, and children who have only their pensions upon which to live.[17]

The king's final statement to the Convention reveals once again his strong sense of compassion. With only a day or two left to live, he could forget his own difficult position long enough to worry about those whom his death might deprive of their livelihood.

As the officers were about to leave, Louis XVI gave them the address of Abbé Edgeworth de Firmont, whom he wished to have serve him as priest during his final hours. Firmont was of Irish origin but had been a priest in France for many years. He had been Madame Elisabeth's confessor during her last months in the Tuileries, and it was she who had recommended him to her brother as a nonjuring priest still residing in Paris.

The Convention refused to grant the king's request for a delay of three days before his execution, but it did agree that he could receive the ministrations of Abbé Firmont and could see his family for a final leave-taking. In its reply to the king's inquiries about the future of his family, the Convention simply said, "The nation, ever great and ever just, would take into consideration the state of his family."[18] It was fortunate that Louis XVI could not foresee the outcome of that statement.

27

Final Hours and Execution

Late on the afternoon of January 20 a messenger went to the lodgings of Abbé Firmont to take him to meet with the council of ministers. In his account of this period, Firmont remarked upon the looks of consternation he saw upon the faces of the ministers. (Most of them were Girondists who had not voted for the king's death.) When the priest assured them that he was willing to serve the king, he was then accompanied to the Temple by Garat, the minister of justice. Firmont recorded the brief remarks that Garat made during that carriage ride: "Good God!" he exclaimed. "What an awful commission I am charged with! What a man! What resignation! What courage!"[1] Firmont debated whether he should respond to these words and converse with Garat. He decided, however, that it was safest to say nothing for fear of jeopardizing his crucial mission.

Firmont climbed the long, winding stairway to the king's apartment about six o'clock in the evening. He was horrified to find that most of the guards manning the checkpoints along the stairway were drunk and later recorded his reaction, "Their terrible cries, echoing through the vaulted ceilings of the tower, had a terrifying effect."[2] Firmont was particularly struck by the scene he found upon entering the king's apartment, where a group of officials had just informed the king that the Convention had denied his request for three days during which to prepare himself for death. According to Firmont, "He was in the middle of them, calm, tranquil, gracious even, and not one of them who surrounded him had the air of assurance he possessed."[3] After the delegation had departed, Firmont could no longer restrain his emotions and fell at the king's feet in tears. Firmont later recorded in the account he wrote of his attendance on Louis XVI in his last hours:

> This sight moved him a thousand times more than the decree that had just been read to him. At first he responded to my tears only by his own, but soon he regained all his courage. "Excuse me," he said to me, "for this moment of weakness, if I may call it that. For a long time I have been living in the midst of my

enemies, and I have become accustomed to that. The sight of a faithful subject touches my heart in a completely different way. It is a sight to which my eyes are no longer accustomed, and that touches me deeply in spite of myself."[4]

After the king and Firmont had talked together for a while, the municipals came to tell him that he could at last see his family. It had been arranged that this meeting was to take place in the dining room so that the municipals could observe the family through a glass window in the door without actually being present at the interview. Cléry described the scene:

> The king sat down; the queen was on his left hand, Madame Elisabeth on his right, Madame Royale nearly opposite, and the young prince stood between his knees. All were leaning on the king, and often pressed him in their embraces. This scene of sorrow lasted an hour and three quarters, during which it was impossible to hear anything. It could, however, be seen that after every sentence uttered by the king, the agitation of the queen and princesses increased, lasted some minutes, and then the king began to speak. It was plain from their gestures that they received from him the first intelligence of his condemnation.[5]

In her account of the scene, Madame Royale stated that when her father told her mother about the trial, he excused those who had condemned him. He also told the queen that he did not believe that the appeal to the primary assemblies would have been a good idea because it might have led to civil war. Then he gave religious advice to the dauphin and urged him to forgive those who had condemned his father to death.[6] Cléry related the end of the interview:

> At a quarter past ten, the king rose first; they all followed. I opened the door. The queen held the king by his right arm. Their majesties each gave a hand to the dauphin. Madame Royale, on the king's left, had her arm round his body; and, behind her, Madame Elisabeth, on the same side, had taken his arm. They advanced some steps towards the entry-door, breaking out into the most agonizing lamentations. "I assure you," said the king, "that I will see you tomorrow morning, at eight o'clock." "You promise?" said they all together. "Yes, I promise." "Why not at seven o'clock?" said the queen. "Well! yes, at seven," replied the king, "farewell." He pronounced "Farewell" in so impressive a manner that their sobs were renewed, and Madame Royale fainted at the feet of the king, round whom she had clung. I raised her, and assisted Madame Elisabeth to support her. The king, willing to put an end to this agonizing scene, once more embraced them all most tenderly, and had the resolution to tear himself from their arms. "Good-by! Good-by!" said he, and went into his chamber.[7]

Firmont recorded what happened when the king rejoined him after this final meeting with his family: "He returned to me in a state of agitation that showed a soul profoundly wounded. Throwing himself upon a chair, he exclaimed: 'What a meeting I have just had! To think that I love so tenderly and am so tenderly loved!'"[8] He then turned his attention, however, to the vital time he wished to spend with the priest to prepare his soul for death. Firmont disclosed to the king his hopes that it might be possible for him to say a mass in the tower the next morning. Louis XVI found it hard to believe that his guards would allow him this privilege but agreed that Firmont should try to make the arrangements. Initially there were some difficulties with the authorities, who feared that the priest might provide the king with poison in the bread or wine, but at last he obtained the requisite permission and sent to a neighboring church for the objects needed for the mass.

Louis XVI and Firmont discussed various spiritual matters until 12:30 A.M., when they retired for the night. Cléry asked the king if he wished him to roll his hair as usual, but he replied, "It doesn't signify." Firmont spent the night in Cléry's bed, while the latter prayed and slept in a chair beside the king.[9] Cléry and Firmont both attest to the fact that the king demonstrated his usual ability to fall asleep readily in tense circumstances. He slept soundly until 5 A.M., when Cléry awakened him as requested. Upon awakening he said, "I have slept soundly. I stood in need of it; yesterday was a fatiguing day to me."[10]

At six o'clock Firmont celebrated mass. Cléry recorded in his journal that Firmont said to him after the mass: "With what resignation and fortitude does he go to meet death! He is as calm and composed as if he had been hearing mass in his own palace, surrounded with his court."[11] After the ceremony had been completed, Louis XVI sat down by his stove to warm his hands on this cold January morning and said, according to Firmont's account: "How happy I am that I have kept my principles! Without them, where would I be now? But with them, death does not seem frightening! Yes, there exists on high an incorruptible judge who will render me the justice that men have refused to me here below."[12] As they were sitting there by the stove, they heard the drums beating the call to arms throughout Paris. Firmont later wrote that the sound "turned my blood to ice in my veins," but the king simply said with no visible emotion, "That must be the National Guard assembling."[13]

The king then decided that it was time to see his family again as he had promised. Firmont, however, persuaded him that he should not do so because the queen would be unable to bear the trauma of another leave-taking. Perhaps he also believed that it was essential for Louis XVI to devote all his attention in these last few hours to preparing his soul for death without another wrenching scene with his family. In his account Firmont described the king's response: "He stopped for a moment and with an expression of profound sorrow, said to me: 'You are right; it would be giving her a death blow. It is better that I deprive myself of this sweet consolation and let her live in hope for a few minutes more.'"[14]

In his account of the king's last hours, Firmont related that from seven to eight o'clock that morning people knocked on the door of the king's room several different times. Each time this happened Firmont trembled to think that it might be the final call, but the king quietly and calmly responded to each knock. Firmont was shocked to hear one of these men say to the king in a mocking tone, "Oh, that was all very well when you were king, but you're no longer king." Louis XVI made no reply but shrugged his shoulders and said to Firmont, "You see how these people treat me."[15]

At last Santerre arrived at the door with his soldiers to take the king to the guillotine. Louis XVI requested that they wait for him a moment, and shutting the door of the room, he asked Firmont to give him a last blessing and to pray that God would sustain him to the end. Then he rejoined Santerre and his men, holding his will in his hand. Addressing the municipal nearest to him, he said, "I beg you to give this paper to the queen," but then he corrected himself and said, "to my wife." This man happened to be Jacques Roux, a radical priest who had taken the oath. Refusing to take the paper, he said: "It is no business of mine. I am come here to conduct you to the scaffold." Finding a more receptive municipal, the king handed him the will. He announced to the municipals that he hoped that Cléry would be allowed to serve the dauphin henceforth. Then, turning to Santerre, he said, "Lead on."[16]

The last words that the king spoke before he left the tower offer yet another measure of the man. When he reached the door to the staircase, he saw Mathey, the warden who had monopolized the fireplace two days earlier, and said to him, "I spoke with some little quickness to you the day before yesterday, do not take it ill."[17]

Firmont rode with the king and two soldiers in a carriage that took them to the Place Louis XV (the present Place de la Concorde) through streets lined with thousands of soldiers and armed citizens. Various of the king's supporters had planned to rescue him that morning or die in the attempt. The authorities succeeded, however, in preventing any suspect people from leaving their houses, so only a handful of men arrived at the designated rendezvous. Firmont had heard of this plot and maintained some hope of its success right up to the foot of the scaffold.

At last, after a trip lasting over an hour, the carriage arrived at the Place Louis XV, where Santerre had assembled 100,000 men to ensure that the king would be executed as planned. Some were unwilling participants in the scene, however. A prominent doctor named Philippe Pinel was present and later stated in a letter to a friend, "I greatly regret that I was obliged to attend the execution bearing arms with the other citizens of the section, and I write to you now with my heart filled with grief and my whole being stunned by the shock of this dreadful experience.[18]

One of the executioners opened the carriage door for the king. Before Louis XVI got out, however, he asked the guards in the carriage to be sure that no harm would befall Abbé Firmont after his execution. After the king descended from the carriage, three executioners surrounded him to take off his outer garments, but he insisted on doing this for himself. Then they started to tie his hands. The king was outraged at this indignity, and Firmont feared that a terrible scene would result:

> He appeared to fear this himself and turning toward me, he looked directly at me, as if to ask my advice. Alas, it was impossible for me to counsel him; at first I replied to him only by my silence. But as he continued to look at me, I said through my tears, "Sire, in this new outrage I see only a last feature of resemblance between your majesty and the God who will be your reward."
>
> At these words, he raised his eyes to heaven with an expression of sorrow I could never convey. "Assuredly," he said, "his example makes it clear that I must submit to such an affront." And turning to his executioners, he said, "Do what you want, I will drink the chalice to the dregs."[19]

Firmont helped the fettered king climb the steep stairs to the scaffold. Stepping forward toward the crowd, Louis XVI then said, over the rising sound of drums: "I die innocent of all the crimes imputed to me. I pardon those who have sought my death, and I pray to God that the blood you are about to shed never returns to plague France."[20]

Epilogue

Albert Camus was one of the many noted French writers of various political persuasions who were impressed with the grace with which Louis XVI met his death:

> But from the moment that he suspected or knew his fate, he seemed to identify ... with his divine mission, so that there would be no possible doubt that the attempt on his person was aimed at the King-Christ ... and not at the craven flesh of a mere man.... The calmness and perfection that this man of rather average sensibility displayed during his last moments, his indifference to everything of this world ... give us the right to imagine that it was not Capet who died, but Louis appointed by divine right, and that with him, in a certain manner, died temporal Christianity.[1]

The king's death left a devastated family mourning him in their bleak tower prison. Unlikely as the union of Louis and Marie Antoinette had originally seemed, they had over the years developed a deep affection for each other. In her memoirs Madame Royale relates that after her father's execution, her mother would no longer go down to the garden because she could not bear to pass the apartment where the king had spent his last months. After his death she sank into a depression, caring little whether she lived or died. Her daughter writes that she sometimes would look at her children "with a pity that made me tremble."[2] The queen's suffering soon became almost unbearable, as Madame Royale relates:

> On July 3 we were read a decree from the Convention stating that my brother was to be separated from us and lodged in the most secure apartment in the tower. The moment he heard this, he threw himself into my mother's arms, screaming and asking not to be separated from her. For her part, my mother was overwhelmed by this cruel order. She did not want to give up my brother and tried to keep the municipals from approaching the bed where she placed him. These men, adamant in their desire to have him, threatened to use violence and to bring up a detachment of guards. My mother told them they might as well kill

her before taking away her child, and an hour passed thus in resistance on her part and insults and threats on the part of the municipals.... Finally, they threatened so unmistakably to kill him as well as me, that she had to give in, out of love for us. My aunt and I got him up, for my poor mother had no strength left. After he was dressed, she took him and gave him to the municipals, covering him with her tears, foreseeing that in the future she would never again see him. This poor little one kissed us all tenderly and left with the municipals dissolved in tears.[3]

Marie Antoinette's sorrow became even more intense when she learned that a municipal by the name of Simon, a former shoemaker, was to be in charge of her son. The family's previous experience with this man in the tower gave them no cause for optimism. Cléry noted in his journal, "This man whenever he appeared in the presence of the royal family always treated them with the vilest insolence."[4] Subsequent events only confirmed the family's fears. Through the sporadic information they obtained from Tison, they learned that the dauphin had cried for two days after leaving his family, until Simon at last frightened him into stopping. In his desire to turn the child into a good revolutionary, Simon in effect brainwashed this helpless eight-year-old boy, destroying his health and converting a lively and gay child into a dull and terrified little boy who within a year became mute. Although the dauphin hated wine, Simon insisted he drink it. Soon he became very overweight and his health began to suffer in other ways. Simon taught him revolutionary songs, which his family could hear him singing as he went up to the tower roof for exercise. Marie Antoinette would sit near a window for hours hoping to get a glimpse of her son as he walked on the roof.[5]

Before many months had passed, Simon had the child cursing his family, the aristocrats, and God. But in what must surely be one of the most abominable acts of the Revolution, he succeeded in wrenching from the child a signed statement accusing his mother and aunt of having had illicit sexual relations with him. This accusation was one of many brought against Marie Antoinette in her trial. On August 2 she was moved from the tower of the Temple to the Conciergerie prison. During the weeks she spent there, a daring attempt by royalists to help her escape failed when she mistakenly spoke to the wrong guard. Her trial began on October 15, and she was executed on October 17, 1793, at the age of 37.

The day before she died Marie Antoinette wrote a letter to her sister-in-law, Madame Elisabeth, asking her to take care of her children. Madame Elisabeth had only six more months to spend with her niece in the tower, however. She was executed on May 10, 1794, at the age of thirty.

After her aunt was taken away, the fifteen-year-old Madame Royale was left entirely alone in her tower room. The guards now simply locked her into her room, only bringing her meals three times a day. For a year and a half she did not even know if her mother and aunt were dead or alive because the municipals always evaded her questions about their fate. Whenever the drums beat, she was terrified that another prison massacre would claim them as victims, little realizing that they were already dead.

Madame Royale was well off compared to her brother, however. In January 1794 Simon departed, and the eight-year-old child was then left constantly alone in a locked room. His sister describes the unbelievable conditions in which the heir to the French throne was forced to live:

> He slept in a bed that had not been changed for over six months.... Fleas and bed bugs covered it, and his clothes and body were also full of them. It had been more than a year since anyone had given him a clean shirt or stockings. His excrement remained in his room; no one threw it out during all this time. His window, closed with a padlock and bars, was never opened; no one could remain for long in his room because of the foul odor.... He passed the day with nothing to do and was given no light.... It is not surprising that he sank into a frightening apathy.[6]

Robespierre fell to the guillotine in late July 1794, and with his death the Reign of Terror soon subsided. In the resulting change of power new, more sympathetic men took charge of the royal children. They were shocked to see the squalid conditions under which the dauphin existed, and one of these men by the name of Gomier did everything he could to help the boy. Each day he spent several hours entertaining the dauphin, taking him to the garden or other rooms in the tower. The child soon became attached to the man who was treating him with such kindness.[7] Gomier saw at once that the child's joints were badly swollen and obtained medical attention for him. It was too late, however. On June 8, 1795, the ten-year-old dauphin died of tuberculosis of the bones. Ironically enough, there had recently been a certain amount of movement toward reestablishing a limited constitutional monarchy with the dauphin on the throne.

In December 1795 Madame Royale was exchanged for several prisoners held by Austria, among them Drouet, the man who had prevented the royal family's escape at Varennes. The Restoration in 1815 brought her uncle Provence to the throne as Louis XVIII, and she returned to France with him. During Napoléon's brief but unsuccessful attempt to regain power during the Hundred Days, she rode out on her horse to help rally royalist forces at Bordeaux, earning from Napoléon the remark that she was "the only man of the family."[8]

Among its many thousand victims, the guillotine claimed Barnave, Bailly, the duke of Orléans, Danton, Robespierre, Saint Just, Brissot, Vergniaud, Mme. Roland, Desmoulins, and Hébert.

Chapter Notes

The author has modernized capitalization and punctuation in some of the texts from the late eighteenth and early nineteenth centuries.

PREFACE

1. John M. S. Allison, *Lamoignon de Malesherbes: Defender and Reformer of the French Monarchy, 1721–1794* (New Haven: Yale University Press, 1938), 129.

2. Susan Dunn, *The Deaths of Louis XVI: Regicide and the French Political Imagination* (Princeton: Princeton University Press, 1994), 140.

3. Albert Camus, *The Rebel: An Essay on Man in Revolt* (1951; New York: Knopf, 1956), 120, as quoted in Dunn.

4. Bailey Stone, *Reinterpreting the French Revolution: A Global-Historical Perspective* (Cambridge: Cambridge University Press, 2002), 1.

5. Derek Beales, *Joseph II: In the Shadow of Maria Theresa, 1741–1780* (Cambridge: Cambridge University Press, 1987), 9–10.

6. Gouverneur Morris, *A Diary of the French Revolution*, ed. Beatrix Cary Davenport, 2 vols. (Boston: Houghton Mifflin, 1939), 2:571–72.

CHAPTER 1

1. Public Record Office, London, dispatch from Lord Stormont, British ambassador to France, SP 78/292.

2. Alfred Cobban, *A History of Modern France*, 3 vols. (Harmondsworth: Penguin, 1961–65), 1:113.

3. Louis-Auguste, Dauphin (Louis XVI), *Réflexions sur mes entretiens avec M. le duc de La Vauguyon*, avec une introduction de M. de Falloux (Paris: J.-P. Aillaud, 1851), xi.

4. Pierrette Girault de Coursac, *L'Educa-*

tion d'un Roi: Louis XVI (Paris: Gallimard, 1972), 18.

5. David Hume, *The Letters of David Hume*, ed. J.Y.T. Grieg (Oxford: Clarendon Press, 1932), 1:416.

6. Girault de Coursac, *L'Education*, 69–70.

7. Mme. [Jeanne-Louise-Henriette] de Campan, *Memoirs of the Private Life of Marie Antoinette*, 2 vols. (Philadelphia: Small, 1823), 1:45.

8. Alfred d'Arneth and M. A. Geffroy, *Correspondance secrète entre Marie-Thérèse et le comte de Mercy-Argenteau, avec les lettres de Marie-Thérèse et de Marie-Antoinette*, 2 vols. (Paris: Firmin-Didot, 1874).

9. Louis-Auguste, *Réflexions sur mes entretiens avec M. le duc de La Vauguyon*, par Louis-Auguste, Dauphin (Paris, J.-P. Aillaud, 1851), xxii–xxiii.

10. Girault de Coursac, *L'Education*, 89.

11. Louis-Auguste, *Réflexions*.

12. *Ibid.*, 18.

13. *Ibid.*, 19.

14. *Ibid.*, 17.

15. *Ibid.*, 16.

16. Abbé de Véri, *Journal de l'Abbé de Véri*, 2 vols. (Paris: Jules Tallandier, 1928–30), 1:110.

17. George Androutsos, "The Truth about Louis XVI's Marital Difficulties: Could the Phimosis of Louis XVI (1754–1793) Have Been Responsible for His Sexual Difficulties and His Delayed Fertility?" *Progres en Urologie* 12 (2002): 132–37.

18. Arneth, *Correspondance*, 1:36.

19. Duc de Croÿ, *Journal inédit du duc de Croÿ: 1718–1784* (Paris: Flammarion, 1906–07), 4:192.

20. Campan, *Private Life*, 1:113.

21. Jean-Baptiste Cléry, *A Journal of Occurrences in the Tower of the Temple During the Confinement of Louis XVI, King of France* (London: Baylis, 1798), 134–35.

22. Arneth, *Correspondance*, 2:10.

23. Coursac, *L'Education*, 199–200.

24. Arneth, *Correspondance*, 1:466.

25. *Ibid.*

26. *Ibid.*, 1:458.

CHAPTER 2

1. Public Record Office, London, dispatch from Lord Stormont, SP 78/292.

2. Véri, *Journal*, 1:119.

3. *Ibid.*, 1:93.

4. Campan, *Private Life*, 1:302.

5. Véri, *Journal*, 1:185.

6. *Ibid.*, 1:186.

7. Public Record Office, London, dispatch from Lord Stormont, SP 78/292.

8. Véri, *Journal*, 1:109.

9. *Ibid.*, 2:9.

10. Paul and Pierrette Girault de Coursac, *Louis XVI A la Parole: Autoportrait du Roi Très Chrétien: Lettres, discours, écrits politiques* (Paris: François-Xavier de Guibert, 1997), 9.

11. M. J. Sydenham, *The French Revolution* (New York: Putnam's, 1965), 19.

12. Véri, *Journal*, 1:204.

13. Allison, *Malesherbes*, 31.

14. Pierre Grosclaude, *Malesherbes, témoin et interprète de sons temps* (Paris: Librairie Fischbacher, 1961), 165–66.

15. *Ibid.*, 105.

16. Véri, *Journal*, 1:317.

17. Allison, *Malesherbes*, 83.

18. Grosclaude, *Malesherbes*, 333.

19. Allison, *Malesherbes*, 93–94.

20. *Ibid.*, 94.

21. Hepworth Dixon, *John Howard and the Prison World of Europe* (New York: Robert Carter, 1850), 195.

22. Allison, *Malesherbes*, 91.

23. Véri, *Journal*, 1:379.

24. Sydenham, *French Revolution*, 19.

25. Alexis Tocqueville, *The Old Regime and the Revolution*, ed. François Furet and Françoise Mélonio, trans. Alan S. Kahan (Chicago: University of Chicago Press, 1998), 2 n. 4.

26. *Ibid.*, 225.

27. *Ibid.*

28. Véri, *Journal*, 1:287–88.

29. *Ibid.*, 1:319.

30. Croÿ, *Journal*, 186.

31. Sydenham, *French Revolution*, 19.

32. Allison, *Malesherbes*, 161.

CHAPTER 3

1. J. B. Ebeling, ed., *Louis XVI, extraits des mémoires du temps* (Paris: Plon, 1939), 94.

2. Horace Walpole, *The Yale Edition of Horace Walpole's Correspondence*, ed. W. S. Lewis and A. Dayle Wallace, 48 vols. (New Haven: Yale University Press, 1965), 32:254.

3. *Ibid.*, 34:98.

4. Véri, *Journal*, 1:240–41.

5. Campan, *Private Life*, 1:89.

6. Arthur Young, *Travels in France* (London: Bell, 1890), 102.

7. Campan, *Private Life*, 1:92.

8. Arneth, *Correspondance*, 2:359.

9. *Ibid.*, 2:360.

10. *Ibid.*, 2:362.

11. *Ibid.*, 3:50.

12. *Ibid.*, 1:313–14.

13. *Ibid.*, 3:80.

14. Derek Beales, *Joseph II: In the Shadow of Maria Theresa, 1741–1780* (Cambridge: Cambridge University Press, 1987), 374.

15. Arneth, *Correspondance*, 3:50.

16. *Ibid.*, 3:56.

17. Alfred Ritter von Arneth, *Marie Antoinette, Joseph II, und Leopold II: Ihr Briefwechsel* (Leipzig: K. F. Köhler, 1866), 4–12.

18. Arneth, *Correspondance*, 3:48.

19. *Ibid.*, 2:404.

20. *Ibid.*, 3:55.

21. Joseph II entry in Wikipedia, citing Norman Davies, *Europe a History.* New York: HarperPerennial, 1998), no page number given, accessed September 12, 2012.

22. Beales, *Joseph II*, 5.

23. Véri, *Journal*, 2:76.

24. *L'Ancien moniteur*, 31 vols. (Paris: Plon, 1857), 18:124.

25. Michel de Lombares, *Enquête sur l'échec de Varennes* (Paris: Librairie Académique Perrin, 1988), 27.

26. *Ibid.*

27. *The Letters of Marie Antoinette, Fersen and Barnave*, ed. O. G. de Heidenstam, trans. Winifred Stephens and Mrs. Wilfrid Jackson (London: John Lane, 1926), 19.

28. *Ibid.*, 18.

CHAPTER 4

1. Count de Ségur, *Memoirs and Recollections of Count Segur, Ambassador from France*

to the Courts of Russia and Prussia, etc. (Boston: Wells and Lilly, 1825), 103.

2. *Ibid.,* 106.
3. *Ibid.,* 109.
4. *Ibid.,* 106.
5. *Ibid.,* 111.
6. Véri, *Journal,* 2:204.
7. William Doyle, *Origins of the French Revolution* (Oxford: Oxford University Press, 1980), 48.
8. Cobban, *History,* 124.
9. Doyle, *Origins,* 43.
10. Campan, *Private Life,* 1:182.
11. Véri, *Journal,* 1:242.
12. *Ibid.,* 2:180.
13. Vincent Cronin, *Louis and Antoinette* (New York: Morrow, 1975), 123.
14. Ségur, *Memoirs,* 157–58.
15. Duke de Cröy, *Journal,* 3:221–24.
16. Ebeling, *Louis XVI,* 115–16.
17. Comte Jean-Françoise de Galaup de La Pérouse, *Voyage de Lapérouse autour du monde pendant les années 1785, 1786, 1787, 1788* (Paris: Club des Libraires de France, 1965), 17.

CHAPTER 5

1. Pierre Jolly, *Necker* (Paris: Oeuvres Françaises, 1947), 186.
2. Doyle, *Origins,* 49.
3. Jolly, *Necker,* 191.
4. Cobban, *History,* 1:125.
5. Véri, *Journal,* 2:92–93.
6. Doyle, *Origins,* 56.
7. Arneth, *Correspondance,* 1:458.
8. Frances Mossiker, *The Queen's Necklace* (New York: Simon and Schuster, 1961), 197–98.
9. *Mémoires du Baron de Besenval* (Paris: Firmin-Didot, 1857), 126.
10. *Ibid.,* 129.
11. Mossiker, *Queen's Necklace,* 520–21.
12. Cobban, *History,* 1:118.

CHAPTER 6

1. Young, *Travels,* 120.
2. Doyle, *Origins,* 43.
3. Tocqueville, *Old Regime,* 221.
4. John Hardman, *Louis XVI* (New Haven: Yale University Press, 1993), 123–24.
5. J. M. Roberts, ed., *French Revolution Documents,* vol. 1 (Oxford: Basil Blackwell, 1966), 20.
6. Stone, *Reinterpreting,* 55.
7. François Furet and Denis Richet, *La Révolution: Des Etats Généraux au 9 Thermidor* (Paris: Hachette, 1965), 1:76.
8. Cobban, *History,* 1:137.

CHAPTER 7

1. Pierre Andre Sayous, ed., *Mémoires et Correspondance de Mallet du Pan,* 2 vols. (London: Bentley, 1852), 1:167.
2. Abbé Sieyès, *Qu'est-ce que le Tièrs-Etat?* 3d. ed. (1789), 7.
3. *Ibid.,* 25–26.
4. Georges Lefebvre, *The Coming of the French Revolution,* trans. R. R. Palmer (Princeton: Princeton University Press, 1947), 7.
5. Furet and Richet, *Révolution,* 1:34.
6. Sydenham, *French Revolution,* 26.
7. Tocqueville, *Old Regime,* 229.
8. *Ibid.*
9. Greg Neale, "How an Icelandic Volcano Helped Spark the French Revolution," Guardian News and Media Limited, April 15, 2010, accessed September 2, 2012, http://www.guardian.co.uk/world/2010/apr/15/iceland-volcano-weather-french-revolution.
10. William Doyle, *Oxford History of the French Revolution* (Oxford: Oxford University Press, 1989), 86.

CHAPTER 8

1. Ebeling, *Louis XVI,* 124 n.
2. De Staël, *Considérations,* 140.
3. Morris, *Diary,* 1:66.
4. *L'Ancien moniteur,* 1:1.
5. Morris, *Diary,* 1:66.
6. Sydenham, *French Revolution,* 45.
7. *L'Ancien moniteur,* 1:95.
8. Sydenham, *French Revolution,* 45.
9. Young, *Travels,* 182–83.
10. Tocqueville, *Old Regime,* 222–23.

CHAPTER 9

1. Baron de Besenval and Ghislain de Diesbach, *Mémoires du Baron de Besenval sur la Cour de France* (Paris: Mercure de France, 1987), 500.
2. Morris, *Diary,* 1:145.
3. Cobban, *History,* 1:149.
4. Simon Schama, *Citizens: A Chronicle of the French Revolution* (New York: Alfred A. Knopf, 1989), 398.
5. *Ibid.,* 391–92.
6. *Ibid.,* 392.
7. *Ibid.,* 399.
8. Georges Pernoud and Sabine Flaissier, *The French Revolution* (Greenwich, Conn: Fawcett, 1965), 35–36.
9. Morris, *Diary,* 1:148.

CHAPTER 10

1. *L'Ancien moniteur*, 1:161–62.
2. Furet and Richet, *Révolution*, 116.
3. De Staël, *Considérations*, 162.
4. Pernoud and Flaissier, *French Revolution*, 48.
5. *Ibid.*, 49–50.
6. Campan, *Private Life*, 2:67.
7. Morris, *Diary*, 1:158–59.
8. Lefebvre, *Coming of the French Revolution*, 118.
9. Doyle, *Oxford History*, 115.
10. Ebeling, *Louis XVI*, 1:77.

CHAPTER 11

1. Morris, *Diary*, 1:243.
2. Mme. de Tourzel, *Memoirs*, 2 vols. (London: Remington, 1886), 1:28.
3. *Ibid.*, 1:27–28.
4. Joseph Weber, *Memoirs of Maria Antoinetta, Archduchess of Austria, Queen of France and Navarre*, trans R. C. Dallas, 3 vols. (London: Rickaby, 1805), 2:196–97.
5. De Staël, *Considérations*, 210.
6. Pernoud and Flaissier, *French Revolution*, 61.
7. Weber, *Memoirs*, 2:203.
8. *L'Ancien Moniteur*, 2:8.
9. Tourzel, *Memoirs*, 1:32.
10. Marquis de Ferrières, *Mémoires du Marquis de Ferrières*, 3 vols. (Paris: Baudouin, 1821), 1:323.
11. *Ibid.*, 1:325.
12. Weber, *Memoirs*, 2:218–19.
13. *Ibid.*, 2:223.
14. Tourzel, *Memoirs*, 1:42.
15. *Ibid.*, 1:43.
16. Campan, *Private Life*, 1:89–90.
17. Tourzel, *Memoirs*, 1:43–44.
18. Morris, *Diary*, 1:246.

CHAPTER 12

1. Allison, *Malesherbes*, 129.
2. Grosclaude, *Malesherbes*, 708.
3. Allison, *Malesherbes*, 129.
4. Tourzel, *Memoirs*, 1:58.
5. *Ibid.*, 61.
6. *L'Ancien moniteur*, 3:297–99.
7. Tourzel, *Memoirs*, 1:129.
8. Cobban, *History*, 1:182.

CHAPTER 13

1. Sydenham, *French Revolution*, 67.
2. De Staël, *Considérations*, 226.

3. Ferrières, *Mémoires*, 3:93–94.
4. J. M. Thompson, *The French Revolution* (New York: Oxford University Press, 1943), 121.
5. Ferrières, *Mémoires*, 95.
6. De Staël, *Considérations*, 227.
7. Tourzel, *Memoirs*, 1:164.
8. *Ibid.*, 1:166–67.
9. *Ibid.*, 1:354.

CHAPTER 14

1. Doyle, *Oxford History*, 140.
2. Tourzel, *Memoirs*, 1:241.
3. Thompson, *French Revolution*, 201.
4. Cobban, *History*, 1:182.
5. Morris, *Diary*, 2:153–54.
6. Tourzel, *Memoirs*, 1:290–91.

CHAPTER 15

1. Tourzel, *Memoirs*, 1:321–23.
2. *Ibid.*, 1:323.
3. *Ibid.*, 1:324.
4. *Ibid.*
5. Pernoud and Flaissier, *French Revolution*, 86.
6. Tourzel, *Memoirs*, 1:325.
7. *Ibid.*
8. *Ibid.*, 1:327.
9. Michel de Lombares, *Enquête sur l'échec de Varennes* (Paris: Librairie Académique Perrin, 1988), 49.
10. Tourzel, *Memoirs*, 1:329.
11. *Ibid.*, 1:327.
12. *Ibid.*, 1:329–30.
13. *Ibid.*, 1:330–33.
14. Lombares, *Enquête*, 81.
15. Pernoud and Flaissier, *French Revolution*, 84–85.
16. *Ibid.*, 87.
17. *Ibid.*, 87–88.
18. Tourzel, *Memoirs*, 1:334.
19. *Ibid.*, 1:333.
20. *Ibid.*
21. *Ibid.*, 335.
22. Lombares, *Enquête*, 193–95.
23. Tourzel, *Memoirs*, 1:343.
24. *Ibid.*, 1:344.
25. *Ibid.*, 1:346–47.
26. *Ibid.*, 1:351.
27. Jérôme Pétion, *Mémoires inédit de Pétion et Mémoires de Buzot & Barbaroux* (Paris: Plon, 1866), 191–92.
28. Tourzel, *Memoirs*, 1:343–58.
29. *Ibid.*, 1:352–55.
30. Pétion, *Mémoires*, 195.
31. Pernoud and Flaissier, *French Revolution*, 92.

32. Pétion, *Mémoires*, 196–97.
33. *Ibid.*, 194.
34. *Ibid.*, 202.
35. Lombares, *Enquête*, 170.
36. Pétion, *Mémoires*, 202.
37. De Staël, *Considérations*, 242.
38. Bernard Fäy, *Louis XVI: or the End of a World* (Chicago: H. Regnery, 1968), 353. Bernard Fäy was a strong proponent of the theory that the Freemasons were responsible for the French Revolution. During World War II, his views about the danger that the Freemasons created as a secret society motivated him to provide the Nazis and the Vichy government, for which he served as director of the Bibliotèque Nationale, with lists of members of the Freemasons. Many were killed or incarcerated as a result. After World War II, Fäy was imprisoned for collaboration with the Nazis.

CHAPTER 16

1. *L'Ancien moniteur*, 9:144.
2. Ferrières, *Mémoires*, 2:456–57.
3. Cobban, *History*, 1:184.
4. *Ibid.*
5. Tourzel, *Memoirs*, 1:398:99.
6. *Ibid.*, 1:406–8.
7. De Staël, *Considérations*, 249–50.

CHAPTER 17

1. Sydenham, *French Revolution*, 87 n.
2. Furet and Richet, *Révolution française*, 1:34.
3. Sydenham, *French Revolution*, 85.
4. De Staël, *Considérations*, 253–54.
5. Sydenham, *French Revolution*, 91.
6. *Ibid.*, 97.
7. *L'Ancien moniteur*, 11:719.
8. Ferrières, *Mémoires*, 3:54.
9. *Ibid.*, 3:55.
10. *Ibid.*, 3:56–57.
11. De Staël, *Considérations*, 270.
12. J. M. Thompson, *Leaders of the French Revolution* (New York: Harper & Row, 1967), 234.
13. Ferrières, *Mémoires*, 3:90–91.
14. Roberts, *French Revolution Documents*, 1:461–63.
15. Ferrières, *Mémoires*, 3:96.
16. A. F. Bertrand-Molleville, *Mémoires particuliers pour servir à l'histoire de la fin du règne de Louis XVI* (Paris: Michaud, 1823), 1:44.
17. Thompson, *French Revolution*, 263.
18. Ferrières, *Mémoires*, 3:103.
19. Morris, *Diary*, 2:449.

CHAPTER 18

1. *L'Ancien Moniteur*, 12:717.
2. P. L. Roederer, *Chronique des cinquante jours du 20 juin au 10 août 1792* (Paris: La Chevardière, 1832), 61.
3. Roberts, *French Revolution Documents*, 1:472.
4. Roederer, *Chronique*, 51–52.
5. Tourzel, *Memoirs*, 2:241.
6. *Ibid.*, 2:135.
7. Roederer, *Chronique*, 49.
8. *Ibid.*, 65.
9. *Ibid.*, 55.
10. *Ibid.*, 56–57.
11. *Ibid.*, 57.
12. Thompson, *French Revolution*, 274.

CHAPTER 19

1. Morris, *Diary*, 2:453.
2. *L'Ancien moniteur*, 12:777.
3. Morris, *Diary*, 2:473.
4. Tourzel, *Memoirs*, 2:178.
5. Staël, *Considérations*, 275–76.
6. Tourzel, *Memoirs*, 2:192–93.
7. *Ibid.*, 2:203–4.
8. *L'Ancien moniteur*, 13:306.
9. Morris, *Diary*, 2:218.
10. *Ibid.*, 2:488.
11. Ferrières, *Mémoires*, 3:159–60.
12. Pernoud and Faissier, *French Revolution*, 107.

CHAPTER 20

1. Roederer, *Chronique*, 350–51.
2. *Ibid.*, 352–53.
3. *Ibid.*, 360.
4. M. Cléry, Jean-Baptiste Cléry, *A Journal of Occurrences in the Tower of the Temple During the Confinement of Louis XVI, King of France* (London: Baylis, 1798), 6–8.
5. Roederer, *Chronique*, 361.
6. *Ibid.* 361–62.
7. *Ibid.*, 362–63.
8. *Ibid.*, 362n-363n.
9. *Ibid.*, 365.
10. *Ibid.*, 368–69.
11. Tourzel, *Memoirs*, 2:213.
12. Roederer, *Chronique*, 370.
13. *Ibid.*
14. *Ibid.*, 371–72.
15. *Ibid.*, 372.
16. *Ibid.*, 373.
17. *Ibid.*, 373–74.

CHAPTER 21

1. Ferrières, *Mémoires*, 3:197–98.
2. Cléry, *Journal of Occurrences*, 25–26.
3. Tourzel, *Memoirs*, 2:275–78.
4. *Ibid.*, 2:222–23.
5. *Ibid.*, 2:228–29.
6. *Ibid.*, 2:231.
7. *Ibid.*, 2:237.
8. *Ibid.*, 2:238.

CHAPTER 22

1. Tourzel, *Memoirs*, 2:247–48.
2. Cléry, *Journal of Occurrences*, 60–61.
3. Marie-Thérèse-Charlotte de France [Madame Royale], "Mémoire," in *Journal de ce qui s'est passé à la tour du Temple par Cléry suivi de dernières heures de Louis XVI par l'Abbé Edgeworth de Firmont et de mémoire écrit par Marie-Thérèse-Charlotte de France*, ed. Jacques Brosse (Paris: Mercure de France, 1968), 136.
4. *Ibid.*
5. Cléry, *Journal of Occurrences*, 61–62.
6. *Ibid.*, 216.
7. David P. Jordan, *The King's Trial: The French Revolution vs. Louis XVI* (Berkeley: University of California Press, 1979), 85–86.

CHAPTER 23

1. Michel Vovelle, *Marat, Textes Choisis* (Paris: Editions Sociales, n.d.), 185.
2. *Ibid.*, 188.
3. Sydenham, *French Revolution*, 118.
4. Thompson, *French Revolution*, 303.
5. Marie-Thérèse-Charlotte, "Mémoire," 137.
6. Staël, *Considérations*, 267.
7. Morris, *Diary*, 2:597–98.
8. P.A.L. Maton de la Varenne, *Les crimes de Marat et des autres égorgeurs* (Paris: Chez Andre, 1795), 70–71.
9. *Ibid.*, 86–87.
10. *Ibid.*, 94.
11. Tourzel, *Memoirs*, 2:284–91.
12. *Ibid.*, 2:293.
13. *Ibid.*, 2:295.
14. *Ibid.*, 2:259–67.
15. *Ibid.*, 2:267–68.
16. Ferrières, *Mémoires*, 3:513.
17. Pernoud and Faissier, *French Revolution*, 154–60.
18. Cléry, *Journal of Occurrences*, 20–23.

CHAPTER 24

1. Cobban, *History*, 203.
2. Cléry, *Journal of Occurrences*, 68–69.

3. Jacques Hébert, *Le Perè Duschesne* 173 (fall 1792), as quoted in *Journal de ce qui s'est passé à la tour du Temple par Cléry*, 205.
4. Cléry, *Journal of Occurrences*, 79.
5. *Ibid.*, 82.
6. Pernoud and Flaissier, *French Revolution*, 209–10.
7. Marie-Thérèse-Charlotte, "Mémoire," 153.
8. Cléry, *Journal of Occurrences*, 115–16.
9. Cléry, *Journal de ce qui s'est* passé, 1968 French edition, 207.
10. Tourzel, *Memoirs*, 2:193.
11. Cléry, *Journal of Occurrences*, 134–35.

CHAPTER 25

1. *L'Ancien moniteur*, 14:465.
2. *Ibid.*, 14:466–67.
3. *Ibid.*, 14:646.
4. Jordan, *King's Trial*, 73.
5. Cléry, *Journal of Occurrences*, 227.
6. *Ibid.*, 149–50.
7. *Ibid.*, 150.
8. *Ibid.*, 151–52.
9. *Ibid.*, 153–54.
10. *L'Ancien moniteur*, 14:720.
11. *Ibid.*
12. De Staël, *Considérations*, 291.
13. *L'Ancien moniteur*, 14:720.
14. Grosclaude, *Malesherbes*, 704.
15. Allison, *Malesherbes*, 138.
16. J. B. Ebeling, *La Révolution française* (Paris: Plon, 1941), 2:111–12.
17. *Ibid.*, 2:112.
18. Allison, *Malesherbes*, 139.
19. Ebeling, *La Révolution française*, 2:112.
20. Cléry, *Journal of Occurrences*, 86–90.
21. Morris, *Diary*, 2:591.

CHAPTER 26

1. Allison, *Malesherbes*, 147.
2. *L'Ancien moniteur*, 14:842.
3. *Ibid.*, 14:844.
4. *Ibid.*, 14:847–48.
5. La Pérouse, *Voyage*, 17.
6. Cléry, *Journal of Occurrences*, 204.
7. *Ibid.*, 180–81.
8. Cronin, *Louis and Antoinette*, 368.
9. *L'Ancien moniteur*, 14:484.
10. Cléry, *Journal of Occurrences*, 213.
11. Allison, *Malesherbes*, 155–56.
12. Cléry, *Journal of Occurrences*, 209.
13. *Ibid.*, 212–13.
14. *Ibid.*, 214.
15. *Ibid.*, 218–19.
16. *Ibid.*, 222–23.

17. *Ibid.*, 226–27.
18. *Ibid.*, 231.

CHAPTER 27

1. Abbé Edgeworth de Firmont, "Les Dernières heures de Louis XVI," in Cléry, *Journal de ce qui s'est* passé, 1968 French edition, 115.
2. *Ibid.*, 117.
3. *Ibid.*
4. *Ibid.*, 118.
5. Cléry, *Journal of Occurrences*, 237–38.
6. Marie-Thérèse-Charlotte, "Mémoires," 145–46.
7. Cléry, *Journal of Occurrences*, 238–39.
8. Firmont, *Dernières heures*, 121.
9. Cléry, *Journal of Occurrences*, 241.
10. *Ibid.*, 242–43.
11. *Ibid.*, 248
12. Firmont, *Dernières herures*, 123–24.
13. *Ibid.*, 124.

14. *Ibid.*
15. *Ibid.*, 125.
16. Cléry, *Journal of Occurrences*, 253.
17. *Ibid.*, 254.
18. Pernoud and Flaissier, *French Revolution*, 202.
19. Firmont, *Dernières heures*, 128.
20. *Ibid.*, 129.

EPILOGUE

1. Camus, *The Rebel*, 120–21.
2. Marie-Thérèse-Charlotte, "Mémoires," 147.
3. *Ibid.*, 154.
4. Cléry, *Journal of Occurrences*, 56.
5. Marie-Thérèse-Charlotte, "Mémoires," 154–57.
6. *Ibid.*, 166.
7. *Ibid.*, 172.
8. Cléry, *Journal de ce qui s'est* passé, 13.

Works Cited

Allison, John M. S. *Lamoignon de Malesherbes: Defender and Reformer of the French Monarchy, 1721- 1794*. New Haven: Yale University Press, 1938.

L'Ancien moniteur, 31 vols. Paris: Plon, 1857.

Androutsos, George. "The Truth about Louis XVI's Marital Difficulties: Could the Phimosis of Louis XVI (1754–1793) Have Been Responsible for His Sexual Difficulties and His Delayed Fertility?" *Progres en Urologie*, 12 (2002).

Arneth, Alfred Ritter von, ed.. *Marie Antoinette, Joseph II, und Leopold II: Ihr Briefwechsel*. Leipzig: K. F. Köhler, 1866.

Arneth, Alfred d,' and M. A. Geffroy, eds. *Correspondance secrète entre Marie-Thérèse et le comte de Mercy-Argenteau, avec les lettres de Marie-Thérèse et de Marie-Antoinette*, 2 vols. Paris: Firmin-Didot, 1874.

Beales, Derek. *Joseph II: In the Shadow of Maria Theresa, 1741–1780*. Cambridge: Cambridge University Press, 1987.

Bertrand-Molleville, A. F. *Mémoires particuliers pour servir à l'histoire de la fin du règne de Louis XVI*. Paris: Michaud, 1823.

Besenval, Pierre-Victor, and Ghislain de Diesbach. *Mémoires du Baron de Besenval sur la Cour de France*. Paris: Mercure de France, 1987.

Campan, Mme. [Jeanne-Louise-Henriette] de. *Memoirs of the Private Life of Marie Antoinette*, 2 vols. Philadelphia: A. Small, 1823.

Camus, Albert. *The Rebel: An Essay on Man in Revolt*. 1951; New York: Knopf, 1956.

Cobban, Alfred. *A History of Modern France*, 3 vols. Harmondsworth: Penguin, 1961–65.

Cléry, Jean-Baptiste. *A Journal of Occurrences in the Tower of the Temple During the Confinement of Louis XVI, King of France*. Translated by R. C. Dallas. London: Baylis, 1798.

_____. Cléry, Jean-Baptiste. *Journal de ce qui s'est passé à la tour du Temple par Cléry suivi de dernières heures de Louis XVI par l'Abbé Edgeworth de Firmont et de mémoire écrit par Marie-Thérèse-Charlotte de France*. Edited by Jacques Brosse. Paris: Mercure de France, 1968.

Cronin, Vincent. *Louis and Antoinette*. New York: Morrow, 1975.

Croÿ, duc de. *Journal inédit du duc de Croÿ: 1718–1784*. Paris: Flammarion, 1906–07.

Dixon, Hepworth. *John Howard and the Prison World of Europe*. New York: Robert Carter, 1850.

Doyle, William. *Origins of the French Revolution*. Oxford: Oxford University Press, 1980.

_____. *Oxford History of the French Revolution*. Oxford: Oxford University Press, 1989.

Dunn, Susan. *The Deaths of Louis XVI: Regicide and the French Political Imagination*. Princeton: Princeton University Press, 1994.

Ebeling, J. B., ed. *Louis XVI, extraits des mémoires du temps.* Paris: Plon, 1939.

———, ed. *La Revolution Française.* 3 vols. Paris: Plon, 1942.

Fäy, Bernard. *Louis XVI: or the End of a World.* Chicago: H. Regnery, 1968.

Ferrières, Marquis de. *Mémoires du Marquis de Ferrières,* 3 vols. Paris: Baudoin, 1821.

Firmont, Abbé Edgeworth de. "Les Dernières heures de Louis XVI." In Cléry, *Journal de ce qui s'est passé à la tour du Temple par Cléry suivi de dernières heures de Louis XVI par l'Abbé Edgeworth de Firmont et de mémoire écrit par Marie-Thérèse-Charlotte de France.* Edited by Jacques Brosse. Paris: Mercure de France, 1968.

Furet, François, and Denis Richet. *La Révolution: Des Etats Généraux au 9 Thermidor.* Paris: Hachette, 1965.

Girault de Coursac, Pierrette. *L'Education d'un Roi: Louis XVI.* Paris: Gallimard, 1972.

Girault de Coursac, Paul and Pierette. *Louis XVI A la Parole: Autoportrait du Roi Très Chrétien: Lettres, discours, écrits politiques.* Paris: François-Xavier de Guibert, 1997.

Grieg, J.Y.T., ed. *The Letters of David Hume.* Oxford: Clarendon Press, 1932.

Hardman, John. *Louis XVI.* New Haven: Yale University, 1993.

Heidenstam, O. G. de, ed. *The Letters of Marie Antoinette, Fersen and Barnave.* Translated by Winifred Stephens and Mrs. Wilfrid Jackson. London: John Lane, 1926.

Hume, David. *The Letters of David Hume.* Edited by J.Y.T. Grieg. Oxford: Clarendon Press, 1932.

La Pérouse, Comte Jean-Françoise de Galaup de. *Voyage de Lapérouse autour du monde pendant les années 1785, 1786, 1787, 1788.* Paris: Club des Libraires de France, 1965.

Jolly, Pierre. *Necker.* Paris: Oeuvres Françaises, 1947.

Jordan, David P. *The King's Trial: The French Revolution vs. Louis XVI.* Berkeley: University of California Press, 1979.

Lefebvre, Georges. *The Coming of the French Revolution.* Translated by. R. R. Palmer. Princeton: Princeton University Press, 1947.

Lombares, Michel de. *Enquête sur l'échec de Varennes.* Paris: Librairie Académique Perrin, 1988.

Louis-Auguste, Dauphin (Louis XVI). *Réflexions sur mes entretiens avec M. le duc de La Vauguyon. Avec une introduction de M. de Falloux.* Paris: J.-P. Aillaud, 1851.

Marie-Thérèse-Charlotte de France [Madame Royale], "Mémoire." In Cléry, *Journal de ce qui s'est passé à la tour du Temple par Cléry suivi de dernières heures de Louis XVI par l'Abbé Edgeworth de Firmont et de mémoire écrit par Marie-Thérèse-Charlotte de France.* Edited by Jacques Brosse. Paris: Mercure de France, 1968.

Maton de la Varenne, P.A.L. *Les crimes de Marat et des autres égorgeurs.* Paris: Chez Andre, 1795.

Morris, Gouverneur. *A Diary of the French Revolution.* Edited by Beatrix Cary Davenport. 2 vols. Boston: Houghton Mifflin, 1939.

Mossiker, Frances. *The Queen's Necklace.* New York: Simon and Schuster, 1961.

Neale, Greg. "How an Icelandic Volcano Helped Spark the French Revolution." Guardian News and Media Limited. April 15, 2010. *http://www.guardian.co.uk/world/2010/apr/15/iceland-volcano-weather-french-revolution.* Accessed September 2, 2012.

Pernoud, Georges, and Sabine Flaissier. *The French Revolution.* Greenwich, Conn: Fawcett, 1965.

Pétion, Jérôme. *Mémoires inédit de Pétion et Mémoires de Buzot & Barbaroux.* Paris: Plon, 1866.

Public Record Office, London, dispatch from Lord Stormont, British ambassador to France, SP 78/292.

Roberts, J. M., ed. *French Revolution Documents.* Vol. 1. Oxford: Basil Blackwell, 1966.

Roederer, P. L. *Chronique des cinquante jours du 20 juin au 10 août 1792.* Paris: La Chevardière, 1832.

Sayous, Pierre Andre, ed. *Mémoires et Correspondance de Mallet du Pan.* 2 vols. London: Bentley, 1852.

Schama, Simon. *Citizens: A Chronicle of the French Revolution.* New York: Knopf, 1989.

Ségur, Count de. *Memoirs and Recollections of Count Segur, Ambassador from France to the Courts of Russia and Prussia, etc.* Boston, Wells and Lilly, 1825.

Sieyès, Abbé. *Qu'est-ce que le Tièrs-Etat?* 3d. ed., 1789.

Stone, Bailey. *Reinterpreting the French Revolution: a global-historical perspective.* Cambridge: Cambridge University Press, 2002.

M. J. Sydenham, *The French Revolution.* New York: Putnam's, 1965.

Tocqueville, Alexis de. *The Old Regime and the French Revolution.* Garden City, N.Y.: Doubleday, 1955.

Thompson, J. M. *The French Revolution.* New York: Oxford University Press, 1945.

_____. *Leaders of the French Revolution.* New York: Harper & Row, 1967.

Tourzel, Mme. de. *Memoirs.* 2 vols. London: Remington, 1886.

Véri, Abbé de. *Journal de l'Abbé de Véri.* 2 vols. Paris: Jules Tallandier, 1928–30.

Vovelle, Michel. *Marat, Textes Choisis.* Paris: Editions Sociales, n.d..

Walpole, Horace. *The Yale Edition of Horace Walpole's Correspondence.* Edited by W. S. Lewis and A. Dayle Wallace. 48 vols. New Haven: Yale University Press, 1965.

Weber, Joseph. *Memoirs of Maria Antoinetta, Archduchess of Austria, Queen of France and Navarre.* Translated by R. C. Dallas. 3 vols. London: Rickaby, 1805.

Young, Arthur. *Travels in France.* London: Bell, 1890.

Index